FRIDA ORUPABO

ON LIES, SECRETS AND SILENCE

FRIDA ORUPABO

ON LIES, SECRETS AND SILENCE

SKIRA

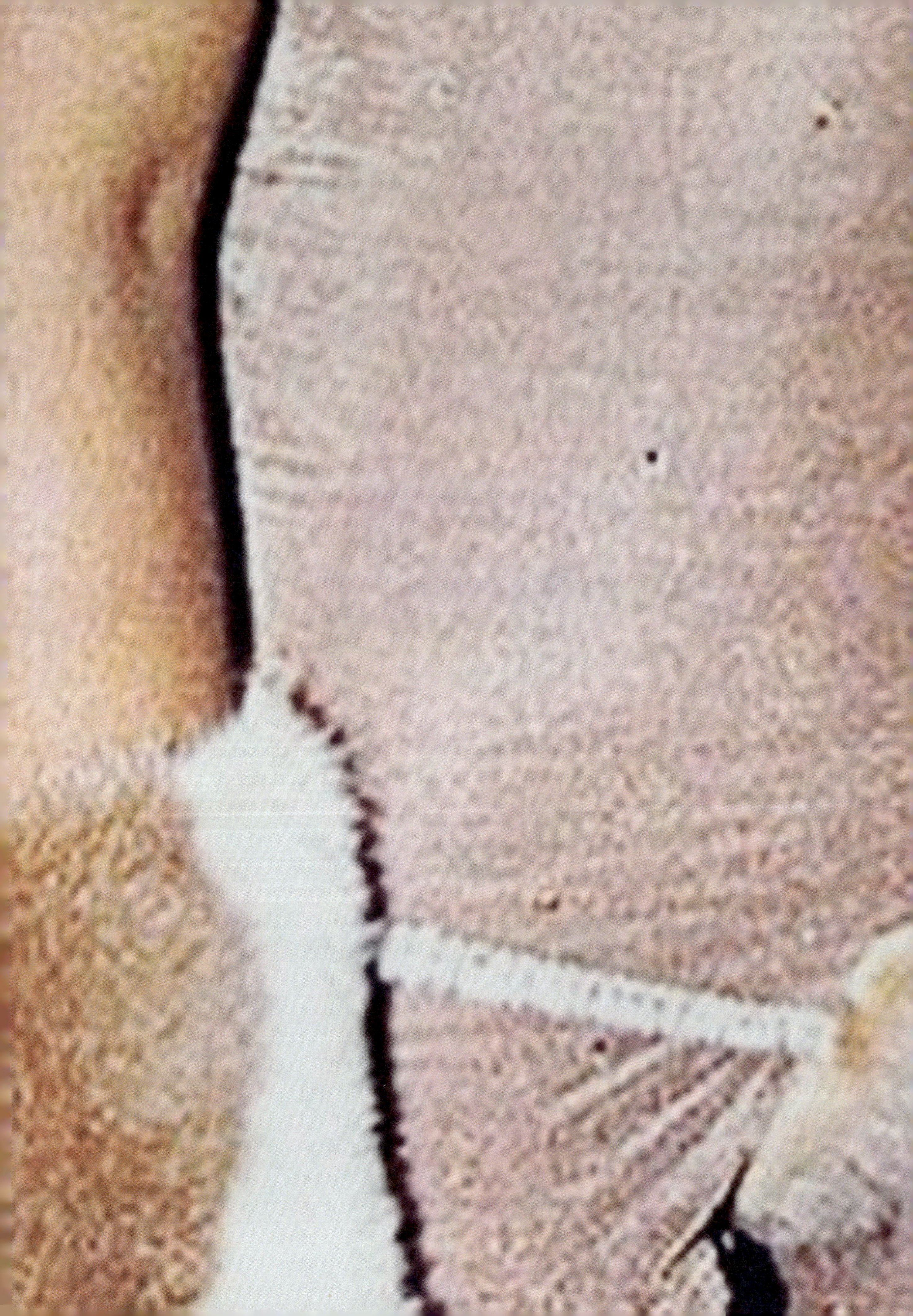

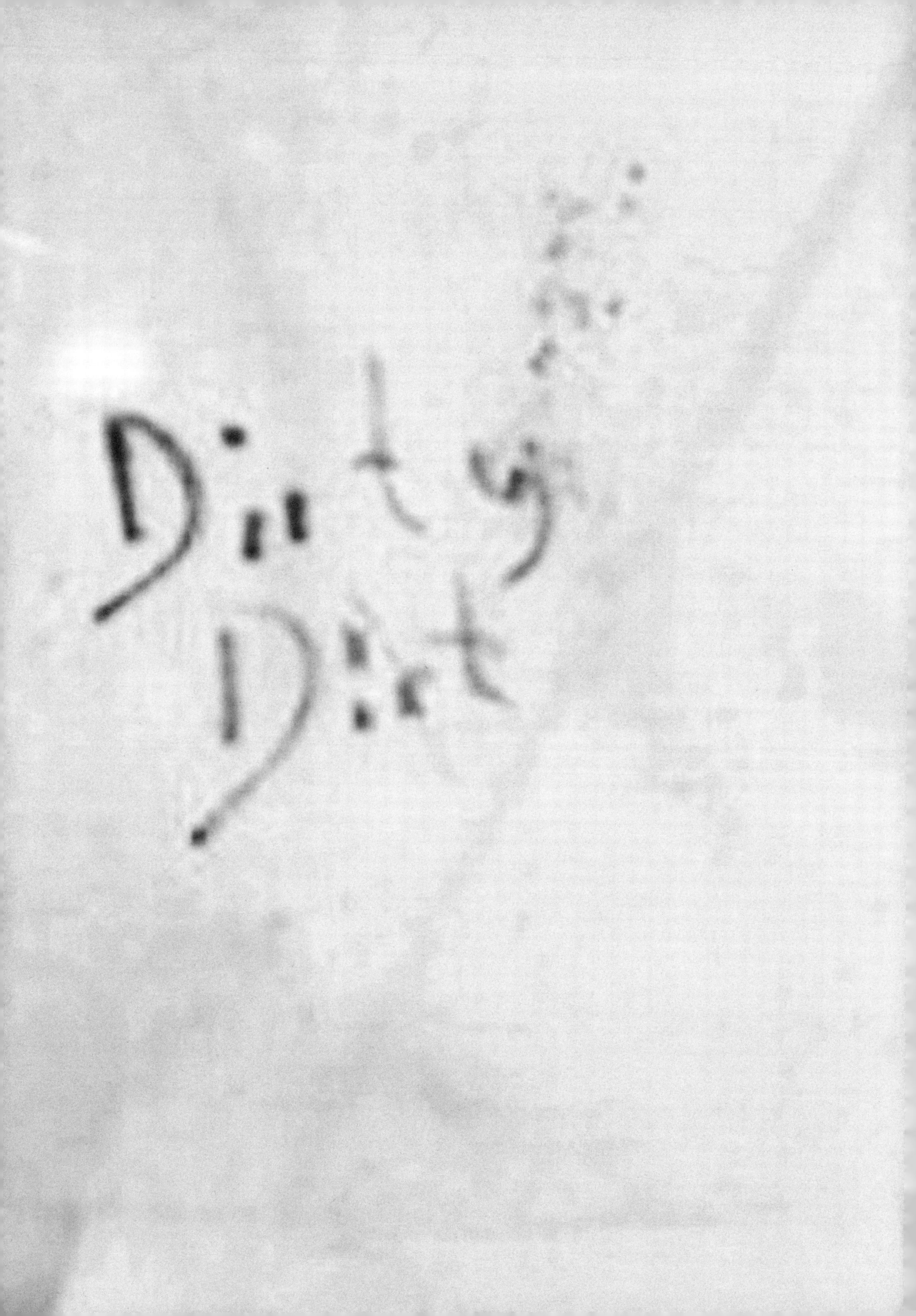
Dirty
Dirt

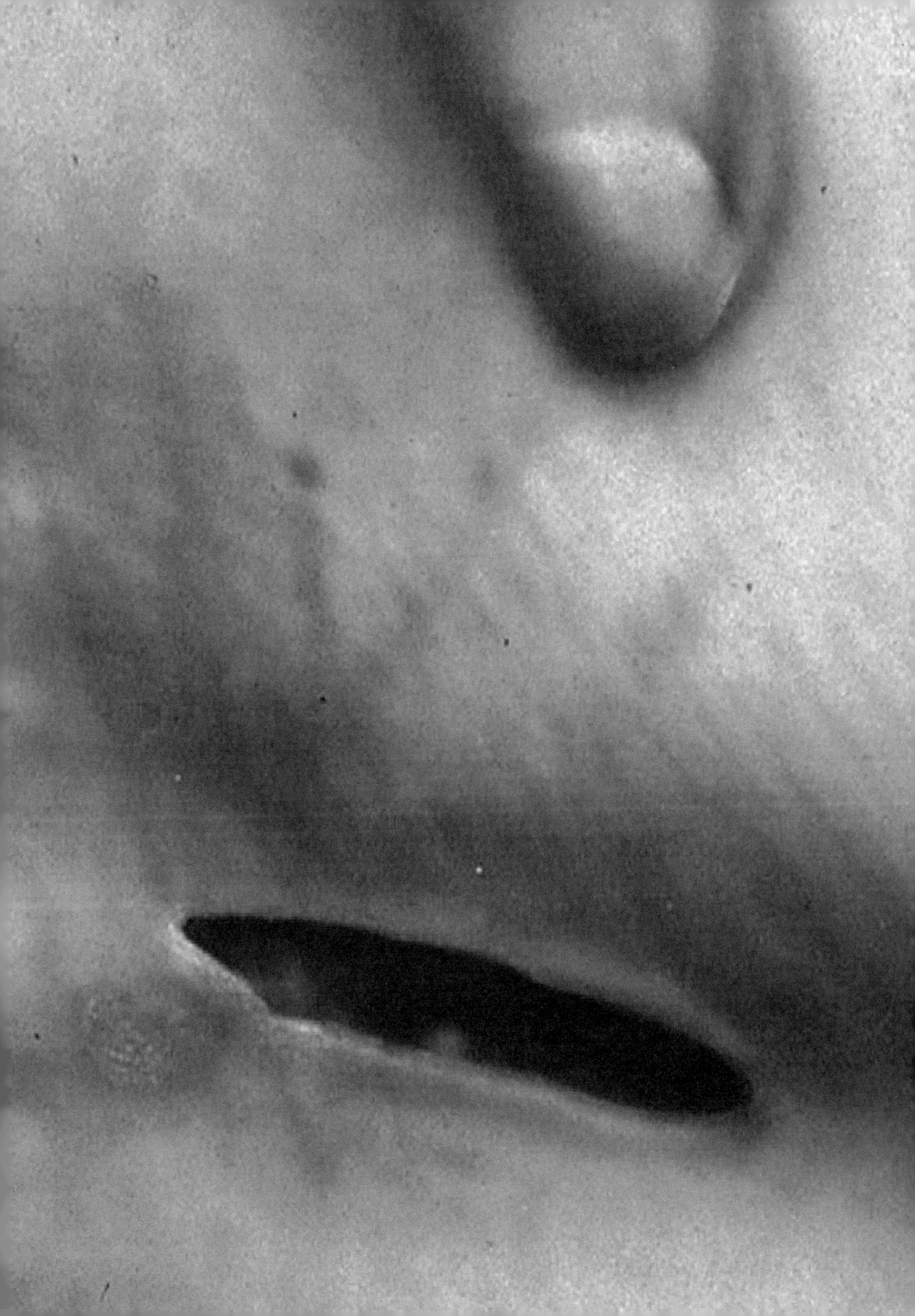

Contents

9 Foreword
Joanna Nordin and Solveig Øvstebø

11 Introduction
Yuvinka Medina and Owen Martin

19 "Everything that is sweet but can soon be rotten"
Portia Malatjie

25 Transgressive Toying
Mai Takawira and Nina Cramer

33 Works

41, 49, 57, 65, 92–93 Poetry by C. LeClaire

129 Just You, Just Me
Hilton Als

143 List of Works
150 Artist's Biography
152 Contributor Biographies
154 Acknowledgments

Foreword

Within a few short years, Frida Orupabo has established herself as a leading figure in contemporary photography. Her incisive practice unearths violences buried in historic photographic and popular archives as well as contemporary digital media. She reimagines these difficult images into otherworldly photomontages, videos, and sculptures. In so doing, she destabilizes rote meanings and draws attention to omissions, opening up new possibilities and insisting that subjects such as race, gender, sexuality, and familial bonds are sensitively examined. She is among a generation of artists whose practice moves fluidly between institutional and digital contexts and transcends the often-fleeting world of social media through a rigorous vision while bringing an urgency and contemporary understanding of how images circulate into museums.

We're very pleased to share Orupabo's particular vision through *On Lies, Secrets and Silence*. This traveling exhibition is the largest solo presentation of the artist's practice to date and is comprised of many new commissions. This includes large-scale sculptures displayed as spatial installations and a video installation, marking an evolution of her distinctive visual language. *On Lies, Secrets and Silence* came about through a close collaboration between the artist, Bonniers Konsthall and Astrup Fearnley Museet. Artists are central to the ethos of both institutions, and we're deeply grateful to Frida Orupabo for trusting us with her practice. She has generously provided her work, making the exhibition and catalog possible—we can't thank her enough.

The contributors to this catalog critically and creatively respond to the exhibition through perceptive texts. It opens with an introduction to Orupabo's practice by the exhibition curators Yuvinka Medina and Owen Martin, which discusses the significance of the artist's early digital work and its relation to *On Lies, Secrets and Silence*. This is followed by an original essay by Dr. Portia Malatjie which considers the connections between race, discomfort, and play. A newly written article by Nina Cramer and Mai Takawira, who together form the Copenhagen-based curatorial platform G/HOSTING, explores the position of Orupabo's work within a Nordic context. Poet C. LeClaire and writer Hilton Als have contributed creative, deeply personal texts that can be read alongside, against, and with the work—opening up new interpretations. The design of the publication is by the talented Gabrielle Guy, who sensitively presents Orupabo's work and the writers' texts and its production was overseen by the dedicated Bettina Schultz. We warmly thank the writers, designer, and project manager! We are grateful to Skira editore for their belief in this catalog. Additionally, we are appreciative of the support and collaboration with Sprengel Museum Hannover and Stiftung Niedersachsen, coinciding with Frida Orupabo receiving the prestigious Spectrum International Prize for Photography in 2025.

We extend our warm thanks to Yuvinka Medina and Owen Martin for their dedicated and thoughtful curatorial and editorial contributions to the exhibition and this accompanying catalog. We sincerely appreciate the support from Galerie Nordenhake, Berlin, Stockholm, Mexico City; Stevenson, Johannesburg, Cape Town, Amsterdam; and Modern Art Gallery, London. We're also deeply grateful to the staff at both institutions—their work and engagement make each project possible. A heartfelt thank-you goes to Bonniers Konsthall's funders, through its Board of Directors, and to Astrup Fearnley Museet's sponsors, funders and Museum Board.

It is our hope that this exhibition and its catalog make a significant impact in our field.

Joanna Nordin
Artistic Director,
Bonniers Konsthall

Solveig Øvstebø
Executive Director and Chief Curator,
Astrup Fearnley Museet

Introduction

Yuvinka Medina and Owen Martin

Many artists use their social media accounts to share the varied outcomes of their practice—in-process experiments, finished works, and inclusion in exhibitions at galleries or museums—or, alternatively, their accounts become a field for which a practice, initiated elsewhere, finds a new grammar and audience. Frida Orupabo has a very different relation to social media. A trained sociologist, she began collecting images from the internet while working at a center for human trafficking and sex workers and this archive found a public expression on Instagram. She only subsequently created works in a material form, first in photomontage, and now in sculpture and video. It is perhaps fitting for someone of a generation that grew up with digital interfaces as the primary means of communication (she was born in 1986), that she entered into a studio practice and the art world more broadly, in this way. It also suggests that the organizing, manipulating, looping, and inverting of images and videos is crucial to understanding her incisive practice; alongside a critical approach to social structures and processes that are informed by her training.

Orupabo opened her Instagram account in 2013 using the handle @nemiepeba [pp. 15–18]. The early posts depict moments with friends and family, as well as self-portraiture, but, among the more conventional images, it's clear that she was testing out the possibilities of the platform and building her own image world. From the very beginning, the format and content of Orupabo's feed is carefully composed, mixing historic archival photographs, alongside more personal, contemporary content and texts from literature, philosophy, and poetry. Image and text brush up against one another, and the friction this creates complicates and nuances the reading of both. As one moves through Orupabo's feed, from the early posts towards the present, colonial-era photographs emerge more prominently and are positioned alongside texts by writers, politicians, and thinkers such as Aimé Césaire and Ama Ata Aidoo. These are joined by excerpts from *The Blood of Jesus* (1941) by director Spencer Williams Junior—a forerunner of Black American cinema—and performances by Malian musician Bouba Sacko and singer Sokona Sacko. Black life and its representations in writing, photography, film, and music are insisted on.

In a 2020 interview with American filmmaker and cinematographer Arthur Jafa, Orupabo describes a deep sense of anger and frustration at growing up in Norway but rarely being seen as Norwegian (she was born in Sarpsborg, in southeast Norway, and now lives in Oslo).[1] From early on, there were persistent questions about where she was from, and her Instagram account became a way to publicly center Black and female subjectivities while prompting discussions about racism and sexism. Yet few artists who seek to represent these

1 Arthur Jafa and Frida Orupabo in Conversation, *Cahiers d'Art* (2020): 134.

experiences and histories have done so in the same way as Orupabo. The images she uses are varied and filtered through her own oneiric vision. She unearths instances of gendered and racially based violence, laying bare prejudiced systems—for example, through the posting of a horrific illustration of the treatment of Black female subjects by J. Marion Sims, a nineteenth-century American surgeon—but follows this with more ambiguous content. A baptism, a snake, and a reference to M. F. K. Fisher's book *How to Cook a Wolf* (1942) appear in close proximity. Context and meaning shift quickly, eliciting empathy and then anger or dread, requiring acute attention and unsettling simplified readings.

From as early as 2016, digitally created photomontages appear as discreet posts alongside found and self-generated content. The collage format of the Instagram feed, with its three square images abreast, is joined by these photomontages, which take the implicit possibilities of the platform's format further. Photographs are manipulated through digitally cutting, arranging, and inverting, drawing upon a long tradition of photomontage. While the technique was used by several artists associated with Dadaism and Russian Constructivism in the first half of the twentieth century, Hannah Höch's work comes to mind as a guidepost. Höch's potent yet intimate collages, thought models rendered visible, troubled conservative gender norms and political conventions—norms and conventions that violently oppressed women and brought a whole continent into conflict with itself and others. Orupabo works in a parallel vein, using the technique in a way that challenges colonial notions still embedded in many social, economic, and political structures.

In 2017, Orupabo was invited by Arthur Jafa to participate in a group exhibition at the Serpentine Gallery in London entitled *A Series of Utterly Improbable, Yet Extraordinary Renditions*. For the first time, she created physical collages instead of the digital photomontages she had previously worked on. Her initial tests involved digitally manipulating images and then printing them to create a complete image, which she found flat. She reverted to a test collage, consisting of many A4 papers pieced together like a puzzle, and realized that this was the right method for her. She did not let the limitations of the printer dictate the scale of the work, allowing her to create large-scale collages while maintaining dynamic materiality, such as the paper's distortion, intentional misalignment, shadows, and the pins holding each element in place. This marked a turning point where two parallel yet distinct directions in her practice, physical and digital, came together. The physical collages are characterized by a scale and context of presentation quite different from Orupabo's digital practice, which is more probing and exploratory. Each format enriches the other, catalyzing new possibilities.

As Orupabo began exhibiting more widely following the Serpentine show, she quickly identified that how a work is displayed impacts its reading and began manipulating this characteristic in her practice. As early as 2019, in *the mouth and the truth*, an exhibition at Portikus in Frankfurt, cut-out photographs were presented on a large, low plinth. In order to view these works, visitors looked down while circulating around the plinth, upending traditional viewing expectations—particularly for lens-based media. This exploration has evolved further in *On Lies, Secrets and Silence* at Bonniers Konsthall and Astrup Fearnley Museet, signaling both a material and conceptual expansion: photomontage and photographs are present, but so too are videos, curtains, and sculptural objects staged as spatial installations. Images are suspended, encouraging visitors to move around and between the works, immersing themselves in the artist's world.

It is striking then, that *On Lies, Secrets and Silence* takes as its starting point our most private and intimate space—the home. As Orupabo's practice becomes more immersive, we are invited into a space that is central to our everyday lives, and she discloses the complex relationships that are contained within it. Through subtle incisions and elisions, what is familiar—a place where one is safe, most "at home"—becomes unnerving, even uncanny. Collages of everyday objects create scenes that convey both proximity and distance. Symbols of childhood and security, such as the doll's house in the video installation *House Party* (2024) [pp. 47–48], become a way of exploring the shadowy sides of the home, and the relationships that are contained therein. We are invited to reflect on how emotions and experiences such as security and anxiety, closeness and distance coexist and shape our identity in-depth, and how we navigate our most intimate spaces.

The exhibition's title is taken from a prose collection by Adrienne Rich, one of America's foremost poets and feminist theorists. In a poetic landscape, Rich's collection *On Lies, Secrets, and Silence, Selected Prose 1966–1978* (1995) addresses a range of topics, including racism, history, motherhood, and the politics of language. For Rich, as for Orupabo, the works become part of the effort to define a female subjectivity that is political, aesthetic, and erotic, and that refuses to be included in a culture of passivity.

Orupabo's work often revolves around the Black female body, which historically has been overlooked, marginalized, and exploited. She highlights these bodies and places them at the center of her works, to show that they extend beyond the limitations imposed by archives. Several of the works are reminiscent of cut-out paper *pantin* dolls, built up layer by layer, loosely pinned together—but rather than amusement and diversion, their scale suggests that they are figures of resistance. Orupabo's reconstructed bodies possess an agency of their own, but at the same time emphasize the multi-layered and malleable nature of the self. Philosopher Judith Butler's theories of gender, queerness, and identity, particularly performativity in *Gender Trouble* (1990), describe how individuals alternate between the roles of subject and object in social contexts. The pantin doll, which is both controlled as an object and expresses itself as a subject, illustrates the ambivalence and the feeling of being imposed upon by bodily prejudices.

The exhibition presents two large-scale collages, *Big Girl I* (2024) [pp. 35–36] and *Big Girl II* (2024) [pp. 39–40], two Amazonian women as pantin dolls gazing down at the viewer. Orupabo uses the gaze as a means to reclaim power and subjectivity. This recalls the work of feminist theorist bell hooks and her ideas on the politics of the gaze, which she discusses in detail in *The Oppositional Gaze: Black Female Spectators* (1992). hooks describes how the resilient gaze can challenge and reshape power structures, and Orupabo channels this power in her works to give Black women a place of power and subjectivity. In so doing, she reshapes and reclaims historical and cultural narratives.

On Lies, Secrets and Silence also includes *Cloud of Confusion* (2024) [pp. 68–69], a group of twelve square images displayed in a rectangle, four horizontally and three vertically. Bridging Orupabo's digital and material work, the format of each image and *Cloud of Confusion* as a whole broadly echoes the format of Instagram. Much like the account @nemiepeba, *Cloud of Confusion* also draws upon an array of sources. Yet unlike Orupabo's feed, where images are captioned, here there are no references, and we are left to search for the origin of each image. This is heightened by their fragmentary quality. Only part of a body or figure is visible: a mouth, a hand, a nostril. The most discernable reference is to an early American cartoon and an open mouth that has a particularly erotic charge. The title is drawn from an American Department of Defense film and details the experience of participants who are exposed to 3-quinuclidinyl benzilate, a mind-altering gas. Over the course of the film, the participants become increasingly disorientated, and the film attempts to mirror their experiences through the use of unusual compositional techniques. This disorientation has a parallel in *Cloud of Confusion*, with the fragmentary quality of the images and the unnamed source material cultivating a sense of instability in the understanding of the work.

Orupabo leans into this instability not only in *Cloud of Confusion* but throughout *On Lies, Secrets and Silence*. Much like her account @nemiepeba, the works in the exhibition urge us to question the images that we encounter and recognize that our understanding of them is always partial. In both its digital and material forms she insists that violences such as racism, sexism, and transphobia are acknowledged, creating a dialogue with feminist and postcolonial theories that prompt critical reflections on societal structures. Despite these violences, she also creates potential by forming counternarratives that move beyond a politics of repair. As we navigate the fragments and layers of Orupabo's art, we are encouraged to confront and question the biases and histories that shape our world, ultimately opening new possibilities for understanding and change.

pp. 15–18 **Instagram reference material from @nemiepeba**

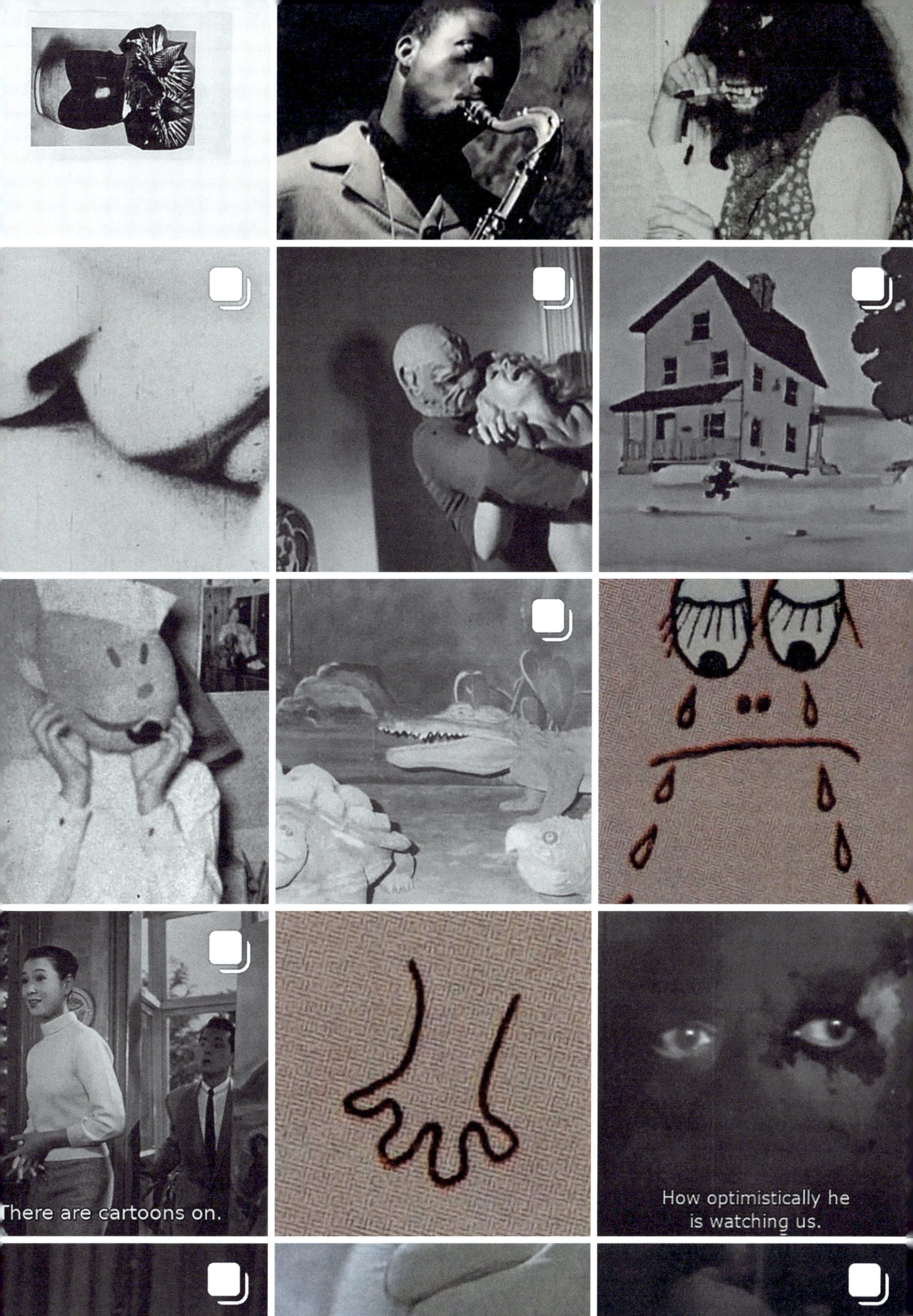
There are cartoons on.
How optimistically he
is watching us.

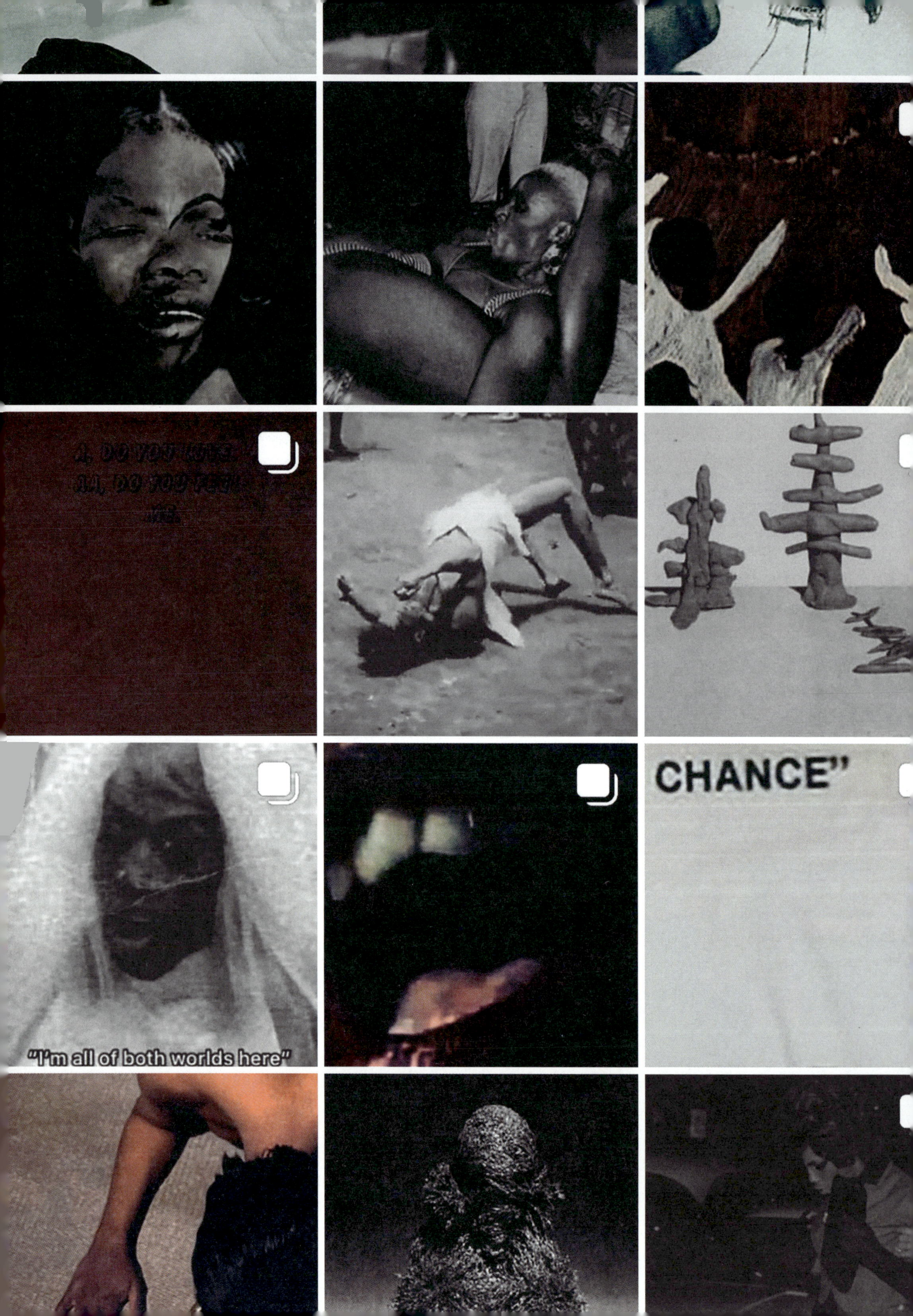
CHANCE”
“I'm all of both worlds here”

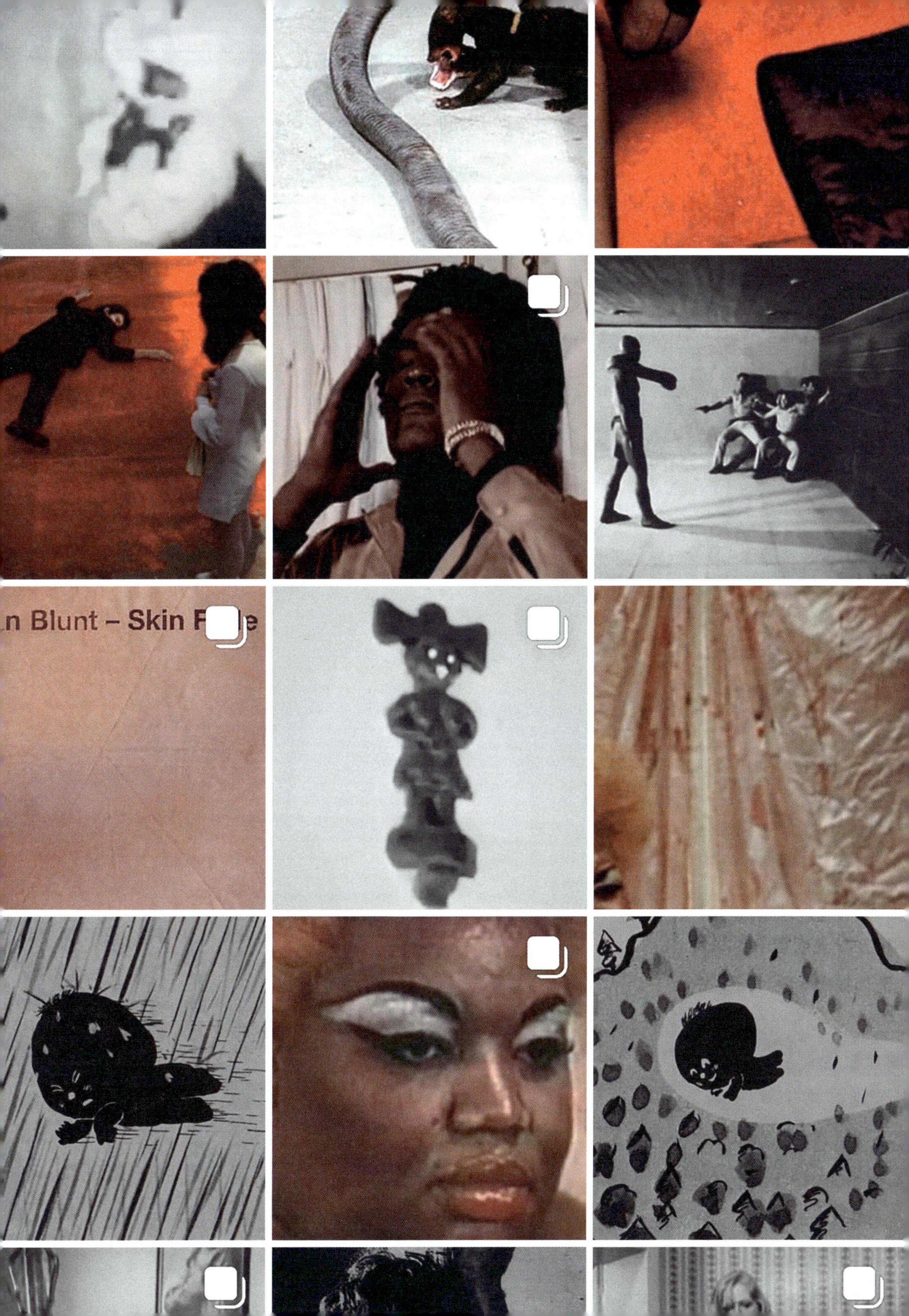
n Blunt – Skin F

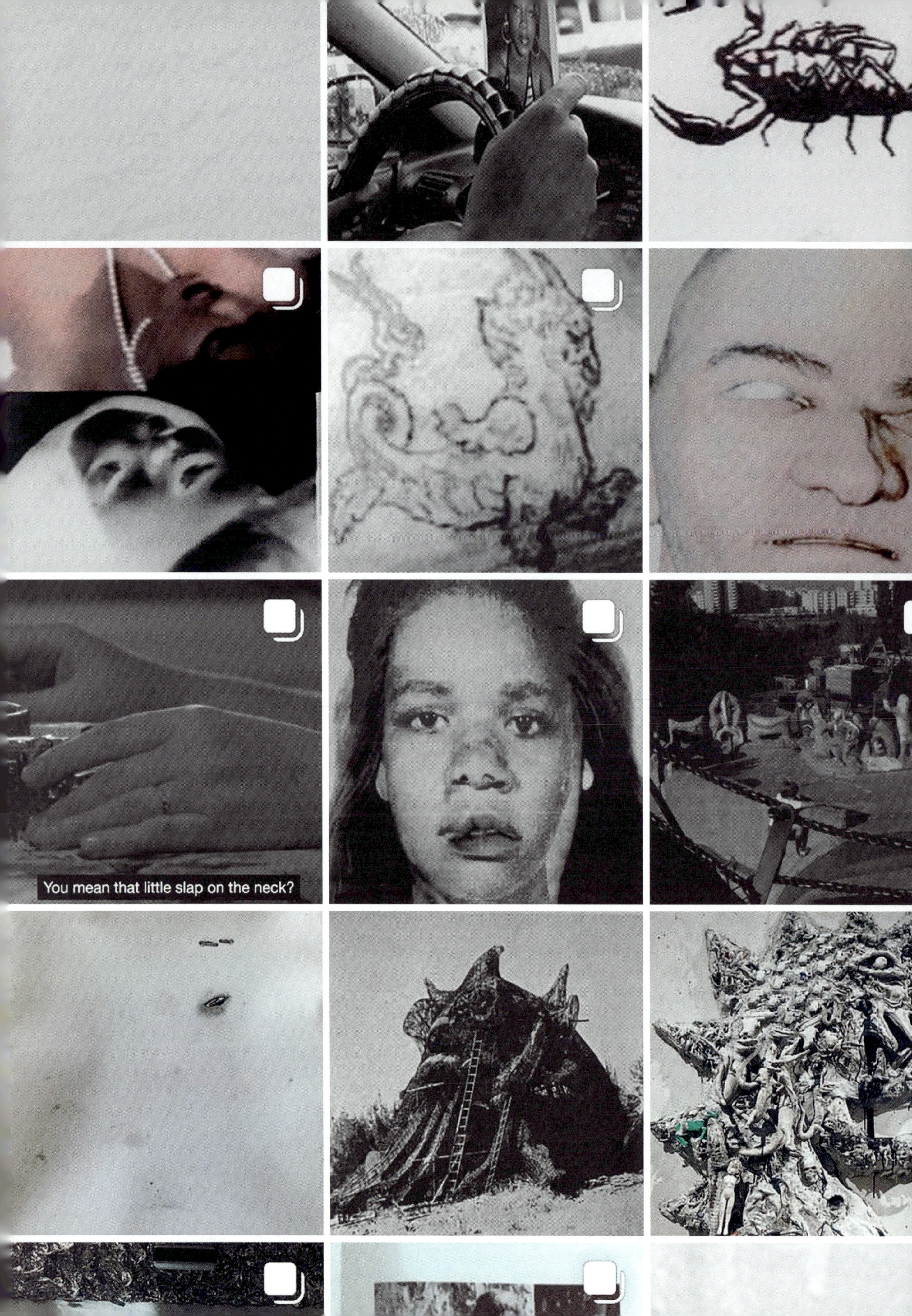
You mean that little slap on the neck?

"Everything that is sweet but can soon be rotten"

Melancholy, Rest, Disquietude

Portia Malatjie

A mood of resignation looms over Orupabo's recent practice. It is a sentiment I share as ecological grief, genocide, war, anti-abortion, and anti-LGBTQI+ laws are passed in a decade where things are meant to be progressing towards full liberation and not regressing astonishingly towards eras where we did not possess the literature, language, tolerance, and justice that we have cultivated in the past few centuries. "This is so Octavia Butler," Orupabo proclaims during our Zoom call.[1] "She was telling us so many years before." We continue to exchange anecdotes of how we feel the world is disintegrating, how humanity is crumbling (while being aware of the colonial politics of humanity), and I begin to wonder if, in my late thirties, I am prematurely enacting the stereotypical "everything is awful" mentality I am meant to have in my old age. On careful examination, I conclude that I am not, and that, as Orupabo portrays in her work, things are surreal at best, and feel apocalyptic most of the time.

This forlorn trope sits comfortably in Orupabo's oeuvre, where she has in the past not allowed discomfort to remain on the margins of her practice but used it as a confrontational aesthetic mechanism. Her practice has continued to work in the same vein as previous works, delving into archival content, distorting the human figure through collage, and working with ideas of grief, rest, concealment and revelation, and the bastardization of all that is meant to be pure and righteous.

It's all fun and games until...

There is a recent trend on social media that asks women if they would rather be stuck in the woods with a bear or with a man (assumed to be a cis-gender heterosexual man). The purpose of the query is to ascertain how safe women feel in society and how vulnerable they feel to violence and assault. An alarming number of women have indicated that they would rather be stuck in the woods with a bear than a man, stating a belief that they are more likely to make it out of the woods unscathed in the presence of a bear. Unable to see the irony of their comments, men have responded by arguing the improbability of encountering a bear in everyday life and that statistics showing that women are more often attacked by men than by bears have an unbalanced frame of reference. Despite the debate that has ensued, the matter of how unsafe women feel in society stands.

What is interesting in Frida Orupabo's sculpture *Jumpy Fits and Facial Tics* (2024) [p. 119] is the juxtapositioning of men and bears. Orupabo, like many of us, grew up coddled by teddy bears, our inanimate and favorite friends who offered companionship and comfort during childhood. But, for Orupabo, the bear also bore more sinister

1 Frida Orupabo, personal communication, 2024.

connotations that are more "real life" than the horrific inanimate teddy bears that come alive to haunt and torment while undermining the refuge that teddy bears offer in (not so critically acclaimed) films such as *The Pit* (1981) and *Imaginary* (2024). Without the startle of the activated lifeless objects, Orupabo's childhood was riddled with warnings of the bear, which in actuality were warnings to be careful of men.[2] Young girls, she recounts, were told stories of the antagonistic and frightening bear (that is, man), which, for Orupabo, was often covertly racialized in a society where young Black girls are frequently oversexualized at a very young age. She links the bear to how desire is often perversely racialized. This leads Orupabo to assert: "I love the bear. But I also fear the bear."[3] Orupabo's *Jumpy Fits and Facial Tics* reveals this fear. Its dark, somber aesthetic does not elicit the comfort of teddy bears, nor the majesty of bears in a forest. It's burnt-like feel repels instead of attracting. Its mood falls neatly into the artist's fascination with and commitment to making the viewer uncomfortable in their viewing process.

The contradiction of the love-fear relationship that bears incite (or the joy-horror that we often derive from watching horror movies, a favorite genre of Orupabo's) appears all too readily, eagerly, and shockingly in children's cartoons, a motif that Orupabo has woven into her work throughout her career. Today, social media is riddled with scenes from children's cartoons that portray sexual innuendo such as arousal, ejaculation, masturbation, oral sex, and, sometimes more ominously, sexual harassment, all for the sake of humor. This once led a close friend to ask, "What were we watching?" and journalist and reporter Elijah C. Watson to proclaim, "Shit gets so crazy out there in the wild west of TV that not even children's programming is safe from the dirty mind of an adult illustrator."[4] While arguments have been made that we were too young to understand the nature of the content,[5] writer Baemisaal argues that "we know that by visual stimuli and exposure we can inject certain ideas and perceptions in the brain from a very young age."[6] Aside from the overtly sexual nature of the cartoons, there was an excessive "sexualization and objectification of women," thus molding children to perceive gender and sexuality in a problematic way from a very young age.[7]

In *The Adventures of the Black Girl in Her Search for God I* (2022) [p. 67] the bunny from *Santa and the Ice Cream Bunny*—a live action 1982 family Christmas movie—appears alongside, among other things, a pair of panties, internal organs, and a high-heeled boot. The innocent imagery of the bunny celebrating a joyous time of the year is corrupted by that of the underwear, an image that conjures up scenes of sexual assault [fig. 1]. Additionally, Porky from the *Porky the Pig's* 1989 Volume 9 episode—while itself not sexualized in nature—finds itself in the gridded company of an open wound, a gaping mouth whose sexual connotation cannot be ignored, colonial and medical archival images, and the term "Dirty Dirt" in the work *Cloud of Confusion* (2024) [pp. 68–69]. Orupabo's insistent inclusion of cartoons that sit appositionally to sexualized and colonial imagery continue to shake our comfort levels while simultaneously showing the tarnished nature of the seemingly pure experiences from our childhoods. Through this offering, she conveys that "everything that is sweet ... can soon be rotten."[8]

Orupabo's art of concealment and revelation, often of sexual conduct and images, runs throughout her practice. *Trauma Catches Up* (2024) [pp. 95–99] sees her playing with ideas of desire and desirability, bringing a different spin on bell hooks's notion of "eating the other" and the cultural and racial consumerism of otherness.[9] *Trauma Catches Up* presents a more urgent, unconcealed

2 Ibid.
3 Ibid.
4 https://www.complex.com/pop-culture/a/elijah-watson/creepiest-sexual-innuendo-moments-in-kids-cartoons (accessed July 3, 2024).
5 Carolyn Ross (cited in Baemisaal, 2020) asks, "If kids don't understand it, how can they be affected by it?"
6 Baemisaal, "Sexual Innuendos in Children's Cartoons: in depth analysis," in *Medium* (2020), https://medium.com/@baemisaalbybae/sexual-innuendos-in-childrens-cartoons-in-depth-analysis-f0138333719f (accessed July 5, 2024).
7 Mariene Mackie cited in Baemisaal (2020).
8 Orupabo, personal communication, 2024.
9 hooks (1992; 310)

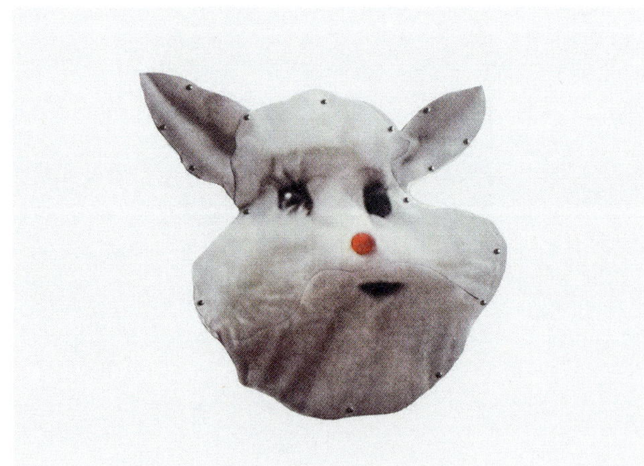

Fig. 1

(and perhaps unconcealable) hunger that emerges, a cannibalistic eating of another. The black-and-white cube sculpture portrays an extract of an image, thus refusing us the immediacy and convenience of completion. What we glean is an image of a gaping mouth, superimposed on that of a woman's torso, with a hand whose source lies outside of the frame firmly clasping the breast. The sculpture resembles a dice, referring to ideas of play and playfulness, despite the harrowing images plastered all over its sides. The recurring gaping mouth alongside the grabbed bosom alludes to an act of consuming the flesh of someone else. Basking in the realm of ambiguity, the scene makes one uneasy, leading one to question whether the actions are of a consensual, passionate, sexual encounter, or of an assault in progress. The representation of sex in Orupabo's practice—often through images borrowed from old-school pin-up magazines—reveals a dark side of desire, which, if not checked, could be the thing of nightmares.

The positioning of *Trauma Catches Up* as an object intended to be viewed from the floor recalls Orupabo's recurring challenging propositions of how to view her works. From putting two-dimensional images on a flat surface, thus refusing a holistic view of works and instead forcing us to view works in parts, to placing TV monitors on the floor at an uncomfortable and sometimes inaccessible angle, Orupabo has always found ways of complicating our viewing process, instead expecting a more active (sometimes labored) engagement. Orupabo, however, does not allow discomfort to remain on the fringes of her practice. She deploys it as a meaningful and generative tool, daring us to exit complacency and soak in the discomfort she presents, whether it is the positioning of two black box television screens on the gallery floor, thus forcing us to either bend over or watch the video diptych *Hand, Bag, Girl* (2022) [fig. 2] from an awkward angle, or the deciphering of the meaning on screen in the video *The Best Kind of Beginning Any Baby Can Have* (2022) [fig. 3]. The latter, a graphic triptych, presents the image of a baby after birth, umbilical cord still attached, another taken from colonial medical archives of a finger penetrating a woman's genitals, seemingly (and yet ambiguously) by a doctor in the process of labor, and a third of a well-manicured Black woman wearing a half-smile, looking attentively, yet uncomfortably, at the activities on the other two screens.

Concealment and revelation continue in Orupabo's use of the curtain, acting more practically in earlier exhibitions, covering a wall whose aesthetics did not appeal to the artist, or darkening a gallery by forbidding the sun's rays from encroaching on it. Sometimes it acts as a mechanism through which one walks to encounter the actual artwork. The theatricality of the curtain elicits feelings of excitement as one can only speculate about the contents of what is concealed. The curtain is intentionally instrumentalized as an object of art whose aesthetics advance a narrative in *Them* (2024) [pp. 120–124] and *Her* (2024) [pp. 125–128], two large-scale images printed on curtains. *Them* is a black-and-white reproduction of a woman and a man kissing, with the man's hand on the woman's breast, and *Her* is a close-up of a woman's face with a green filter washing over it. Despite this revelation of the images—through placing them on the exterior of the curtains instead of using the curtain as a device of concealment—the obviousness of the content begins to crumble on closer inspection. Between the folds of the black-and-white image is a concealed image of a reclining woman touching her genitals. What at first glance appears to be a sweet moment between two people, is soon disrupted as the screenshot from a vintage pornographic film reveals illicit moments. This highly sexual image sits opposite a

Fig. 1 **Detail from *The Adventures of the Black Girl in Her Search for God I*, 2022, collage with paper pins, cotton, paper, installation dimensions variable**
Fig. 2 Left ***Girl*, 2022, digital video, duration 9 min. 56 sec.;**
Right ***Hand, Bag*, 2022, digital video, duration 10 min. 20 sec.**
Fig. 3 ***The Best Kind of Beginning Any Baby Can Have*, 2022, digital video, sound, duration 10 min.**

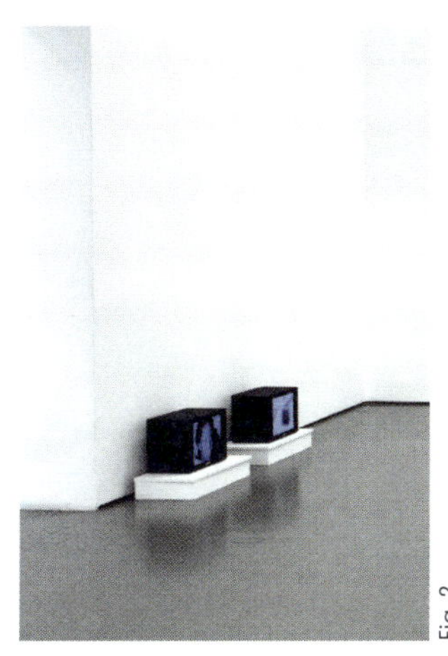

Fig. 2

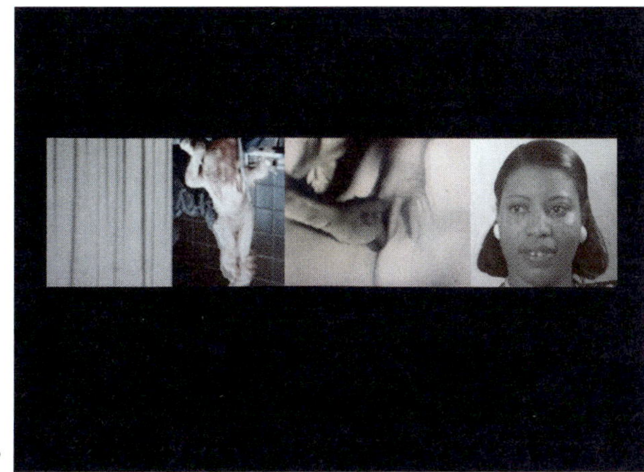

Fig. 3

woman's face pristinely captured in a photographic studio, a 1920s portrait from a US archive. Much like the cartoons of our childhood that are emblematic of innocence, there is a disruption to the unassuming quality of innocence in the studio photograph in its encounter with the illicitness of *Them* that ultimately corrupts it.

Restful disquietude

Orupabo has proclaimed her love of women's bodies, expressing her desire to always find innovative ways of representing them. The two large-scale collages ***Big Girl I*** **(2024)** [pp. 35–36] and ***Big Girl II*** **(2024)** [pp. 39–40] continue this experimentation, landing on a kind of cartoonification of the female body, not as a form of ridicule, but in a quest to push its boundaries and explore its endless possibilities. She plays around with the scale of the works, enlarging them to surpass the size of the average human form. Standing at over three meters tall, the stoic Black women tower over the viewer, imposing their presence and insisting that they be recognized. Making commentary on the invisibility of women, and their inability to be heard unless they shout, to be seen unless they perform something spectacular, Orupabo makes space for these two women who have given themselves permission to unashamedly and unapologetically take up space. She comments on the invisibilized efforts and labors of Black women, whose actions are perpetually erased, and, in this one gesture, insists on aggrandizing Black womanhood, thus demanding visibility and refusing erasure.

Orupabo wishes to find ways of representing Black women's bodies without objectifying them, while simultaneously wanting to "reveal all parts of them," even those parts that may land to a felonious viewer as a site of deviant consumption.[10] Nonetheless, she persists, opting to utilize strategies of concealment and revelation, veiling and unveiling. In *Big Girl II* one of the woman's breasts is surreptitiously concealed with her long hair—assumedly to protect it from objectification—only for the other breast to remain bare, exposed to the viewer. Orupabo lingers in this ambiguity, asking: "Can you show the female body without objectifying it?", sometimes opting to hide parts of it with hair, bags, and other objects when she is unsure how much she wishes to reveal.

While not a continuation of her recurring reference to Western art histories, I cannot help but think of Orupabo's wayward nods to modernism in *Big Girl II*, whose lower legs escape from the wall onto the floor. This conjures images of the reclining figure trope, a genre Orupabo has referenced in works such as ***Mother and Child I*** **(2020)** [fig. 4] and ***Reclining Woman II*** **(2022)** [fig. 5].[11] In the past, her reclining figure has landed as a bastardization, critique, and perverse admiration of the Western genre, a woeful and willful disruption of the visual lexicon from whence it emerged. Her perpetual recourse to the reclining figure—at times as the reclining nude—taps into her interest in ideas of rest.

By borrowing from Renaissance and modernist works, she enmeshes images of reclining white nudes with images of Black women from colonial archives. Sometimes, she weaves together scenes of white nudes in different states of leisure with harrowing footage of Black bodies in states of anguish. By design, the white art-historical nude invites feelings of restfulness. Its reclining stance mimics that of a body in leisure or at rest, not burdened by the need of activity. It is intended to put the largely white male viewer at ease due to its poise and tranquility, and is the epitome of the art of doing nothing. However, due to the expectations already put on it to perform the role of aesthetically

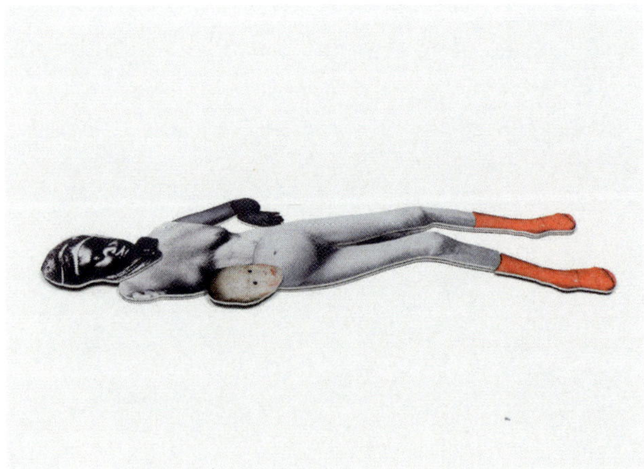

Fig. 4

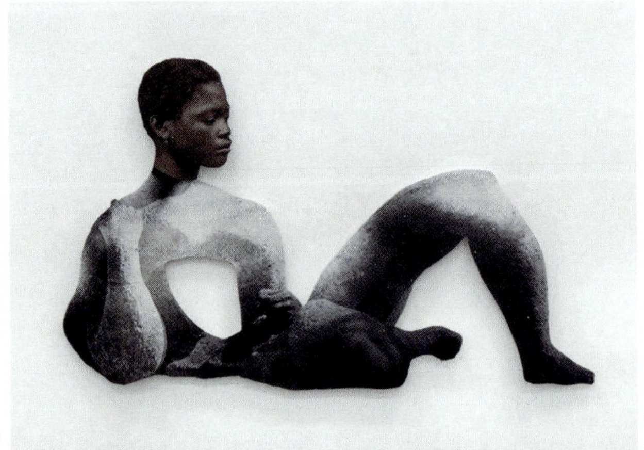

Fig. 5

beautiful object, and the subject of the work having the obligation to epitomize feminine beauty, the nude is an object always already at work, perpetually fulfilling multiple labored roles. By virtue of being instrumentalized and needing to serve a particular purpose and perform its duty as an art object, we come to realize that the reclining nude is never at rest. Orupabo often amalgamates this un-resting and unrestful reclining nude with images of Black people from colonial archives. By tapping into these colonial repositories where images of Black people go to die, Orupabo renders the colonial archive as a graveyard of the trapped souls of the Black people portrayed in the images. But, instead of performing the role of quietude where the dead are laid to rest, these repositories are sites of continued violence and unending subjugation. Orupabo's employment of these images acts as an animation of that which has been refused peaceful rest anyway—and instead of burying the unrest in these repositories, she puts their state of zombification on display, refusing the concealment of the horrors their subjects have had to endure by being enslaved in perpetuity. What we are reminded of in Orupabo's presentation of rest is that rest is never restful, especially when it intersects with race and with gender.

Orupabo's interference with the tranquility of the nude body that is meant to be resting—such as the accumulation of different body parts from different images, thus creating a Frankensteinian figure in *Mother and Child I*, for instance—is an extrapolation and exaggeration of a prevailing fallacy. The three collages ***Woman with Hand***, ***Woman with Dress***, and ***Woman with Dog II*** (all from 2024) [pp. 58–64] are an amalgamation of a woman laying down (perhaps ready for slumber), with a dog and other objects appearing restful. The angelic, inviting, and Eros-like imagery of the three figures begins to crumble the closer you come to them and the more you look—hints that there's something amiss are revealed in moments such as when the *Olympia*-like grope emerges from the shadows between her thighs. *Resting Head* (2020) [fig. 6] is a collage of a Black person's head resting on a pair of white hands where she flirts with the suggestion that this is what is possible when Black bodies are no longer trapped in a cyclical state of unrest and are, finally, allowed to have a moment of repose. Instead of complete and unconditional rest, it is just the head that is resting, not the whole body. In the politics of rest, history has always seen Black bodies as facilitators and never recipients of rest, and in *Resting Head* there is an uncomfortable suggestion that whiteness is facilitating and permitting Black people's rest.

Orupabo's recent work offers cause for pause and an invitation to bask in its affective ambiance. While there is an allusion to silence, there is an undeniable loudness precipitated by the themes and imagery of horror, violence, colonialism, hypersexualization, corrupted innocence, racism, sexism, domination, and erasure. There is loudness in the forlorn and melancholic mood. What might present as restful, serene, silent, may in fact be resignation due to the current state of the world that has resulted in endless iterations of unrest and distress. The silence in Orupabo is not serene, but rather pregnant with melancholy. Orupabo invites us to percolate in this melancholic state, compelling us to sit with the apocalyptic aura and reality prophesized by Octavia Butler decades ago.

10 Orupabo, personal communication, May 2024.
11 Portia Malatjie, "Openings: Frida Orupabo," in *Artforum* (2023): 186.

Fig. 4 *Mother and Child I*, 2020, primed anodized aluminum with digital print, velour foil, 8 pieces, 160 × 54 × 1.5 cm
Fig. 5 *Reclining Woman II*, 2022, collage with paper pins, 108 × 180 cm
Fig. 6 *Resting Head*, 2020, collage with paper pins, 27.5 × 39.5 cm (52.5 × 68 cm framed)

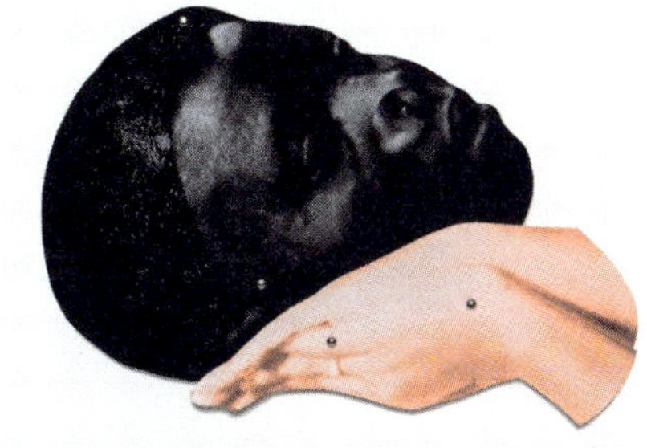

Fig. 6

Transgressive Toying

Mai Takawira and Nina Cramer
of G/HOSTING

"Who dares to enter the hallowed terrain of the European public record? The collection, the archive, the research library, all those repositories of collective memory that preserve artefacts attesting to the fact that we were and are here, on this planet earth. For me this is a battlefield. Past and present shadowboxing a mutual enemy: Silence, forgetting, amnesia."
Temi Odumosu

"I have seen a million pictures of my face and still I have no idea."
Elaine Kahn

We are haunted by a ghostly black presence in the Nordics. Silenced voices, captive bodies, crushed wills and unrealized dreams that refuse to let go of us, that we refuse to let go of.

Our entry point into the colonial archive is our research into the understudied visual and material culture related to the colonial history of Denmark-Norway. This colonial history includes, but is not limited to, Denmark-Norway's extensive participation in transatlantic enslavement, the administration of slave forts on the west coast of Africa and the plantation economy of the former Danish West Indies (today, the US Virgin Islands) as part of the larger Dano-Norwegian empire.[1] Our embodied presence in Denmark has a dis/connected relationship to this history.[2] We are not descendants of the people enslaved by Denmark-Norway. Instead, our diasporic existence results from more recent migration flows from the African continent. Yet we co-exist with the material legacies of Denmark-Norway's colonial history, including its ongoing effects on Nordic cultural logics and in the visual field.

When Frida Orupabo narrates the beginnings of her artistic practice, she describes creating collages out of her family's photographs. Constructing an alternative family photo album, Orupabo worked through the absence of her Nigerian father while growing up in white majority Norwegian society. Collage for Orupabo entails the removal of something, the addition of something else, perhaps in an approximation, but never the attainment, of resolution into wholeness. Later, Orupabo replaced her family photographs with often anonymized imagery of black people past and present, combing digitized colonial archives, auction sites, and the internet at large for imagery to repurpose in her artworks.

In our curatorial and editorial work as G/HOSTING, we question the circulation of colonial

* In this text, we use the lowercase spelling of "black" inspired by Afro-Nordic feminist scholar Oda-Kange Midtvåge Diallo who writes: "I do not capitalize black to come closer to a translation of 'svart', and to make room for the multitudes of blackness in the Norwegian context, that are both removed from and inspired by blackness elsewhere." Oda-Kange Midtvåge Diallo, *Joining in black study*, 2023, PhD thesis, Norwegian University of Science and Technology.

1 The political union Denmark-Norway existed in the years 1536–1814.
2 See also Marronage and Diaspora of Critical Nomads, *Vi vil mere end at overleve: Opgør med en antisort verden* (Copenhagen, 2020).

imagery and other objectifying images of people photographed under duress, in and by Nordic institutions. Orupabo's work and exhibitions challenge some of these assumptions. The excisions, de- and recontextualizations that Orupabo performs in her collages pose a challenge as our usual approaches—searching for historical context, names, provenance—come up short. Instead, Orupabo's interest lies in the juxtaposition and "affective proximity" between images rather than where the images stem from.[3] She seeks to dislodge the figures from the colonial archive, away from easily recognizable surroundings. She explores what the images can mean for us today, rather than in their original contexts and refuses to succumb to the logics of the colonial archive or collection.[4]

On the occasion of Orupabo's exhibition ***On Lies, Secrets and Silence***, we look at representations of play, childhood, caregiving, and mothering in her work. Our discussion is based on critiques of antiblackness in the Nordic region and its cultural and visual terrains. The motif of caregiving between woman and child is a recurring one in Orupabo's practice. In some works, the woman and child motif bears a clear resemblance to (exclusionary, white) Christian iconography. Others represent gestation and childbirth. Still others are concerned with the question of how, as a black parent, to prepare your children to enter the world.

Play

In the prints ***Clover I*** [p. 80] and ***Clover II*** [p. 81] that feature in this exhibition, a translucent veneer like frosted glass is layered over a photographic image of a woman—a still from the horror blaxploitation film *Abby* (1974) in which the formerly pious titular character becomes possessed by a demon of sexuality. Cut out of this layer is a three-leaf clover, recalling the shape of clubs, one of the four suits into which a deck of French-suited playing cards is categorized. Through this clover-shaped puncture, a part of the image below is revealed in full color. Abby wears a pained expression, a frothy white substance trailing from her mouth in the midst of possession. The second print is a closer crop than the first, but with the clover kept in the same dimensions, a different part of Abby's face is framed.

Motifs suggestive of playing cards turn up in several of Orupabo's prints, collages, and sculptures. In the metal sculpture ***On My Hands and Knees*** (2024) [fig. 1] a grainy close-up image of a face is cut into the same graphic shape of a clover. In ***Untitled*** (2019) [fig. 2], the symbol for spades, the other black suit, appears behind an anonymous face.[5] The two are secured to each other with four metal rivets. Protruding from this constellation are crossbones. This amalgamation suggests a symbol of death or danger, and a warning sign.

In the photogravure ***Picnic*** (2024) [fig. 3], a playing card appears at an oblique angle among an implausible assortment of elements. The photogravure's colors are inverted, like a photographic negative, the scene rendered in black, white, and the green of night-vision, chosen for that purpose because it is the color that provides the greatest contrast in low-light conditions for human vision to see through darkness. This near-neon green saturates a voluminous pillow that props up the disembodied head of a black woman. Next to them is an absurd juxtaposition of a plush toy rabbit wedged inside a head of cabbage that the artist found and screenshotted on eBay. The lone playing card in the bottom right of the image is also a screenshot from eBay, taken from a deck of cards with colonial photographs, featuring abstracted representations of black people. These disparate elements are laid

3 Paola Malavassi, "Arthur Jafa: Face It: The 'Affective Proximity' of Imagery" (2020), https://flash--art.com/article/arthur-jafa-face-it-the-affective-proximity-of-imagery/.

4 Our thinking on de- and recontextualization is informed by Robin Coste Lewis, *Voyage of the Sable Venus* (New York: Alfred A. Knopf, 2015).

5 The conjunction of the spades symbol and the black body in such works recalls David Hammons's recurring use of the spades symbol.

Fig. 1 ***On My Hands and Knees***, 2024, CMYK print on anodized aluminum, stainless steel, 50 × 41 × 30 cm
Fig. 2 Detail from *the mouth and the truth*, 2019, collage with paper pins, installation dimensions variable
Fig. 3 ***Picnic***, 2024, photogravure printed on four sheets of Somerset 410 gsm, 140.5 × 199.5 cm

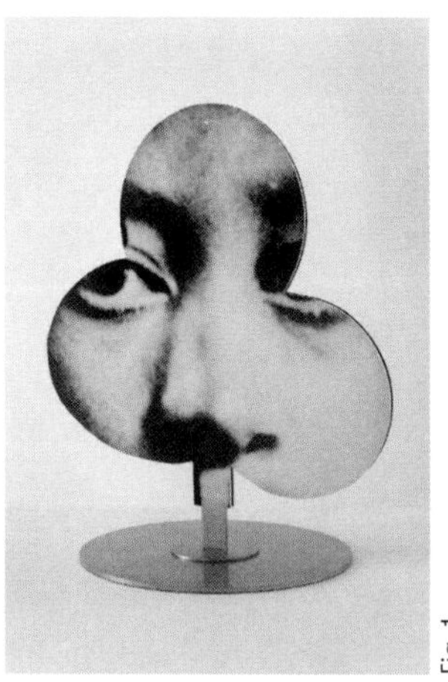

Fig. 1

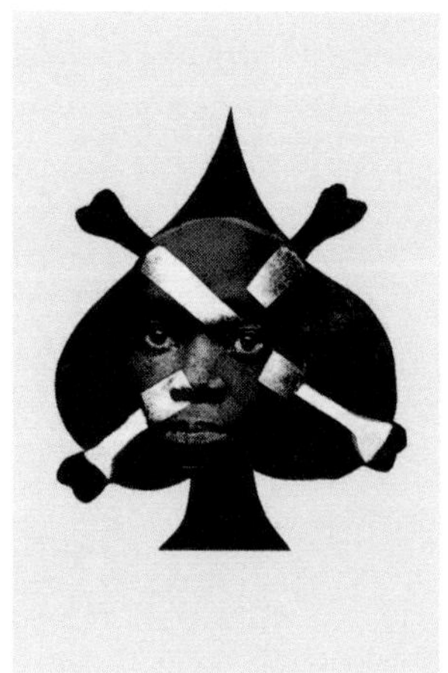

Fig. 2

out on the titular picnic blanket, a reference to lynchings in the United States where gratuitous antiblack terror functioned as an enjoyable pastime for white picnickers who cut off body parts of their victims as keepsakes. This playing card, and the playing card motifs in the aforementioned works, point toward antiblack racism's history as a pleasurable, playful mode of white supremacy.

In the sculpture *Trauma Catches Up* (2024) [pp. 95–99], circular images puncture blurry background imagery in which hands close around a neck. None of the motifs are revealed in their totality. The circles show glimpses of motifs including darkened wounds and orifices—some held open by firm fingers—an excerpt from the book *Yurugu: An African-Centered Critique of European Cultural Thought and Behavior* (1994) and a close-up of natural hair. The circles accumulate like dots on the square faces of six-sided dice. In Orupabo's hands, the small, haptic object of the die is transformed into a sculpture of pornotropes;[6] the overlapping processes of degradation caused by the interplay between antiblack violence, hypersexualization, and the scopic field. The die, as an implement in a game, connotes chance, gratuitousness, a limited but random set of possible outcomes.

These allusions to dice and card games in Orupabo's work bring to mind Toni Morrison's landmark book *Playing in the Dark* (1992), which demonstrates the way cultural products utilize blackness as an open playing field for the white cultural imagination. Morrison examines the normalized "metaphors; summonings; rhetorical gestures of triumph, despair, and closure dependent on the acceptance of the associative language of dread and love that accompanies blackness" in US literary history.[7] Yet her perspective is relevant here, in the study of contemporary Afro-Nordic visual art, as well. In Morrison's account, attraction to and repulsion from blackness is present not only in the United States, but also across postcolonial European cultures as a way of maintaining white cultural hegemony.[8] Blackness becomes "both a way of talking about and a way of policing matters of class, sexual license, and repression, formations and exercises of power, and meditations on ethics and accountability."[9] The metaphorical use of blackness in the white cultural imagination Morrison traces functions much like playing cards or dice whose meanings and values can change at the player's will, depending on the game.

Childhood

A grid of twelve black-and-white images form a monumental unit in Orupabo's work *Cloud of Confusion* (2024) [pp. 68–69]. The images are close-ups of mostly dark skinned bodies, naked dark skin and an open wound, alongside a fearful Disney animated pig, fur enveloping a groin, a ceramic four-legged animal, and a gritty reproduction of the words "Dirty Dirt" scrawled on a white hoodie.[10] Other motifs are more indefinable because, although the work is not a collage, Orupabo has cropped the images in a way that makes several of them difficult to decode. Some appear downright abstract. As is usual in Orupabo's practice, the original images she has dissected are not revealed. But unlike in her collages, the excerpted images are not shaped into a new body. Rather it is up to the viewer to make the connections between the disparate images, to work through the de-formation.

For us, this work sets in motion a number of dis- and counteridentifications and interpretations as the "historical self" erupts into the here and now.[11] That part of our subjectivity, which is conveniently hidden away but emerges when a certain event, encounter, or exchange reminds us that some people

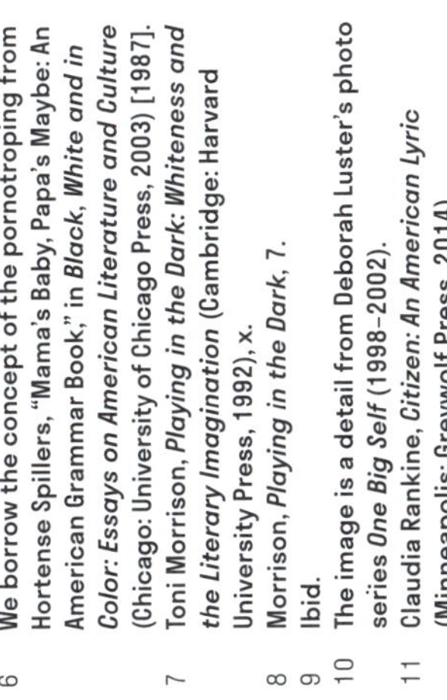

6 We borrow the concept of the pornotroping from Hortense Spillers, "Mama's Baby, Papa's Maybe: An American Grammar Book," in *Black, White and in Color: Essays on American Literature and Culture* (Chicago: University of Chicago Press, 2003) [1987].

7 Toni Morrison, *Playing in the Dark: Whiteness and the Literary Imagination* (Cambridge: Harvard University Press, 1992), x.

8 Morrison, *Playing in the Dark*, 7.

9 Ibid.

10 The image is a detail from Deborah Luster's photo series *One Big Self* (1998–2002).

11 Claudia Rankine, *Citizen: An American Lyric* (Minneapolis: Greywolf Press, 2014).

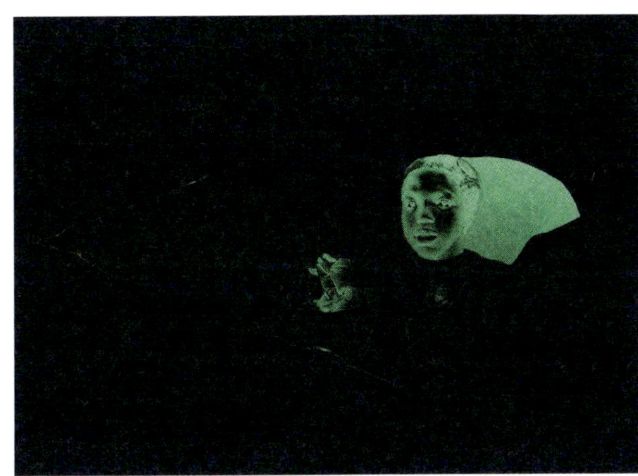

Fig. 3

can trace their ancestral origins back to the enslaved and/or colonized, while others only trace them back to the colonial and slaveholding powers. Some of us can trace our ancestry in both directions.

As mixed-black women who have grown up with Nordic culture, *Cloud of Confusion* put us into painful contact with inherited colonial language and imagery. The work reminds us of a Danish children's song that continues to live a quietly disturbing life in *De små synger* (1948), one of the most canonized Danish children's books, including its latest reprinting in 2018. *Inger Goes to School* (1947) is about the "vain" girl Inger, who "naughtily" wears her lavender blue Sunday dress to school.[12] In the fourth verse, she suffers the consequences:

> Four boys are playing
> fighting with a n****.
> Inger takes a sideways view,
> looks at the lavender blue.
>
> See how they throw dirt about!
> Alas, a mighty splash
> through the air does spew,
> hitting the lavender blue.[13]

It is still unclear to us what "playing/ fighting with a n****" really means, whether this is a real person of African descent, or are we dealing with a "game" where someone has to be the n**** (as in everyone against the n****) or whether it is because the person is a n**** that they have to be covered in mud, and whether this ultimately helps to confirm their position as n****? But the moral of the song is unmistakable: Inger gets dirty just like the n**** is "dirty," and her shameful behavior manifests itself externally, through the mud on her dress, because like the n**** she is "justly" punished.

Orupabo's grid of images opens up a festering historical wound that is still open in the Nordic colonial reality, where blackness continues to be met with equal parts fascination and fear. Black people appear in Danish-Norwegian art and cultural history as foils, as representations of the sides of white subjects they wish to disavow. Black people are tropes, as Morrison describes, through which white subjects understand themselves in the disruption of cultural norms and transgression of taboos. The shameful, aggressive, sexual, the "dirty dirt".

As for Orupabo, who began her practice by cutting up her own family albums and reassembling them, one gets the feeling that *Cloud of Confusion* also recalls or re-enacts the child's exploration of the world, making meaning out of the images and words she encounters and seeking to understand their causality. This feeling is reinforced through the comic book reference, which, like *Inger Goes to School*, traces the presence of racial violence in the child's world.

Critical race studies scholar Ahrong Yang's research on children's racialized becoming in race-evasive Nordic culture notes how ideas about child innocence and white innocence coalesce.[14] "[T]he value of a child's innocence depends on their capacity to be protected, which does not benefit children equally," Yang writes. While innocence sticks to white Nordic bodies, it is still rarely extended to black Nordic subjects, including black mothers and children who instead become figures of culpability in the national imagination.[15] Within this logic, the black child's innocence will always already be compromised. If antiblack racism is something about which children are expected not to know anything, black children fail to live up to this standard of childhood.

How do black children make sense of the meaningless logic of racism, forced to see and understand themselves through a white gaze? *Cloud*

12 See also Mai Takawira, "Under the White Gaze," in *This is Not Africa*, exh. cat. (Aarhus: ARoS, 2021).
13 Hulda Lükten, ed., *De små synger* (Copenhagen: Høst & Søns Forlag, 1948), 92. Our censorship.
14 Ahrong Yang, "Racism suitable for children? Intersections between child innocence and white innocence," *Children & Society* 38, no. 4 (2024), https://doi.org/10.1111/chso.12797.
15 Jan Therese Mendes, "Disciplining the disobedient Black maternal subject: the assimilatory pedagogies of public suffering and punishment," *Feminist Theory* (2024), https://doi.org/10.1177/14647001231223099.
16 Frantz Fanon, *Black Skin, White Masks*, trans. Charles L. Markmann (New York: Grove Press, 2008).

of Confusion activates and mirrors a disturbing black experience, but it also remains an unfinished puzzle. A collection of pieces that cannot be put together. Recalling Frantz Fanon in *Black Skin, White Masks*: "The black man is a toy in the hands of the white man. So in order to break the vicious circle, he explodes."[16] In this way, the artist's de-formations can be experienced as the incomprehensible, the madness and lack of coherence that determines black existence. How can we create meaning out of the fragments left to us by the colonial powers?

In Orupabo's collages we encounter portrayals of black women resembling paper dolls held together by metal rivets, playthings [pp. 35–40]. The visible de- and recontextualization gives the doll-like portrayals the character of a patchwork, assembling different skin tones and proportions of the body parts. In some places, extra body parts and various objects from the original photographs have crept in. As curator Awa Konaté notes, "the metal pins," in Orupabo's collages, "suggest instability, motion and transformation," but the doll motif is also reminiscent of the role-playing games of young children with their dolls, which contribute to their development of empathy and care.[17]

Toni Morrison's novel *The Bluest Eye*, set in a small town in 1940s America, explores the impact of racism on love, desire, beauty, hatred, and self-hatred. In the novel, we get a glimpse into the secret treasured ritual of the narrator, a little black girl: taking apart the blonde, white, blue-eyed dolls that the adults give her for Christmas. The white doll, the adults assume, is her greatest desire, however she reveals to the reader: "I had only one desire: to dismember it. To see of what it was made, to discover the dearness, to find the beauty, the desirability that had escaped me."[18] Something analogous is at play in Orupabo's dissections, as she works her way through antiblack visual material, processing archival images seeking to understand love and beauty, how to give care where there has been none. In Orupabo's case, body parts are cut out of the original images, leaving the unsettling places they were found behind. The disorientation of the cropped images combined with the women's confrontative gazes leaves us with the impression that we as viewers are encountering icons that transcend time and space, even if just for a moment.

Mothering

In *Love at First Site* (2020) [fig. 4], a woman's gaze meets ours. Her expression is serious, her frown emphasized by the shadows on her face. Excised from a black-and-white photograph, the woman's face is dark skinned with African features, juxtaposed with a pale resting body. Unlike the face, the body appears to be painted, but like the rest of the collage it bears the quality of a black-and-white photocopy. In her arms, the woman holds a baby, also composed of photography and painting, rendered in dark and light body parts. The two figures are fastened together with rivets and elevated by black patterned and white draped fabric that flows into lace. This collage plays with the honorific, the idea of giving black subjects a place in art history, but does not fulfill the expectation because of the awkward way the figures are put together. We wonder, was the artist only able to find images of white resting bodies? Or should the discrepancy between the faces and bodies of the figures emphasize the well-known tropes of art history, the white body enjoying the comfort of rest or sleep opposite the serving black body. There is no eye contact between the woman and the child. The child's face is turned away from hers with its neck turned at an awkward angle. Her facial expression conveys skepticism and worry,

17 Awa Konaté, "Frida Orupabo," in *Deutsche Börse Photography Foundation Prize 2023* (London: The Photographers' Gallery, 2023).

18 Toni Morrison, *The Bluest Eye* (New York: Penguin Random House, 1970).

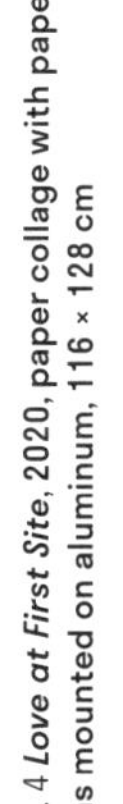

Fig. 4 *Love at First Site*, 2020, paper collage with paper pins mounted on aluminum, 116 × 128 cm

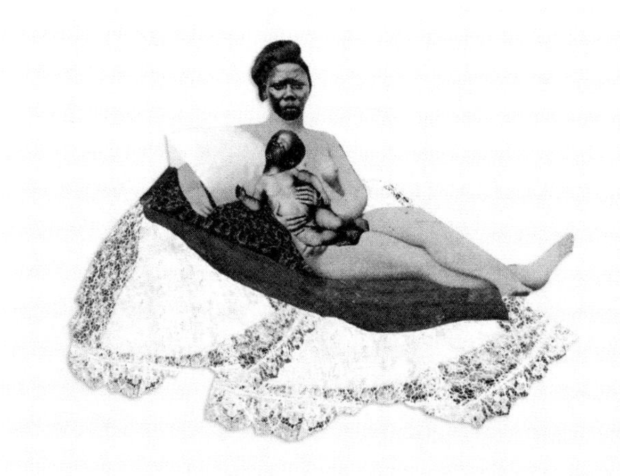

Fig. 4

like someone who needs, but cannot find, rest. The paradox of being at once exhausted and tense.[19] As such the mother-child scene is one of failure, as they both seem out of place, together as well as in their surroundings.

Orupabo's works recall open questions about love, care, and motherhood that black feminists have posed in relation to the colonial archive. Art historian Temi Odumosu writes about the lack of care that characterizes (digitized) colonial photographic archives in Denmark. She does so through an analysis of a photograph of a crying child taken in the former Danish West Indies and currently in the custodianship of the Royal Danish Library.[20] This image was widely distributed in the early twentieth century on postcards with the derogatory caption "A St. Croix Pickney," which Odumosu reads as a reference to the Jim Crow caricature as a dirty child comically impervious to pain in contrast to white children's innocence and need for (white) care. How, Odumosu asks, can we care for this child left unattended in the archive, calling to us from the past?

Another figure in the colonial archive that raises difficult questions about care is the black nanny, a notable presence in Nordic cultural history. The enslaved and later free black nannies in Scandinavian colonies who cared for the children of white families have been represented in literature, painting, and, later, in photography as supports for the white children in their care.[21] The black nanny's labor constitutes coerced caregiving such that, in the words of Saidiya Hartman, "[t]he care extracted from her to tend the white household is taken at the cost of her own. She is the best nanny and the worst mother."[22] This extraction of motherly care from black women can be seen in many other colonial contexts in the Americas, Europe and on the African continent where relationships between black parents and children could be disrupted at the colonizer's whim.

Orupabo's collages create ambivalent affective atmospheres that suggest broken and pieced together lineages and relationships between black children and caregivers. It is as if the pieces could be taken apart and rearranged. As is often the case with Orupabo's works, these figures seem to exist in a continual process of fragmentation and reconnection.

Violent anamnesis

For us, who like Odumosu, hesitate to "enter the hallowed terrain of the European public record," Orupabo's practice seems courageous. She finds her artistic materials by moving through bodies fixed in degrading and coerced positions. She breaks down the images and pieces them together, as in *Trauma Catches Up*, or spreads them out, as in *Cloud of Confusion*. The content of her dis/formations is violent, but her experiments with form are especially disturbing. Bodily integrity is transgressed as black bodies become the surfaces of toys and other domestic objects—clothes hangers, vases, curtains. However, Orupabo reproduces antiblack violence and objectification, with the intention of arriving at something else.

The colonial repression that characterizes the Nordic cultural imaginary makes it possible for many in the white majority to never have to become acquainted with their "historical selves," as the friction this requires has long been eliminated. Monica Miller describes how Nordic colonial repression demands explicit recitation of colonial violence. She exemplifies this using works by Afro-Danish artist Jeannette Ehlers (reproducing the ritual of whipping) and Afro-Swedish artist

19 Here we draw on the idea of tension in colonial photography discussed by Tina Campt, *Listening to Images* (Durham: Duke University Press, 2017).

20 Temi Odumosu, "The Crying Child: On Colonial Archives, Digitization, and Ethics of Care in the Cultural Commons," *Current Anthropology* 61, no. S22 (2020), https://doi.org/10.1086/710062.

21 Temi Odumosu, "Loving in the Colonial Archive: A Short Meditation in Three Parts," *Marronage* 1, 2017. See also Helene Birkeli, "Den svarte 'barnepiken' og rasismens melankoli," *Periskop – Forum for Kunsthistorisk Debat* 25 (2021), https://doi.org/10.7146/periskop.v2021i25.128293 and Ursula Lindqvist, "West Indian women in Danish popular fiction," *African and Black Diaspora: An International Journal* 7, no. 1 (2014), https://doi.org/10.1080/17528631.2013.858919.

22 Saidiya Hartman, "The Belly of the World: A Note on Black Women's Labors," *Souls* 18, no. 1 (2016), DOI: 10.1080/10999949.2016.1162596, 54.

Makode Linde (serving a screaming blackface cake for Swedish politicians). These reproductions of violence are necessary, Miller proposes, for that violence "to be legible and acknowledged, for time to be capable of bending back toward the fullness of [a] shared history."[23]

In G/HOSTING we search for any trace, the smallest clue, that can tell us about the dreams, loving relationships, and inner lives of those whose racial abjection the archive is complicit in cementing, however, Orupabo's search and desire is different. Together, our different positions point toward the variety of Afro-Nordic perspectives and strategies regarding the region's coloniality. We might describe Orupabo's position in relation to the grotesque as formulated by Mikhail Bakhtin:

> To degrade is to bury, to sow and to kill simultaneously, in order to bring forth something more and better. To degrade also means to concern oneself with the lower stratum of the body, the life of the belly and the reproductive organs. Degradation has not only a destructive, negative aspect, but also a regenerating one.[24]

More specifically, Orupabo's work may be commensurate with the black grotesque that takes racialized degradation as its subject:

> As an expressive practice, black grotesquerie infuses the materiality of the black body with the textuality of the art object. Rather than merely signifying excess, dread, or decay black grotesquerie delineates an aesthetic practice of contortion, exaggeration, substitution, inversion, corruption.[25]

The size of Orupabo's works has increased over the course of her career. This is the artist's response to her work being exhibited in institutions with mostly white visitors. With this current exhibition, she says, she wants the works to be so large that the viewer is "eaten up" when they enter the space. In a reversal of the dynamic described by bell hooks as "eating the other," the other eats the viewer.[26] Working with horror and desire, Orupabo promotes an "affective proximity" of disparate images, which, rather than wholeness, creates the disturbance that might be necessary to challenge colonial amnesia. We can glimpse a space where "blackness grasps us even as we seek to grasp it."[27]

23 Monica Miller, "On Having Your Cake and Eating It Too: Black (Diasporic/Nordic) Arts," *Social Text* (2020).
24 Mikhail Bakhtin, *Rabelais and His World*, trans. Hélène Iswolsky (Cambridge: MIT Press, 1968), 21.
25 Aliyyah I Abdur-Rahman, "Black Grotesquerie," *American Literary History* 29, no. 4 (2017): 683.
26 bell hooks, "Eating the Other: Desire and Resistance," in *Black Looks: Race and Representation* (Boston: South End Press, 1992).
27 Tavia Nyong'o, *Afro-fabulations* (New York: NYU Press, 2018), 3.

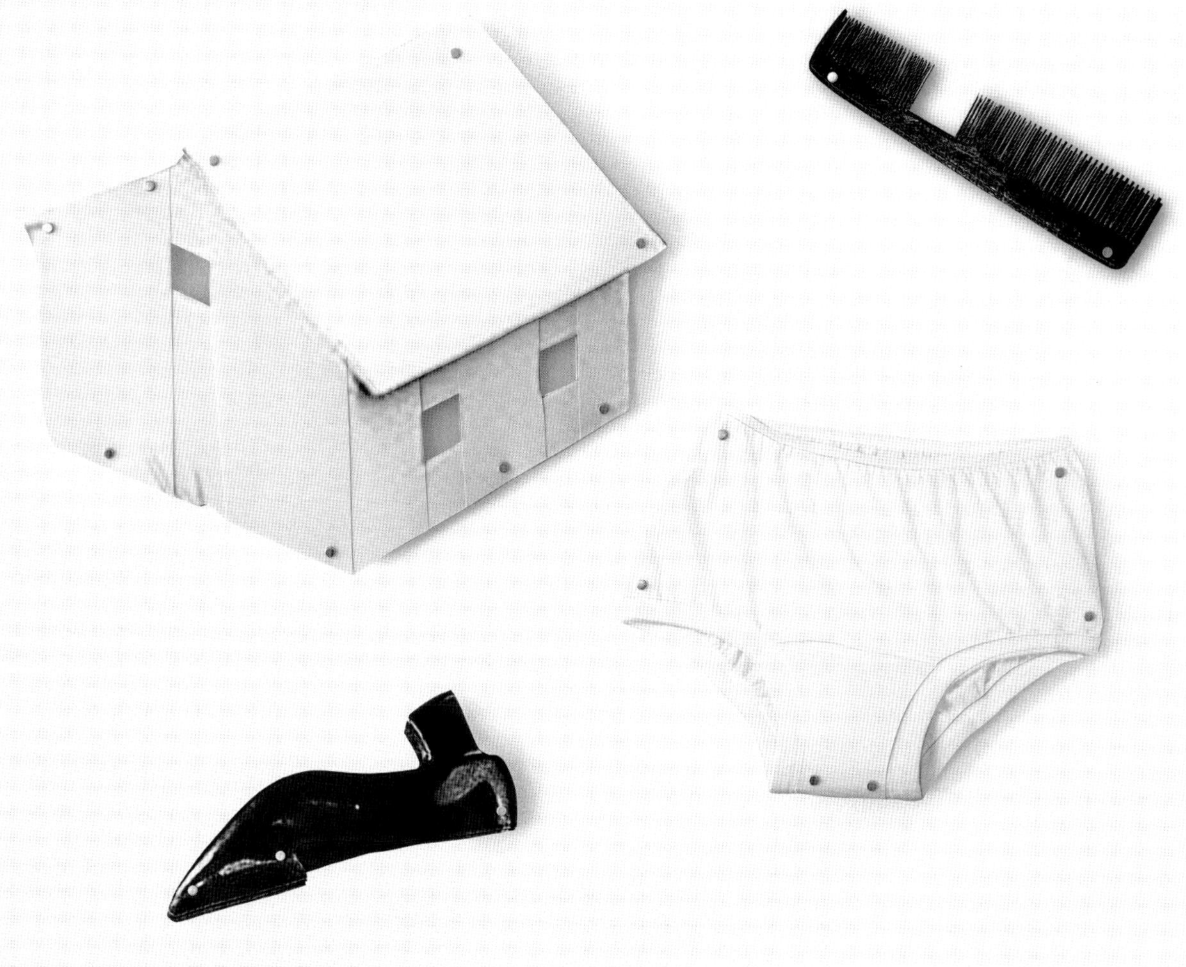

Object I, II, III, IV

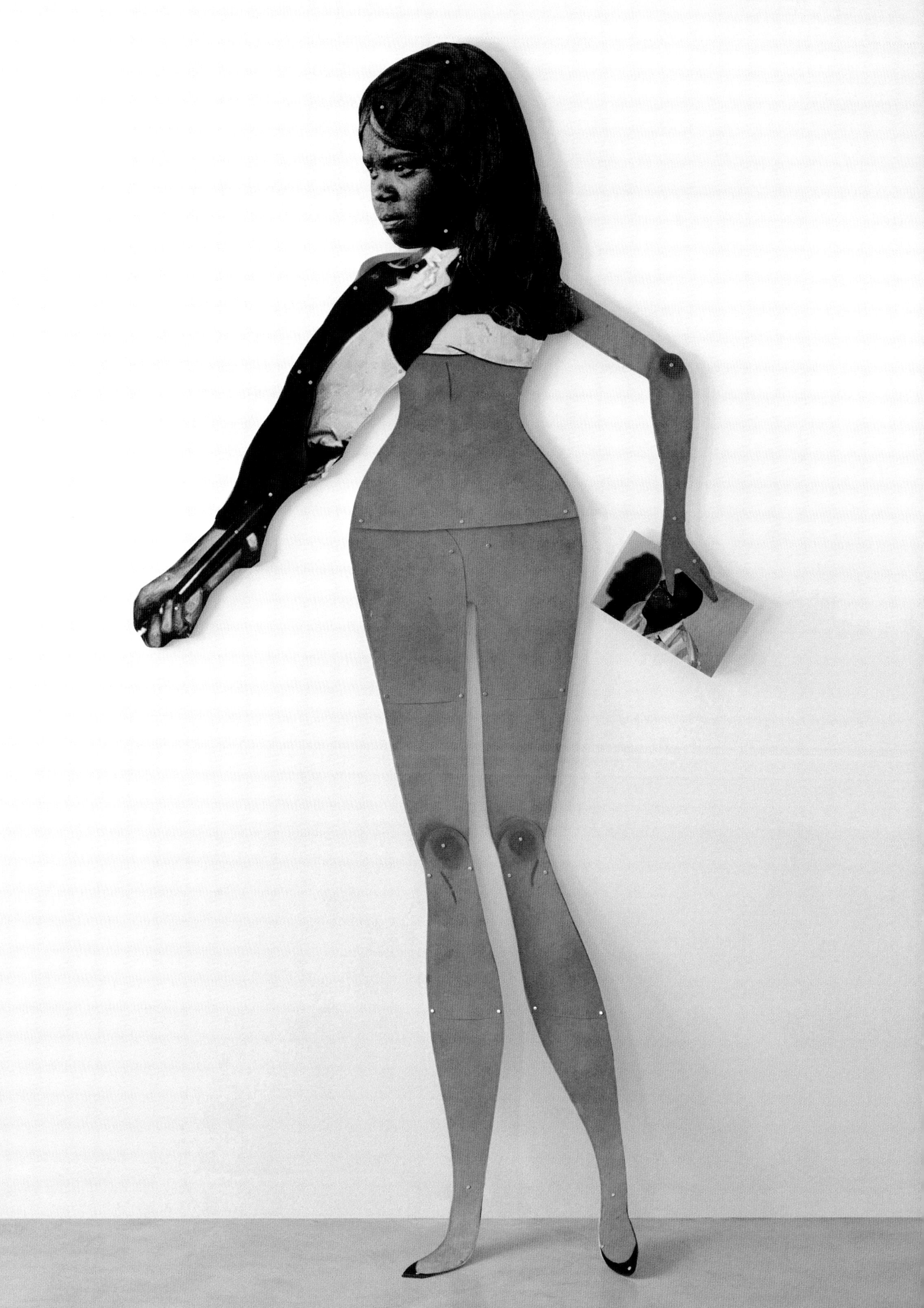

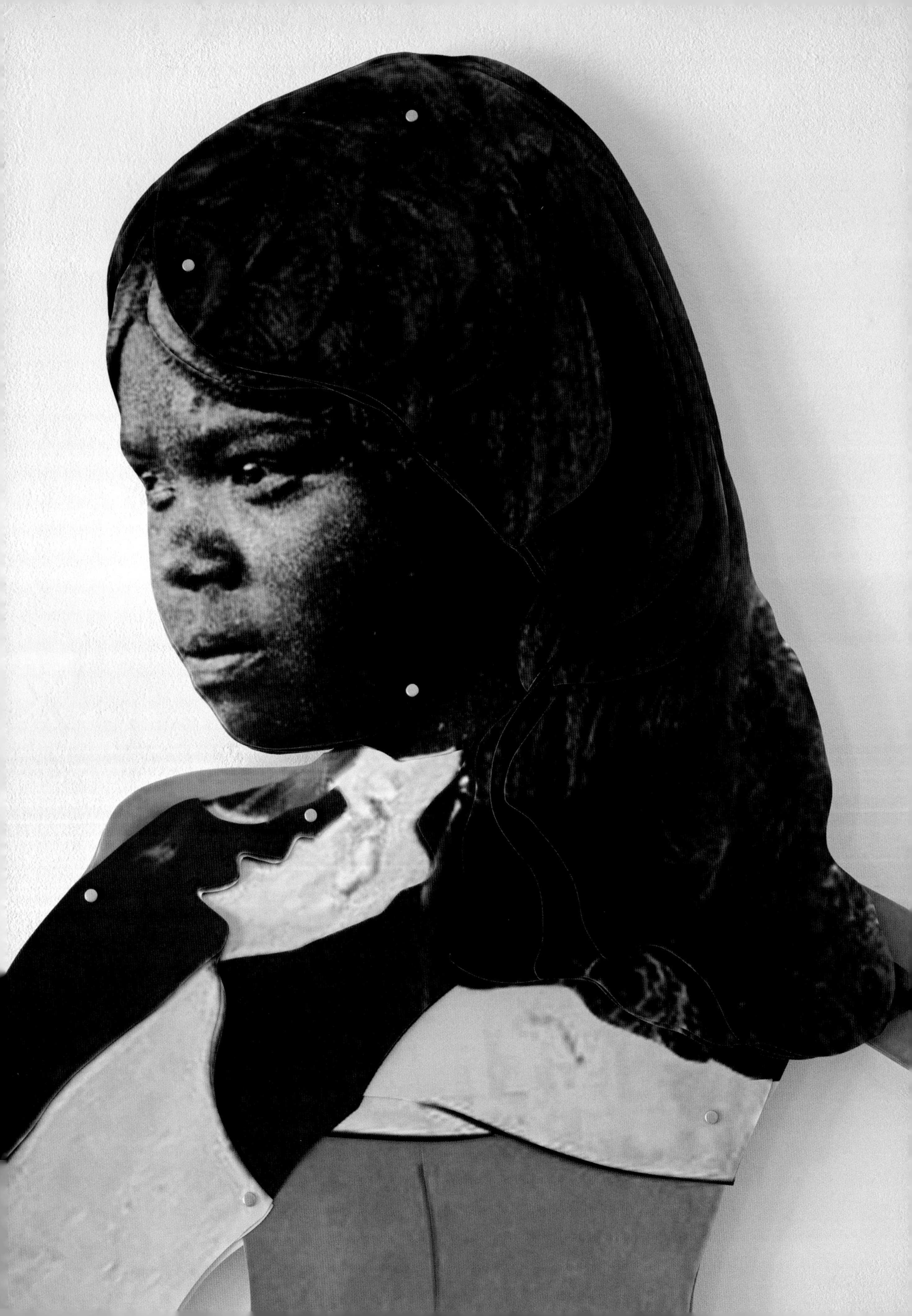

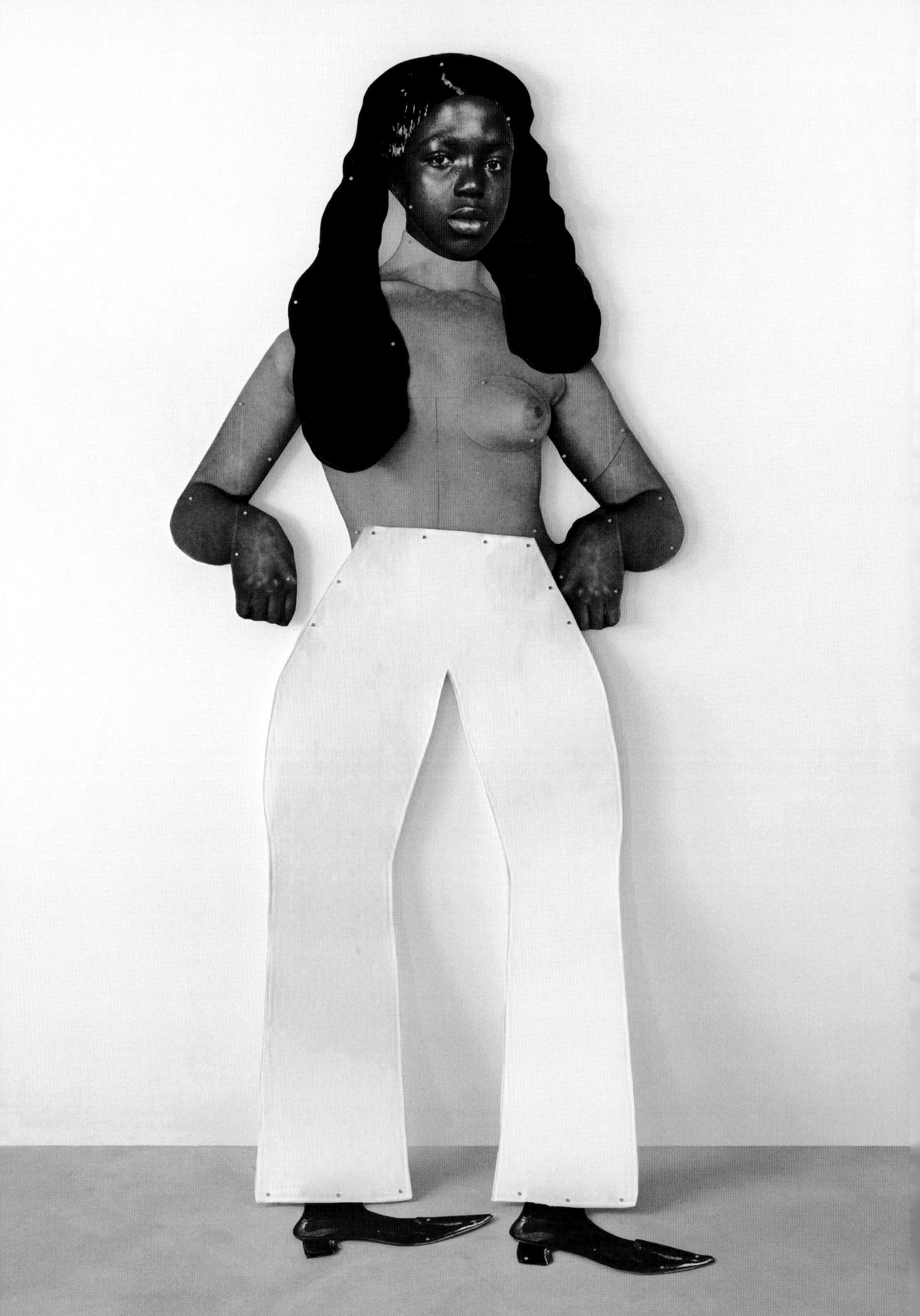

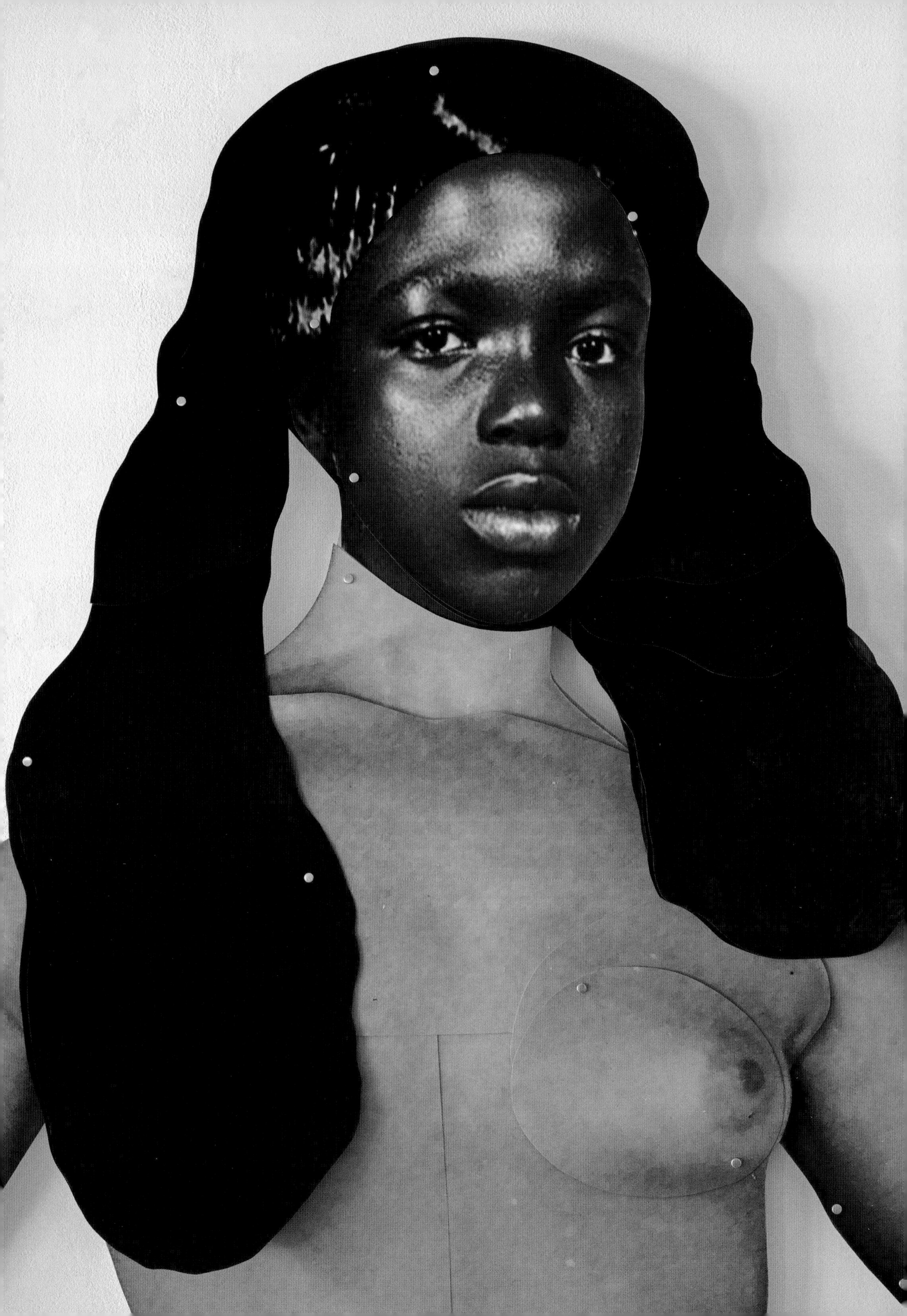

dear nina,
by the time the news reached us, the mud was too thick to swallow. we were girls, tall like lightning bolts, tough like potato peels, but young in music. we counted to seventy with our fingers and toes and missing teeth. we searched for your crown in the pockets of our overalls. they said to handle you like hot coals or fine china. where in heaven are you? how violent have you become? have you damned the blues? how many hours do you practice now? is your body any more black as a dead and sweet thing than it was alive and bitter? and when will you return?

C. LeClaire

Opposite **On My Hands and Knees II**
Overleaf **Lead by the Nose**

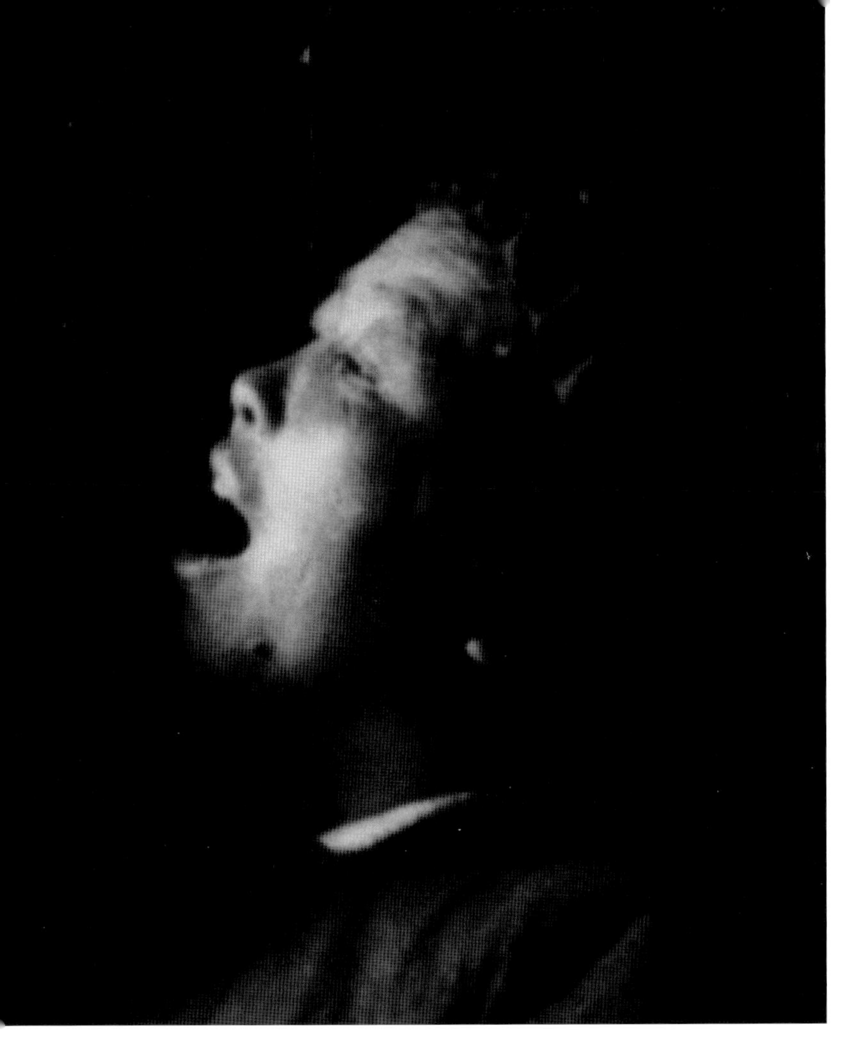

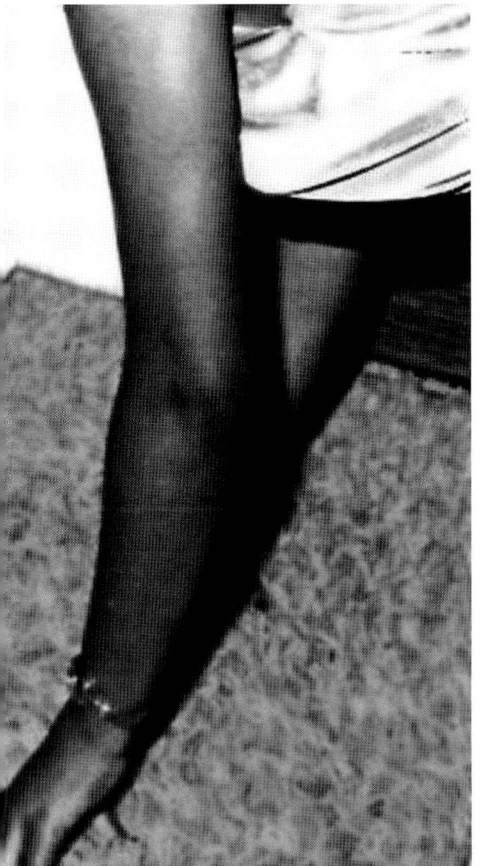

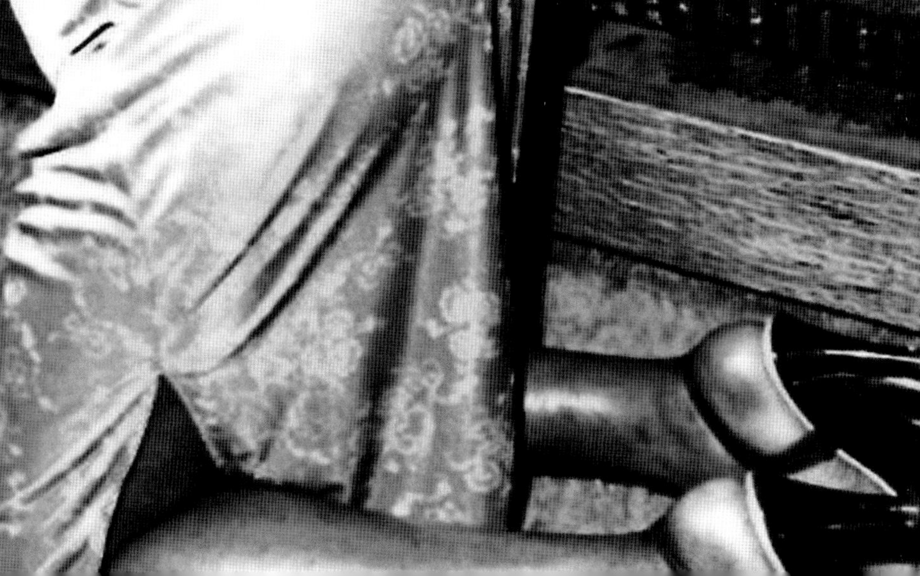

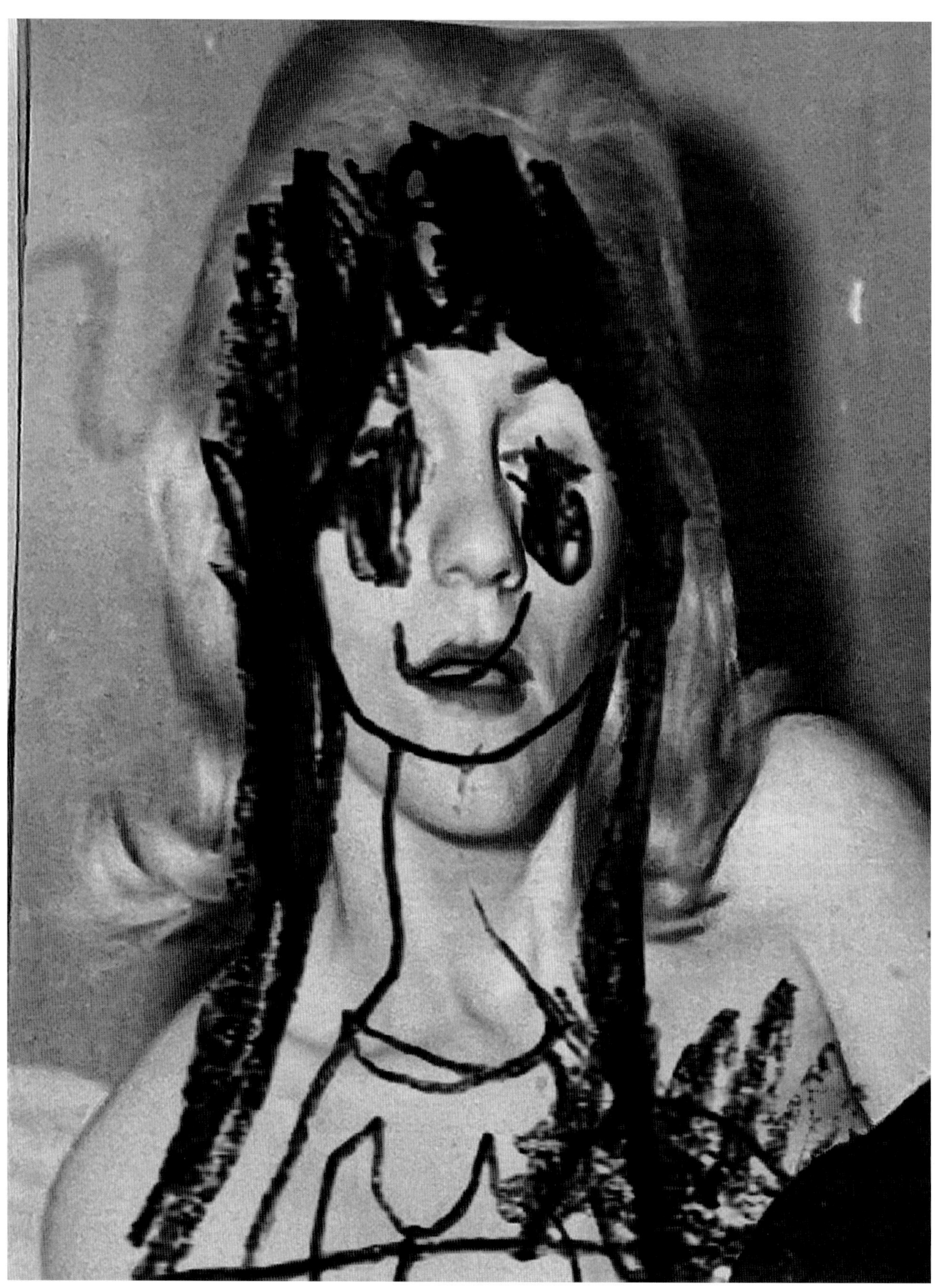

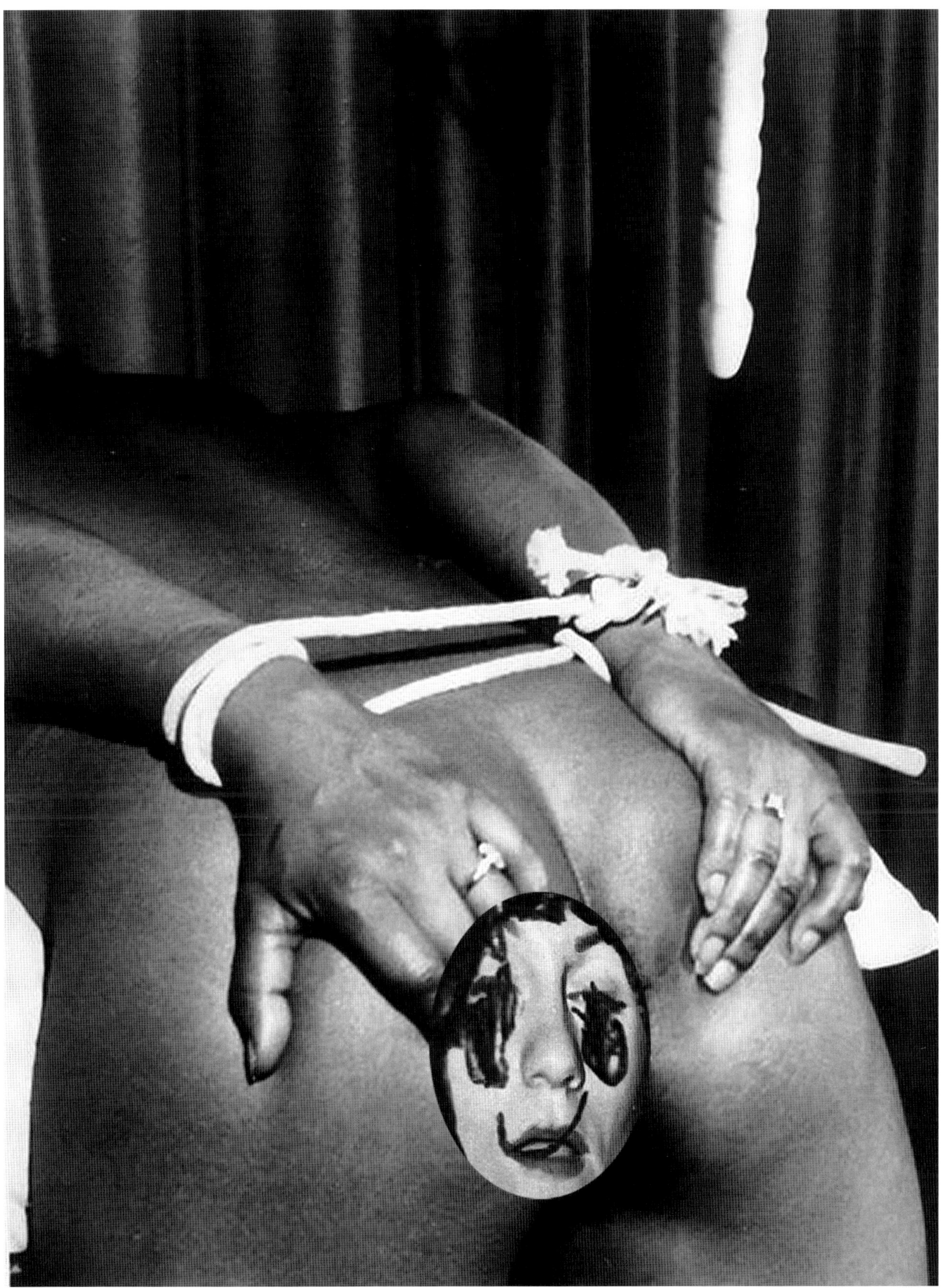

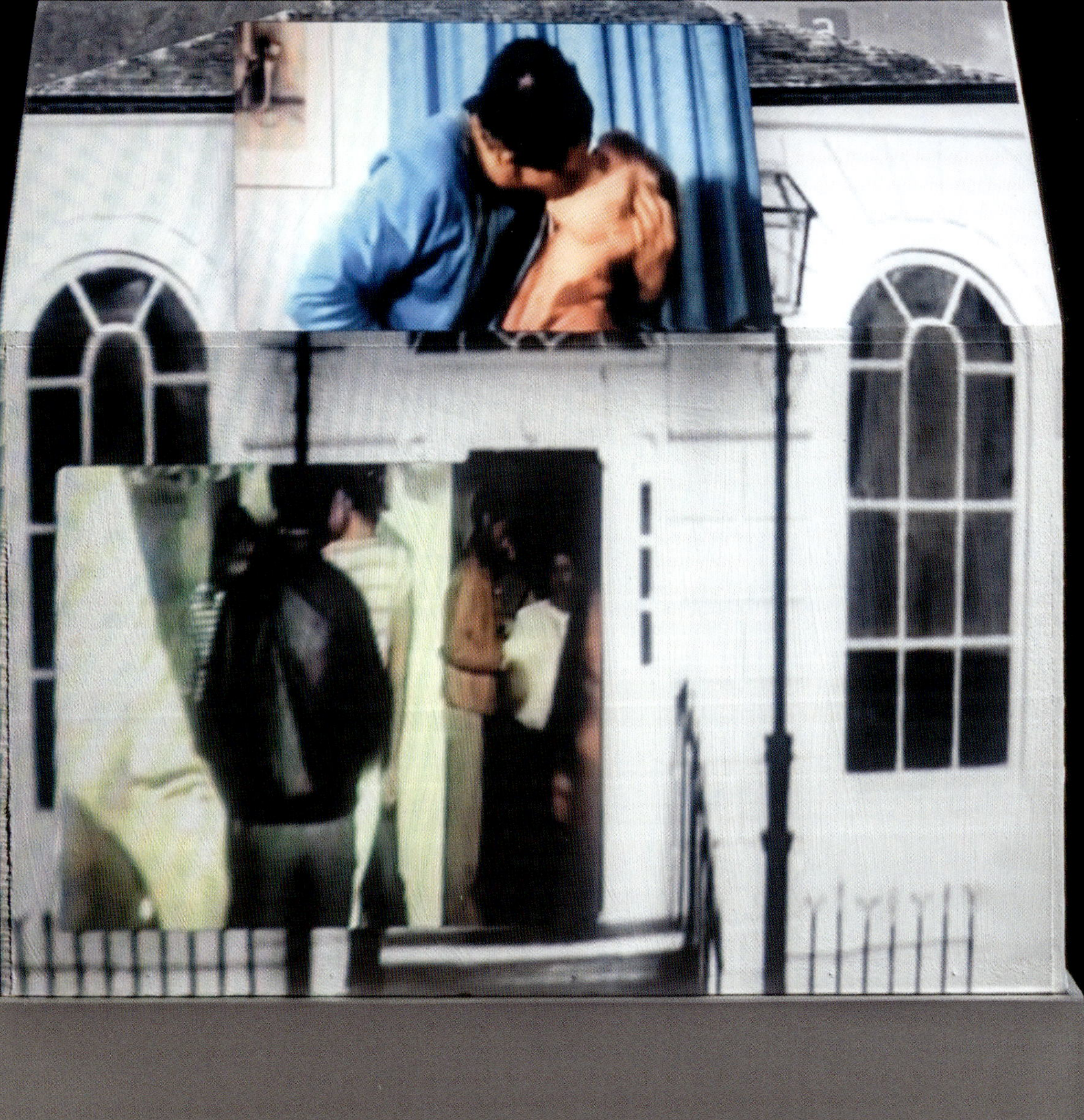

dear nina,
summer is thick with your salt. the tables are empty.
i feed grass to the dog and dance the dance of
helplessness. starving still, i am the hem of your dress.
i am your number runner, your cold-cocked memory.
i carve your drum into my knees and pray the sun tells
the truth next time.

C. LeClaire

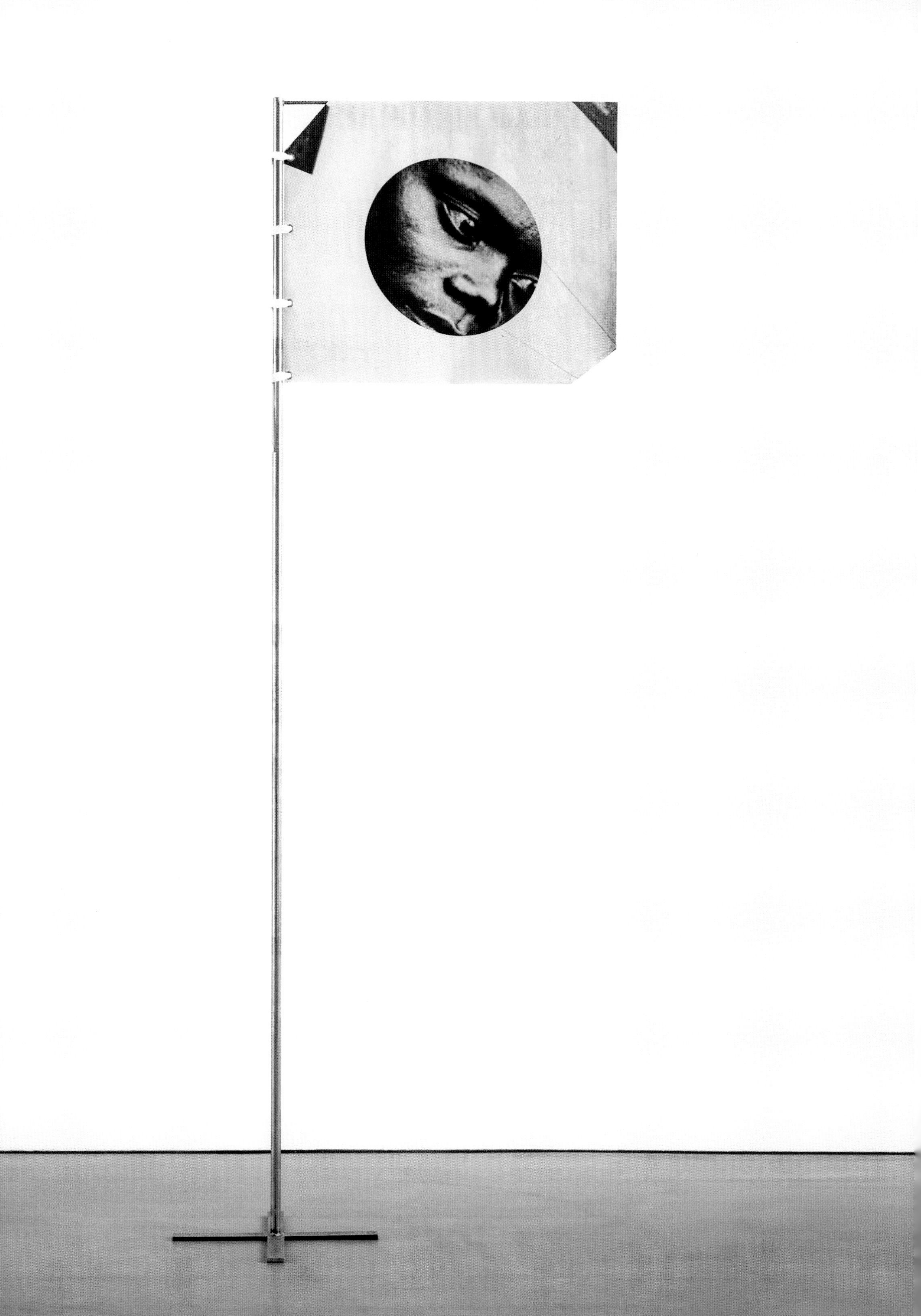

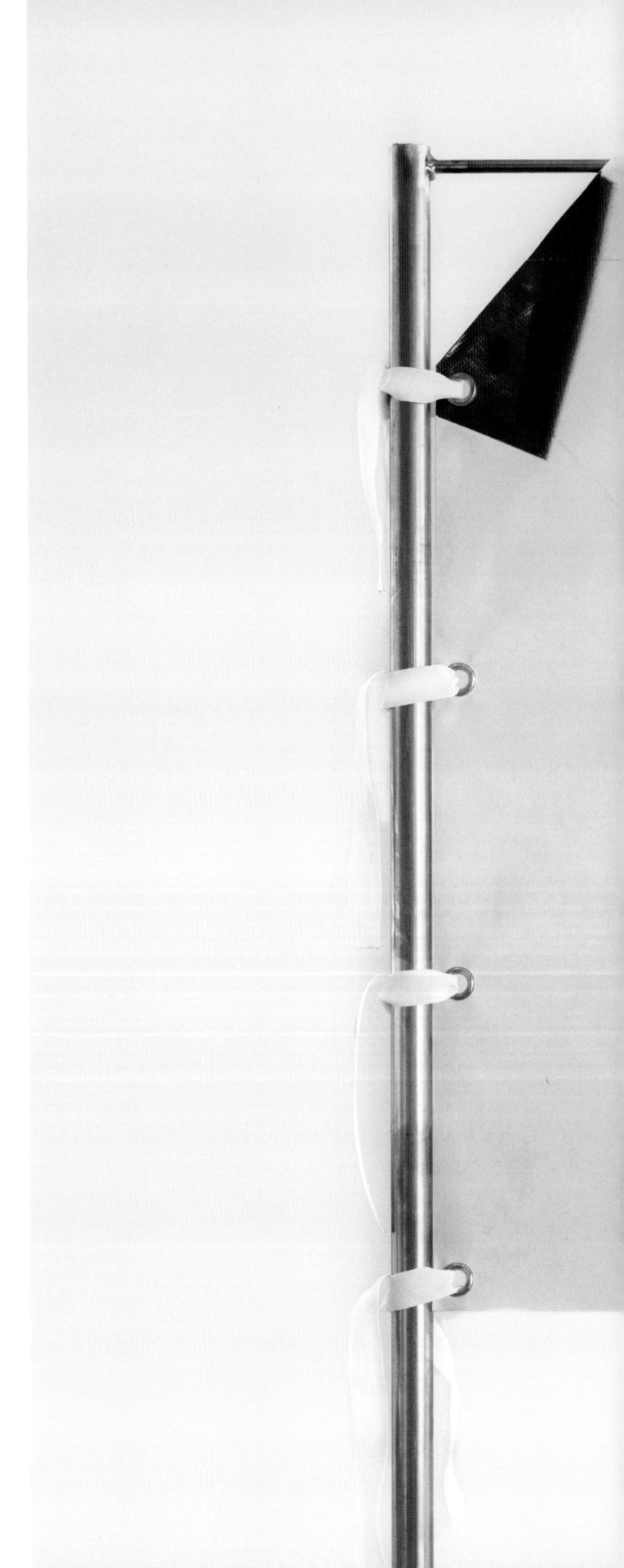

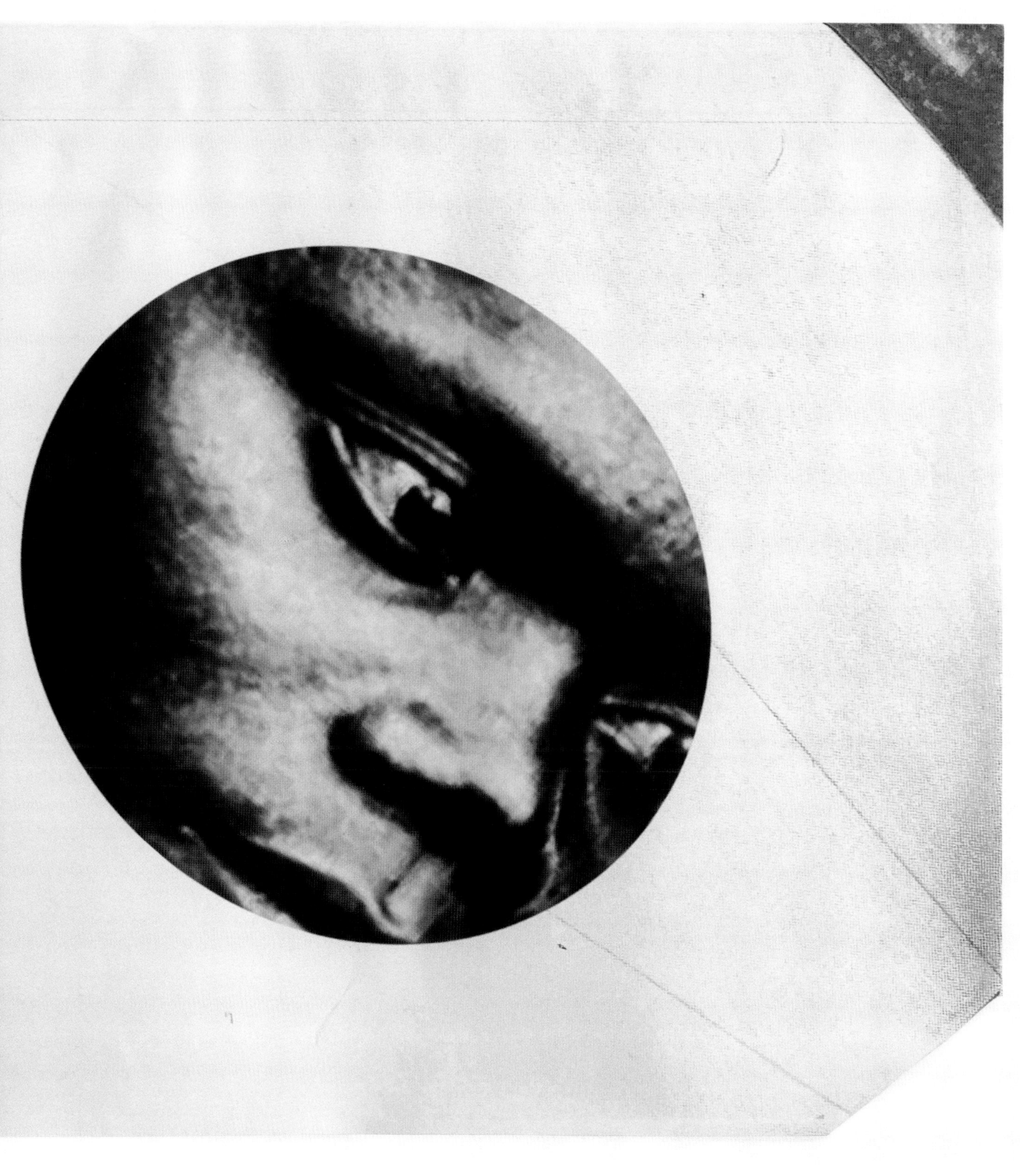

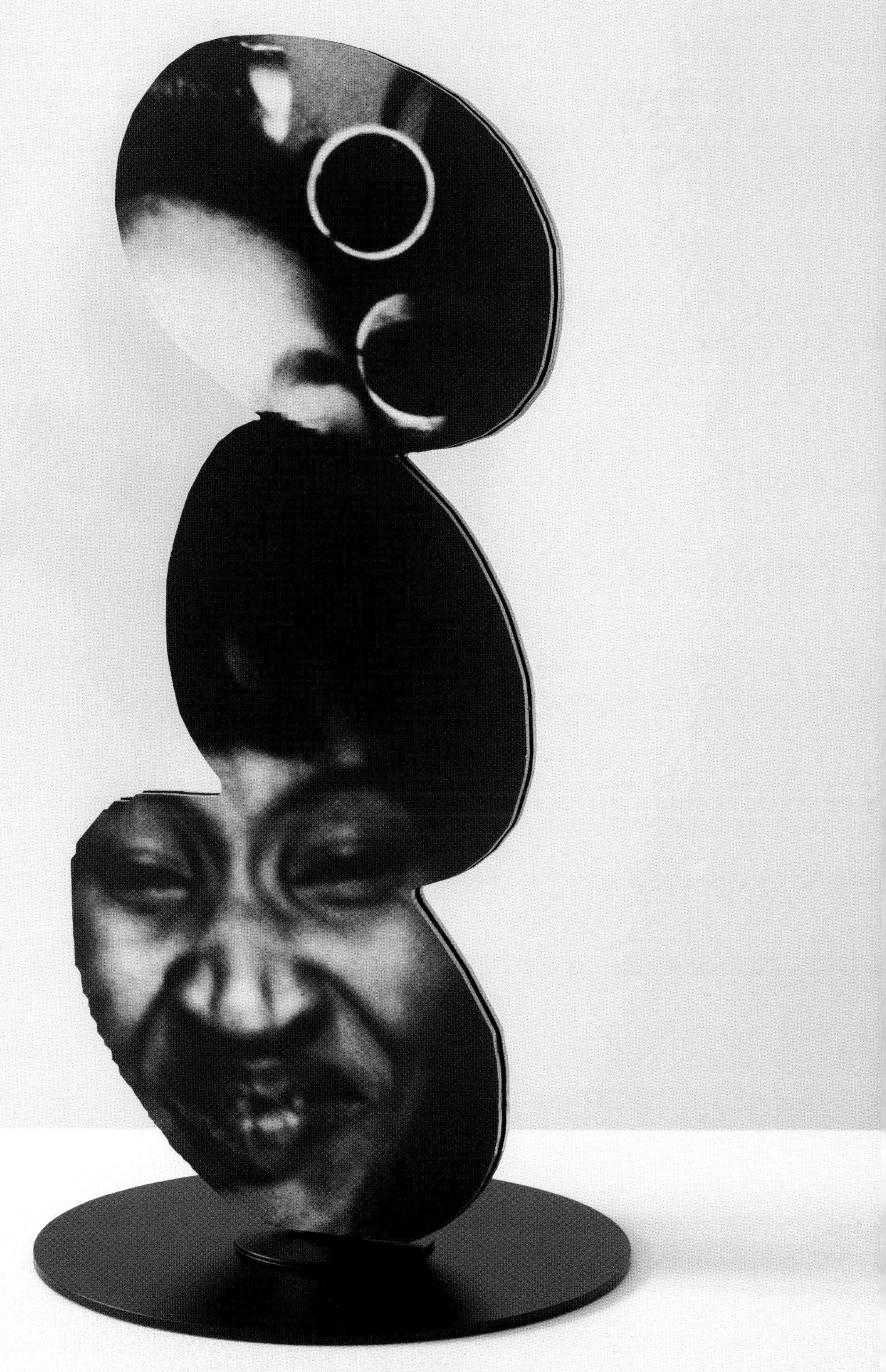

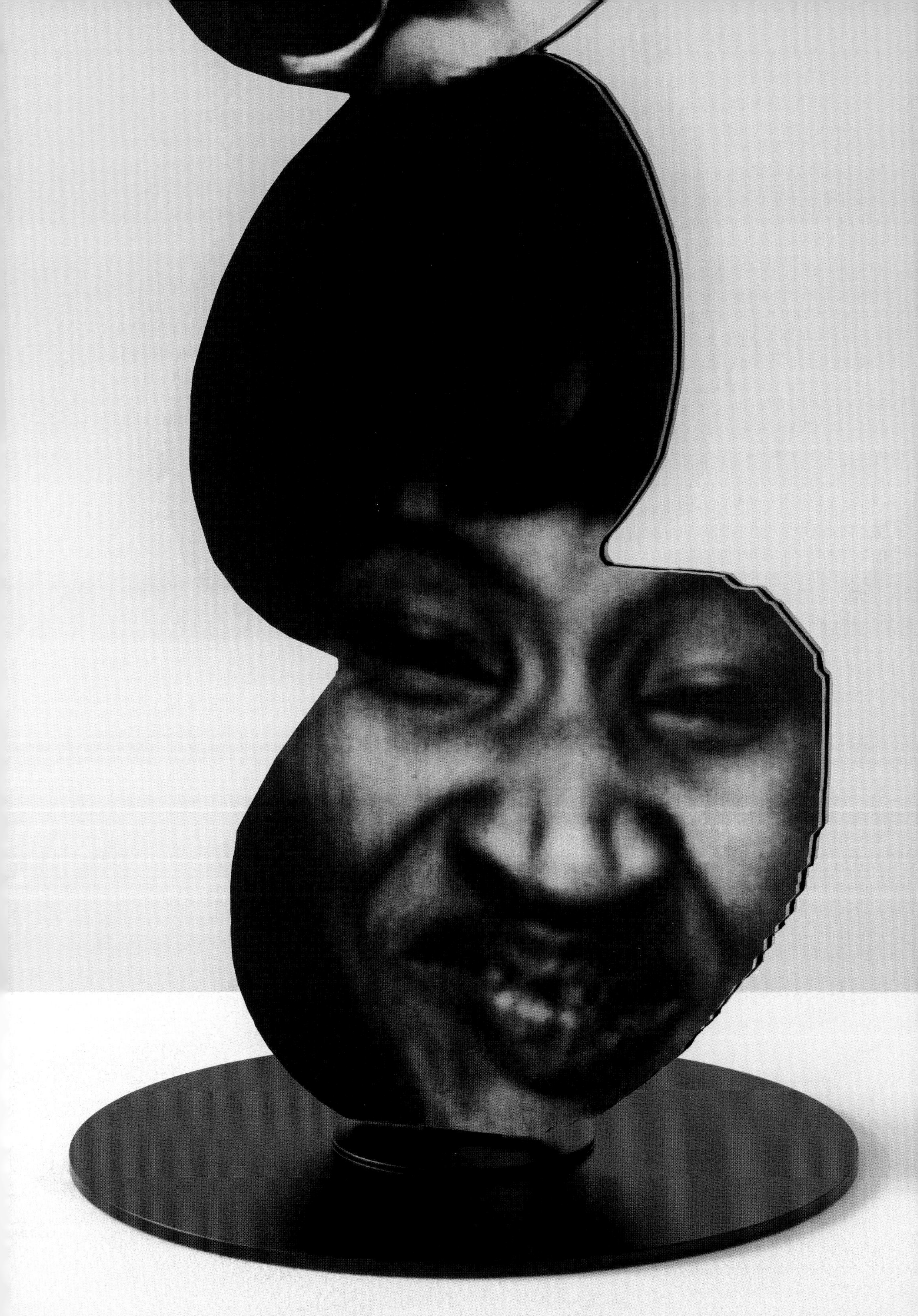

dear eleanora,
the lipstick is mother’s. as is the bitterness. as is the denial.
she keeps pulling our lips. she is brittle like candelilla wax.
we bribe the back roads to take us anywhere and everywhere.
in red, we are lovesick nightbirds. in plum, we are pigeon-toed
girls wrecked by tradition. we are painted bullets waiting to
be kissed. and for all we know we may die this way.

C. LeClaire

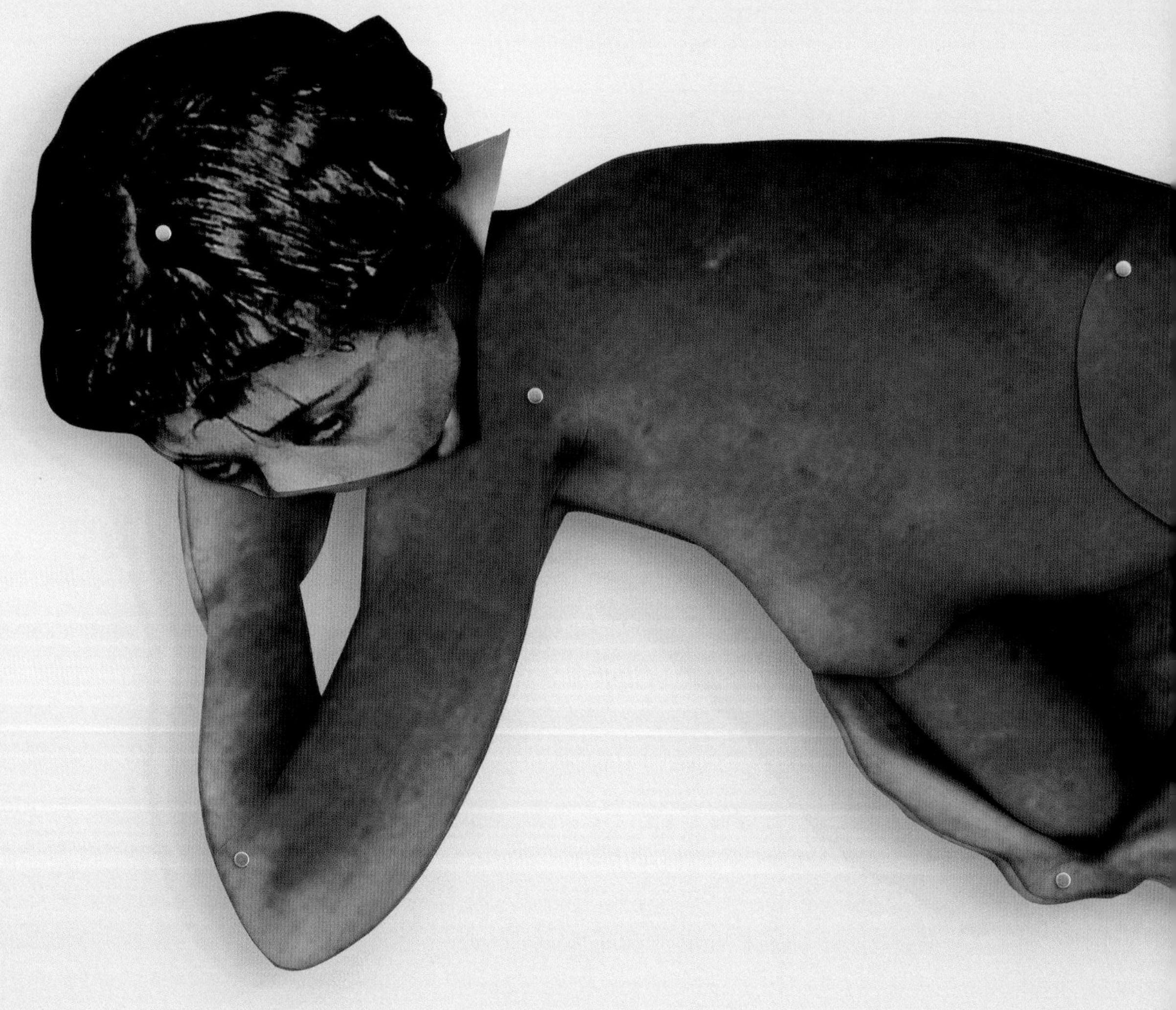

Woman with Hand

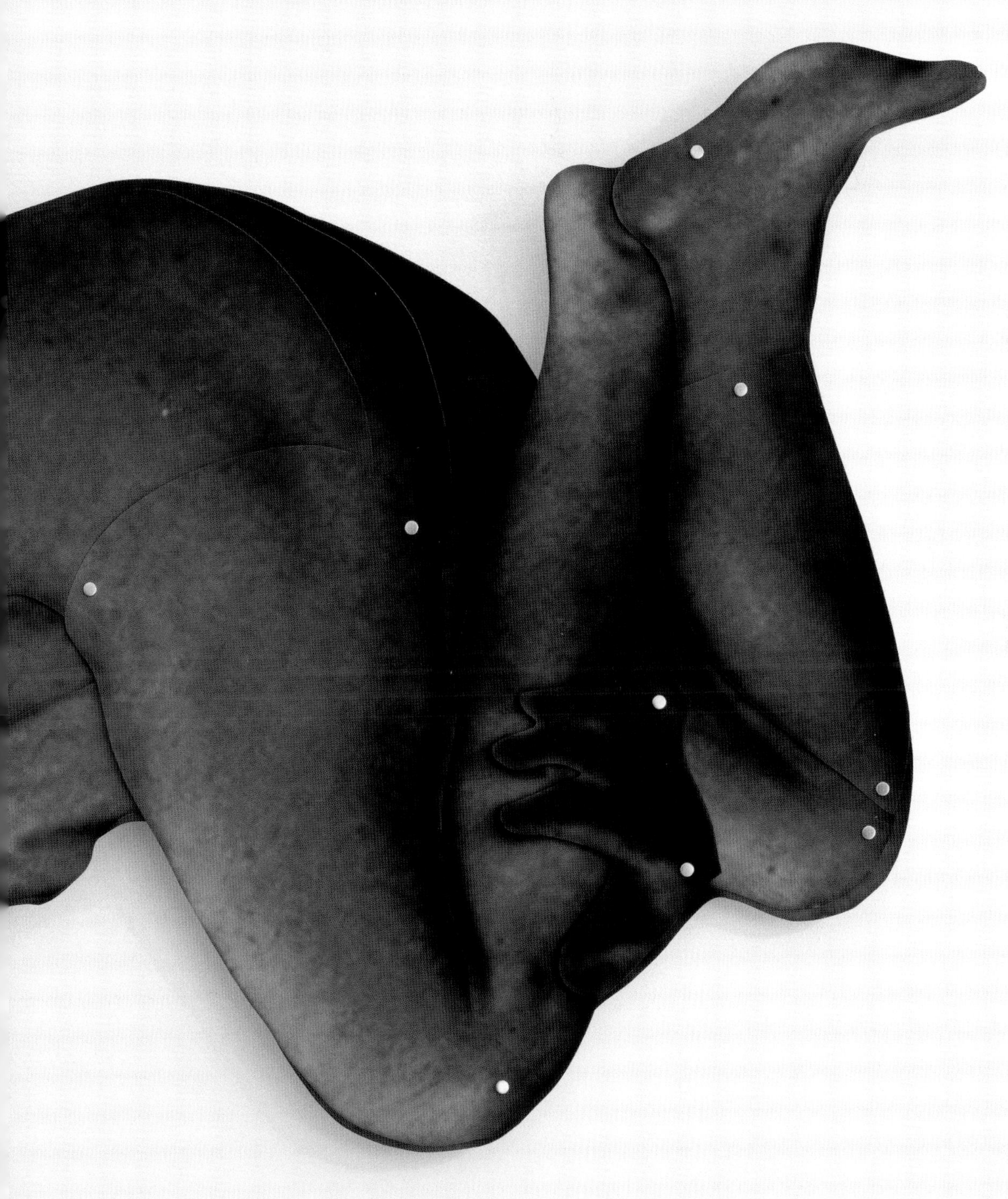

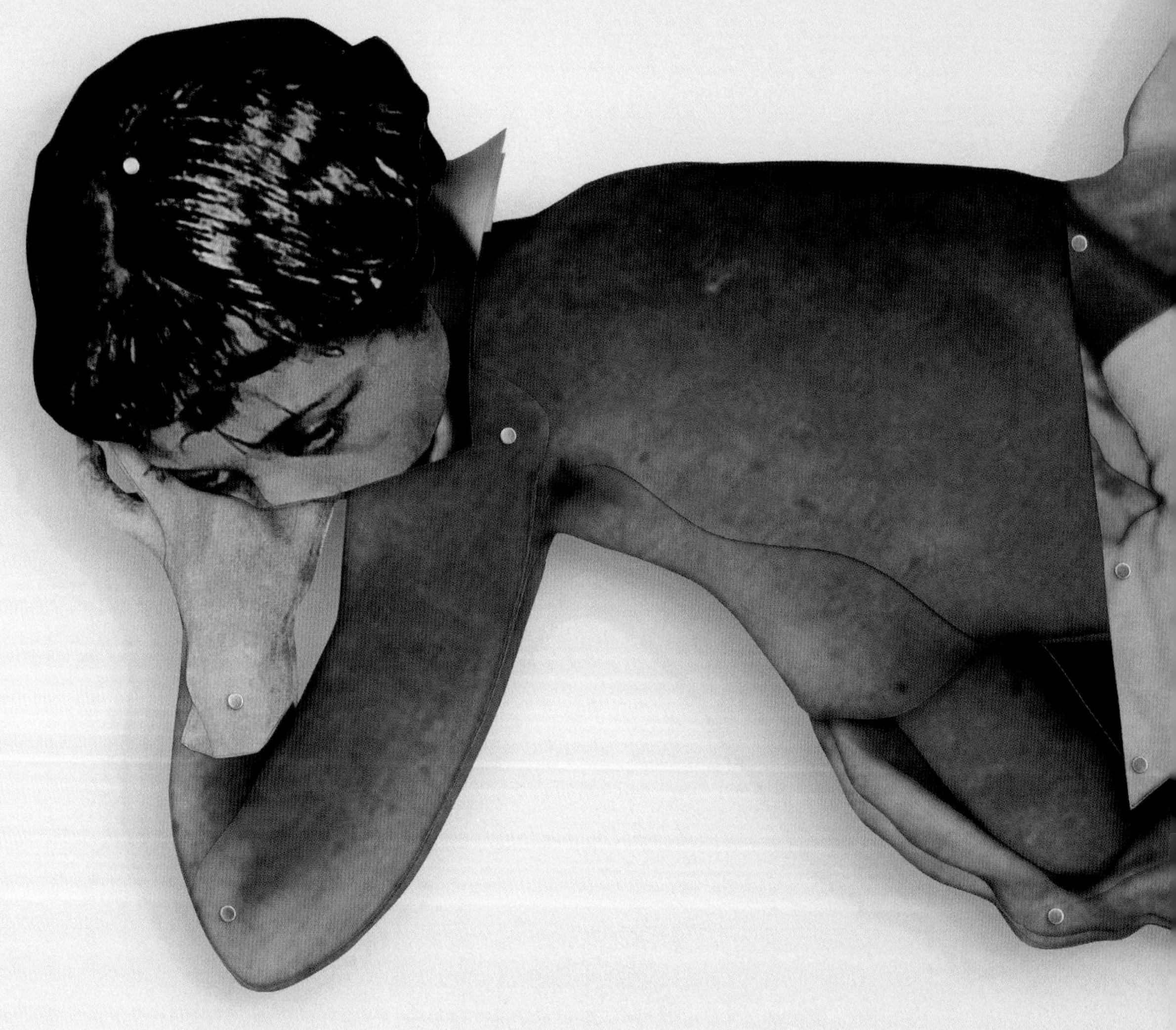

Woman with Dress

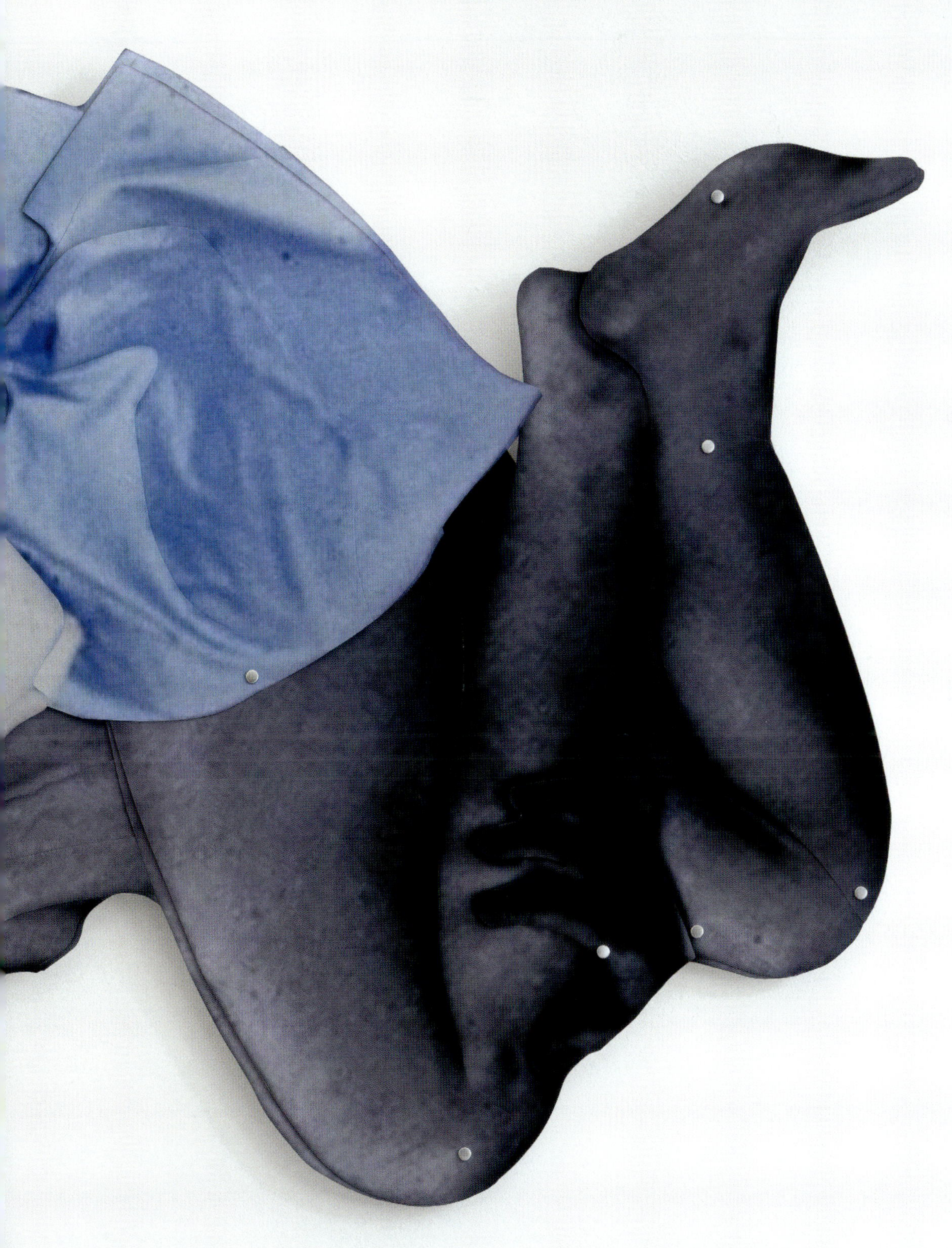

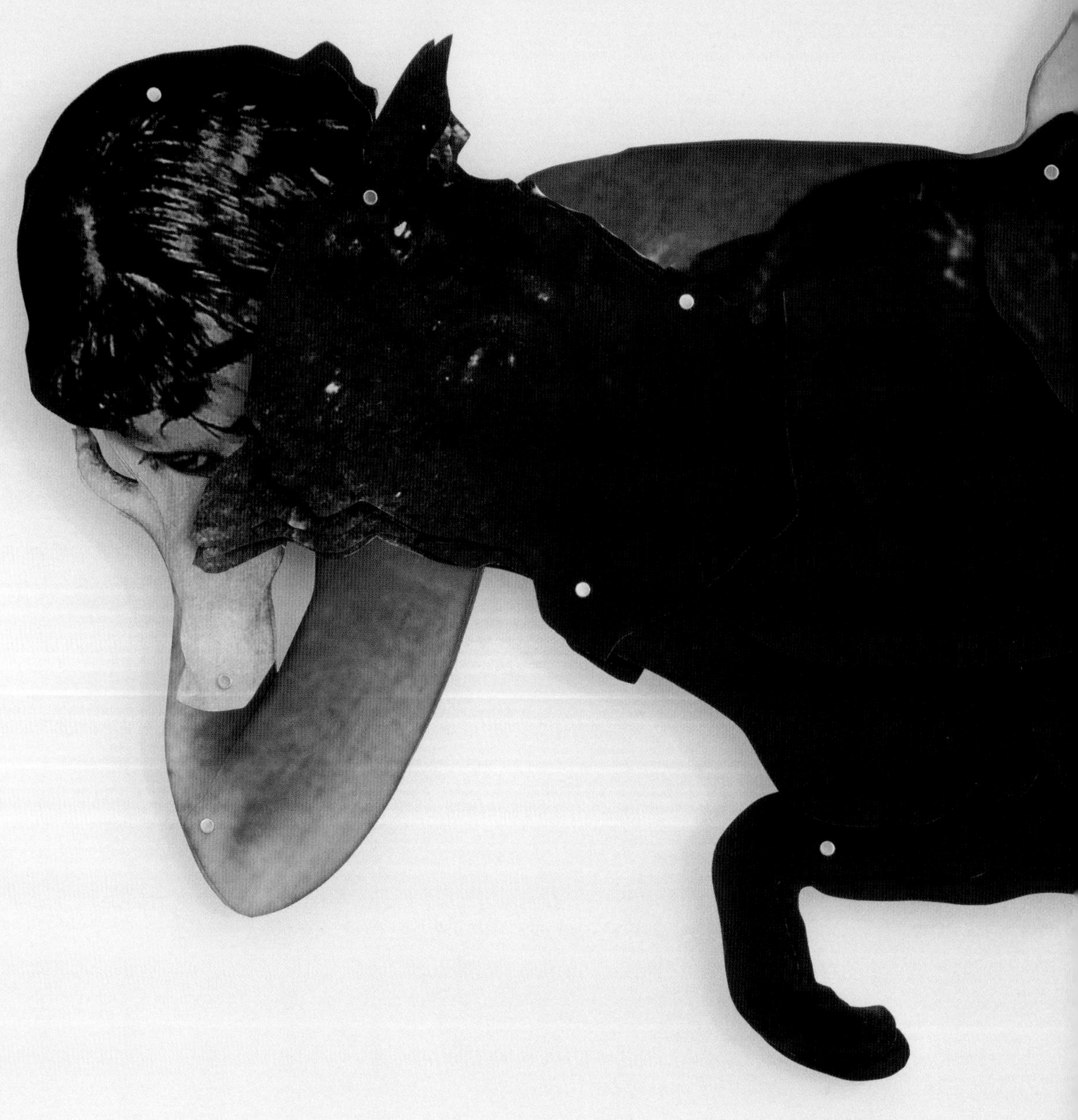

Woman with Dog II

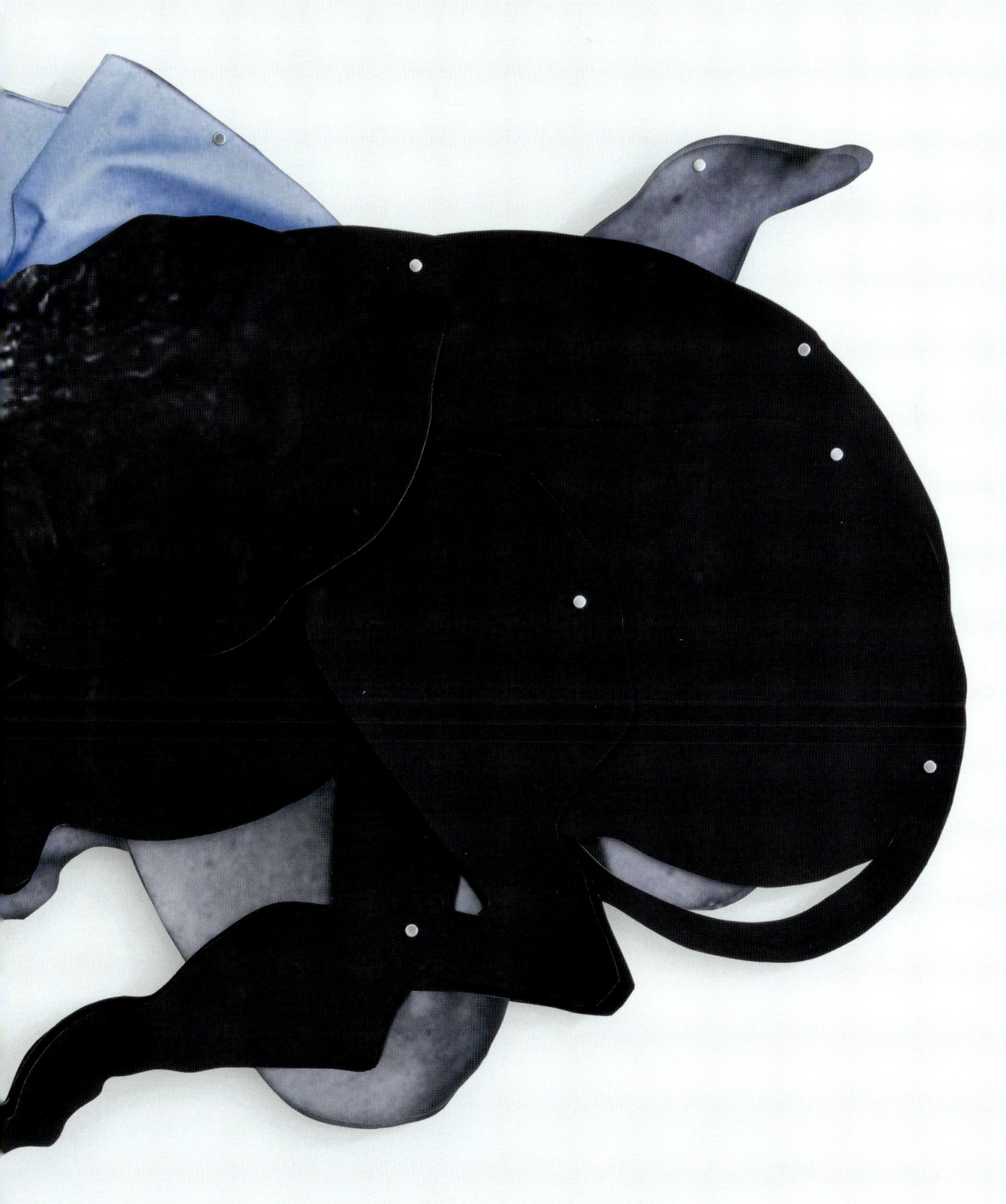

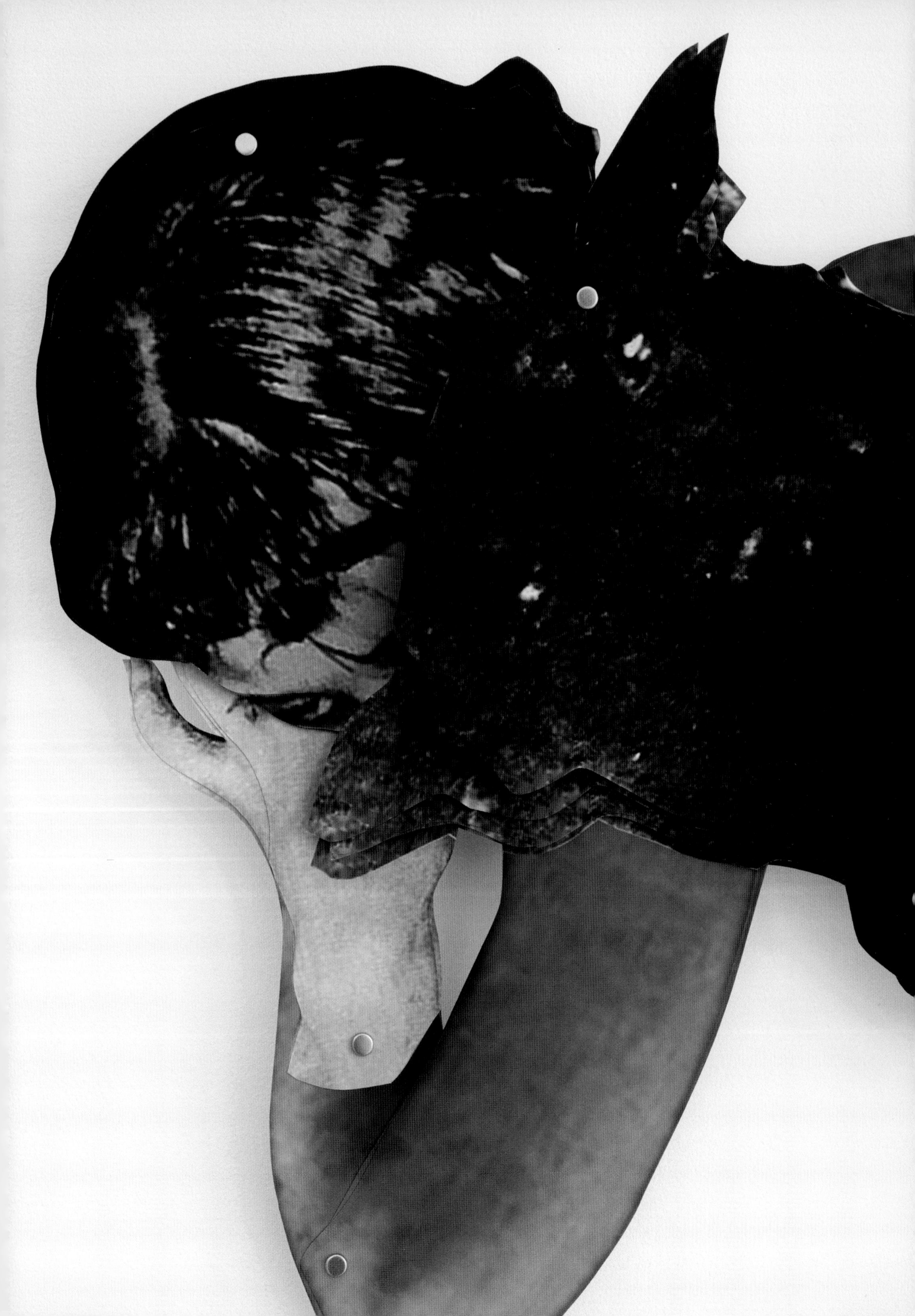

dear anna marie,
when the spirit is a distillery the body does not respond to tambourines or drums or hand-holding. i watch the whiskey drop and wait for you. i fall into the glass with braided hair and a dying face. i wait for you to rescue my wants from exhaustion. where is this world you promised me? where can i separate my drunkenness from the living steam?

C. LeClaire

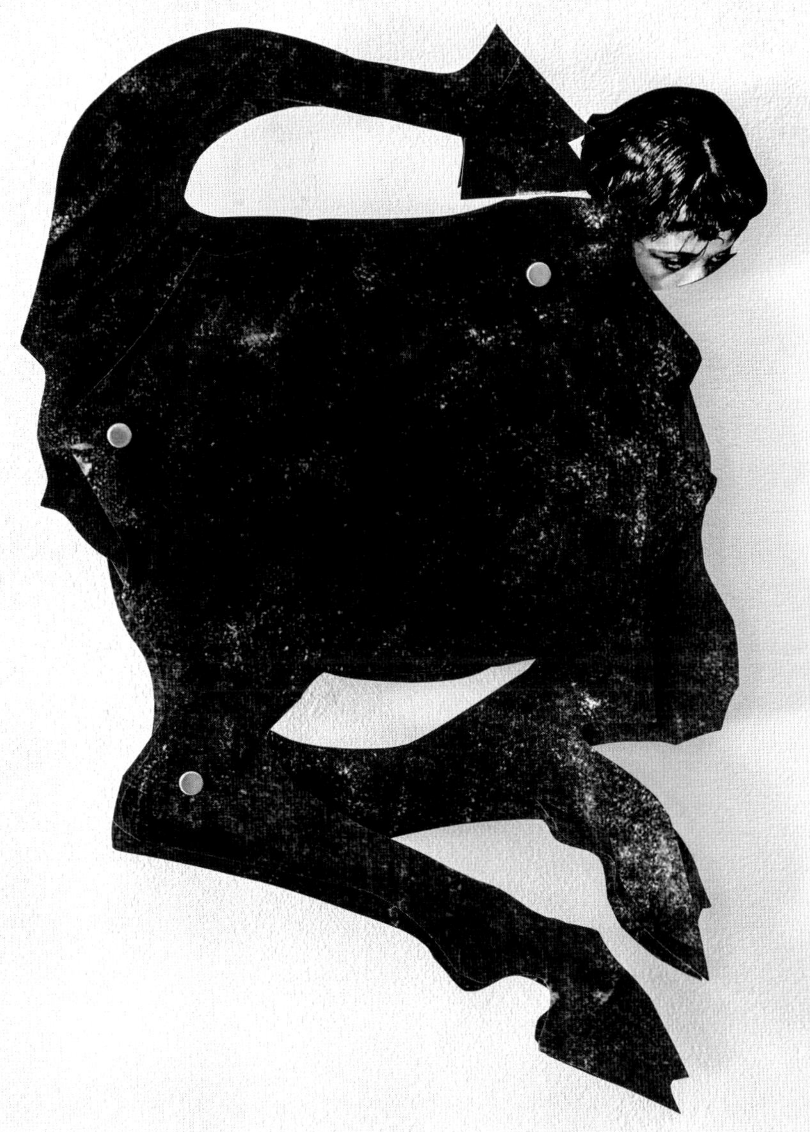

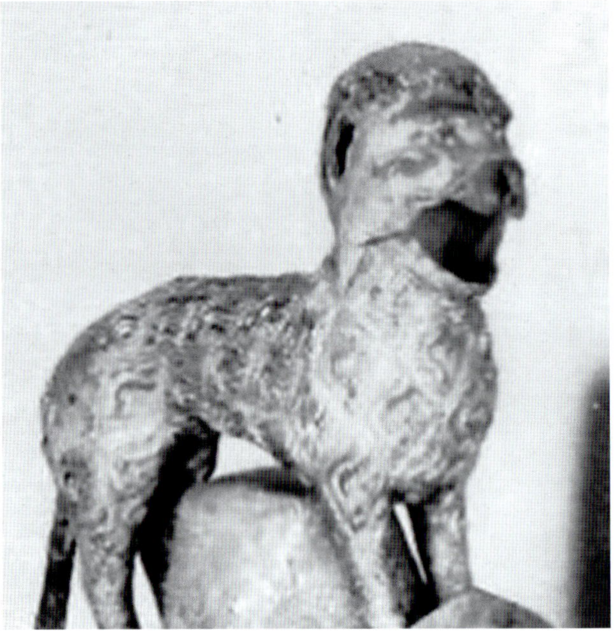

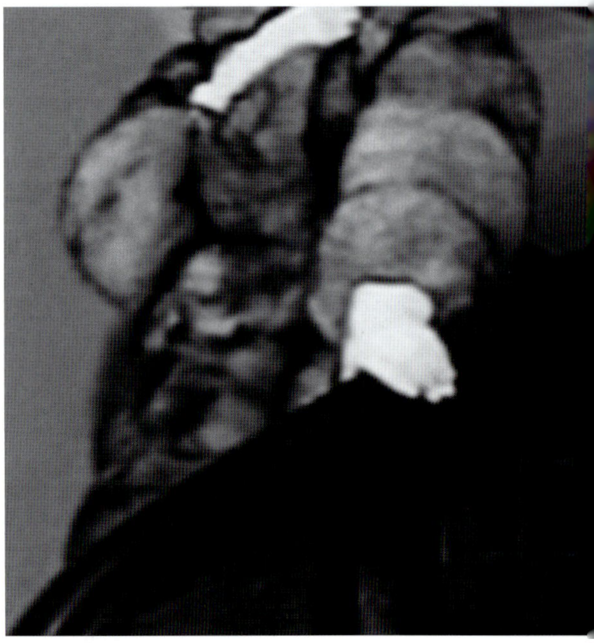

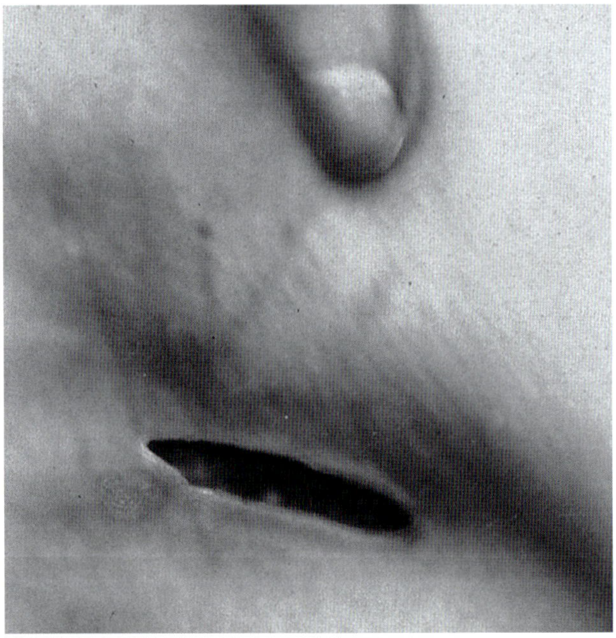

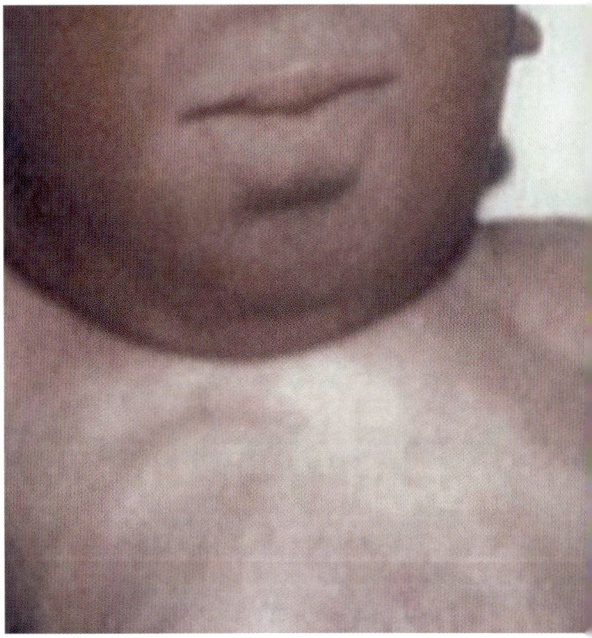

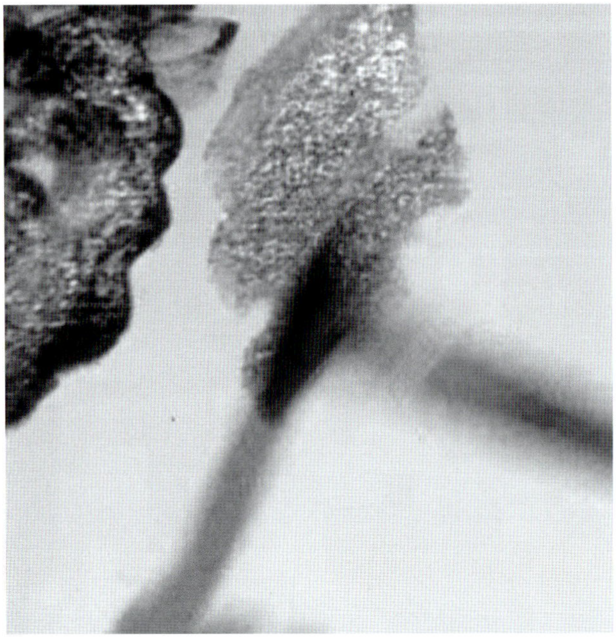

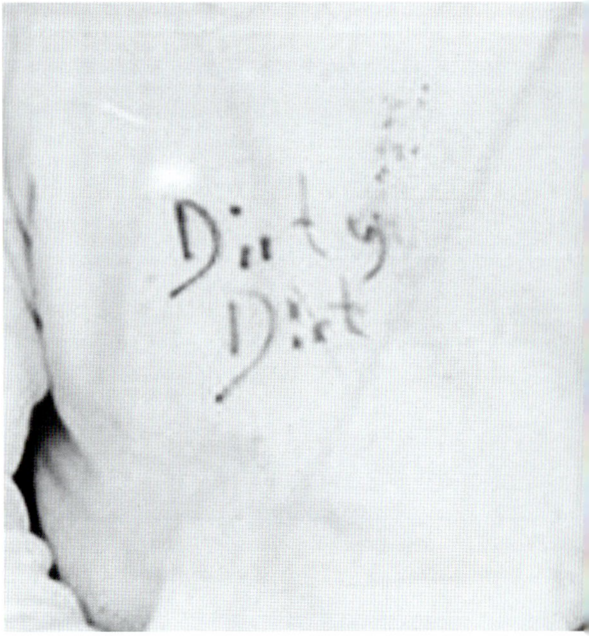

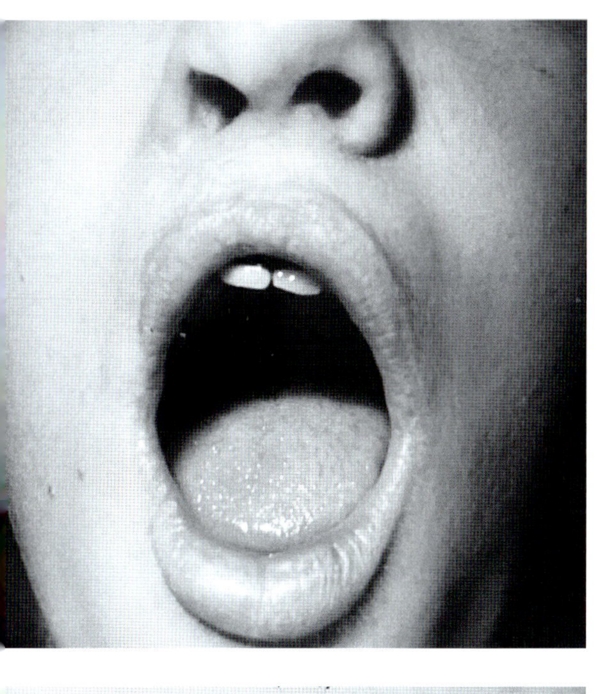

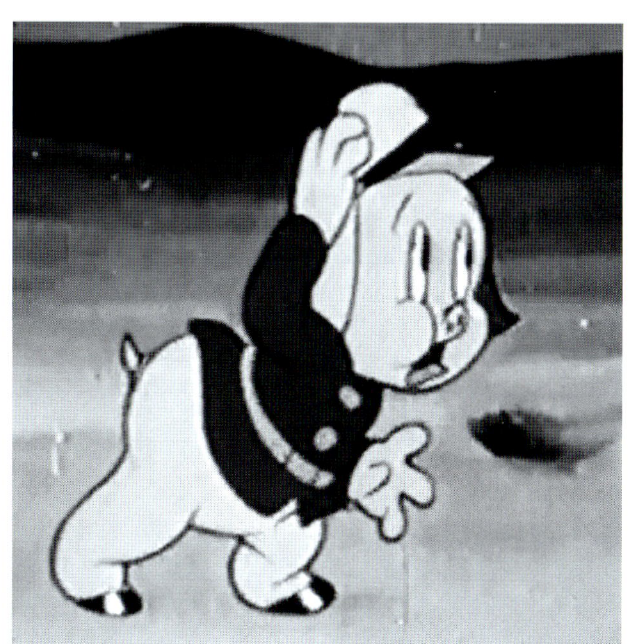

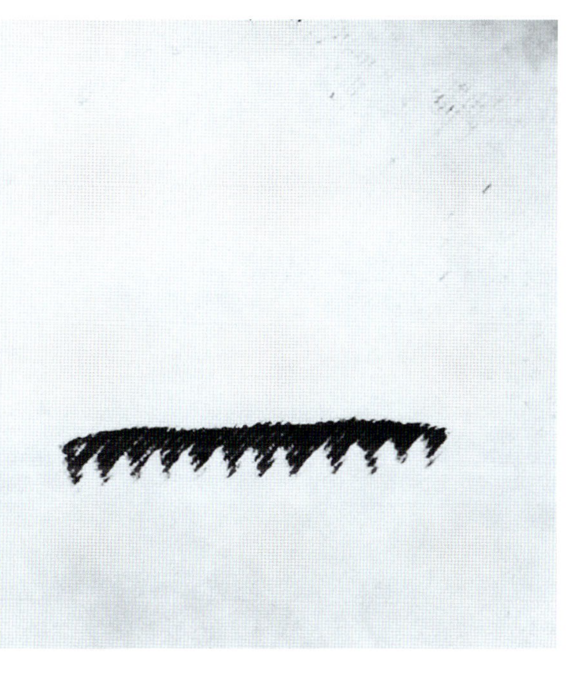

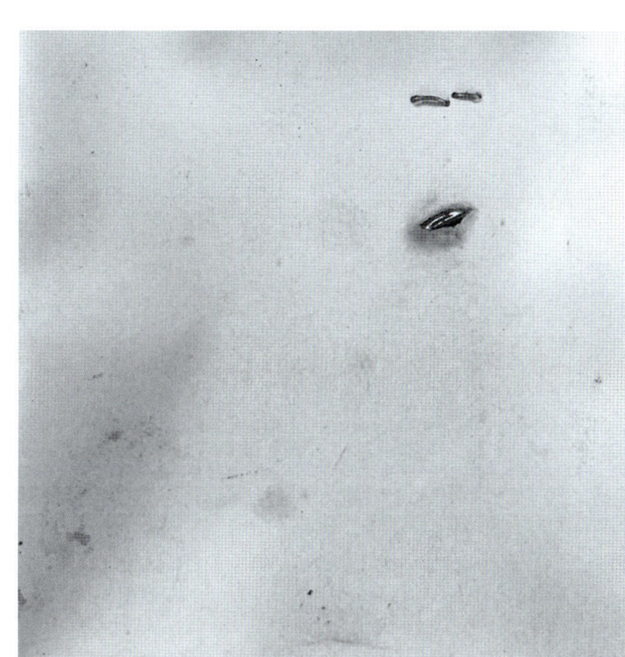

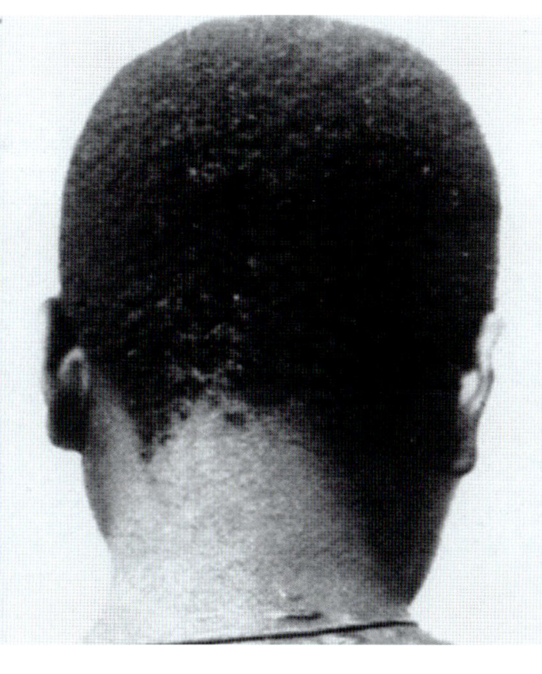

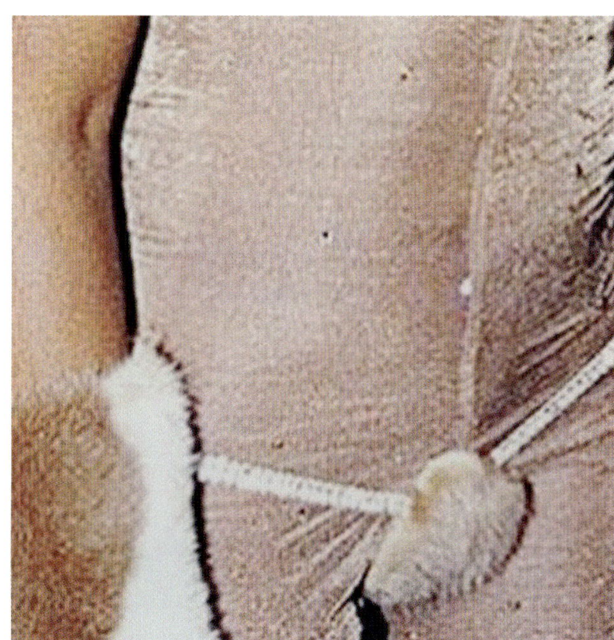

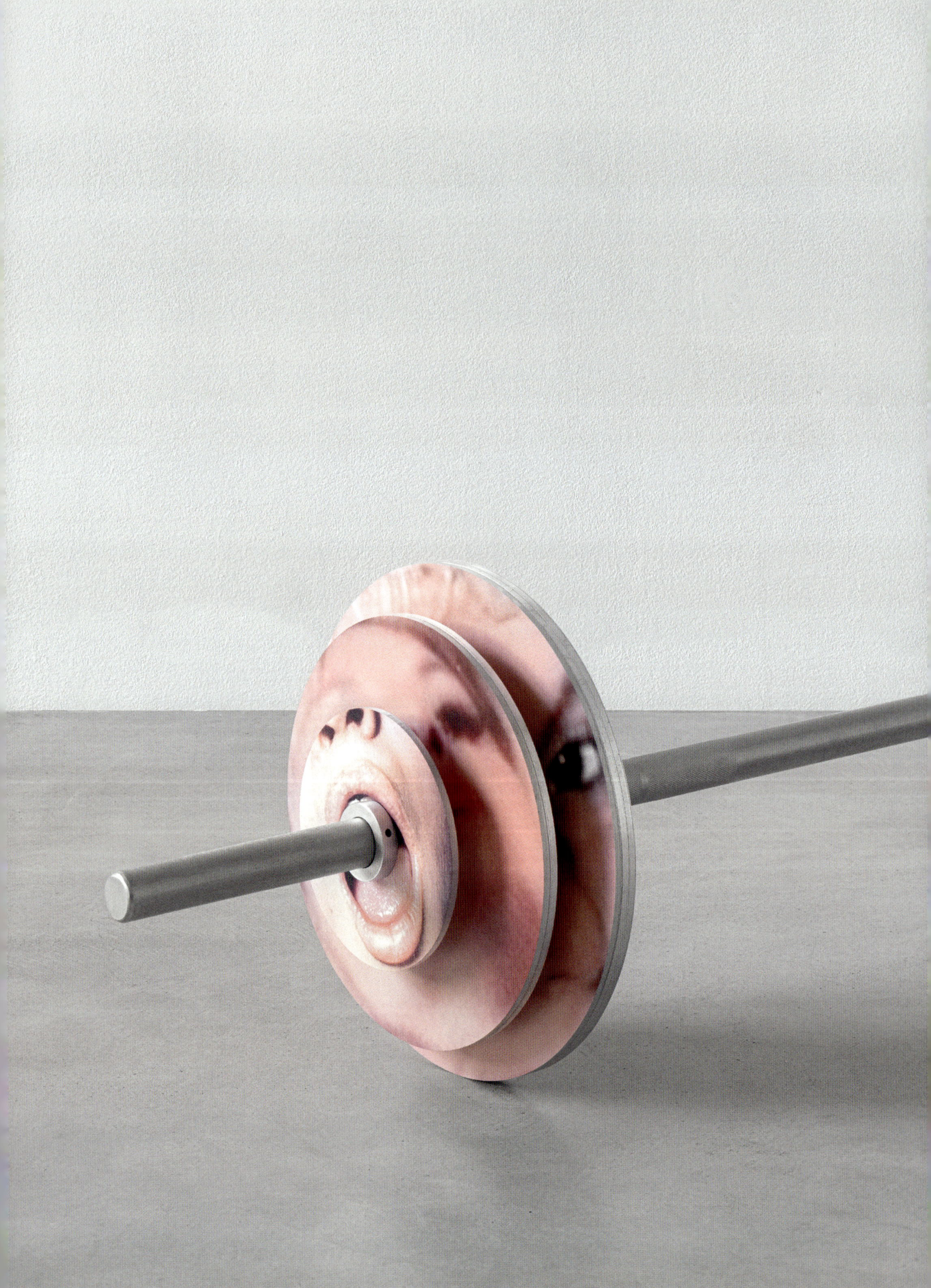

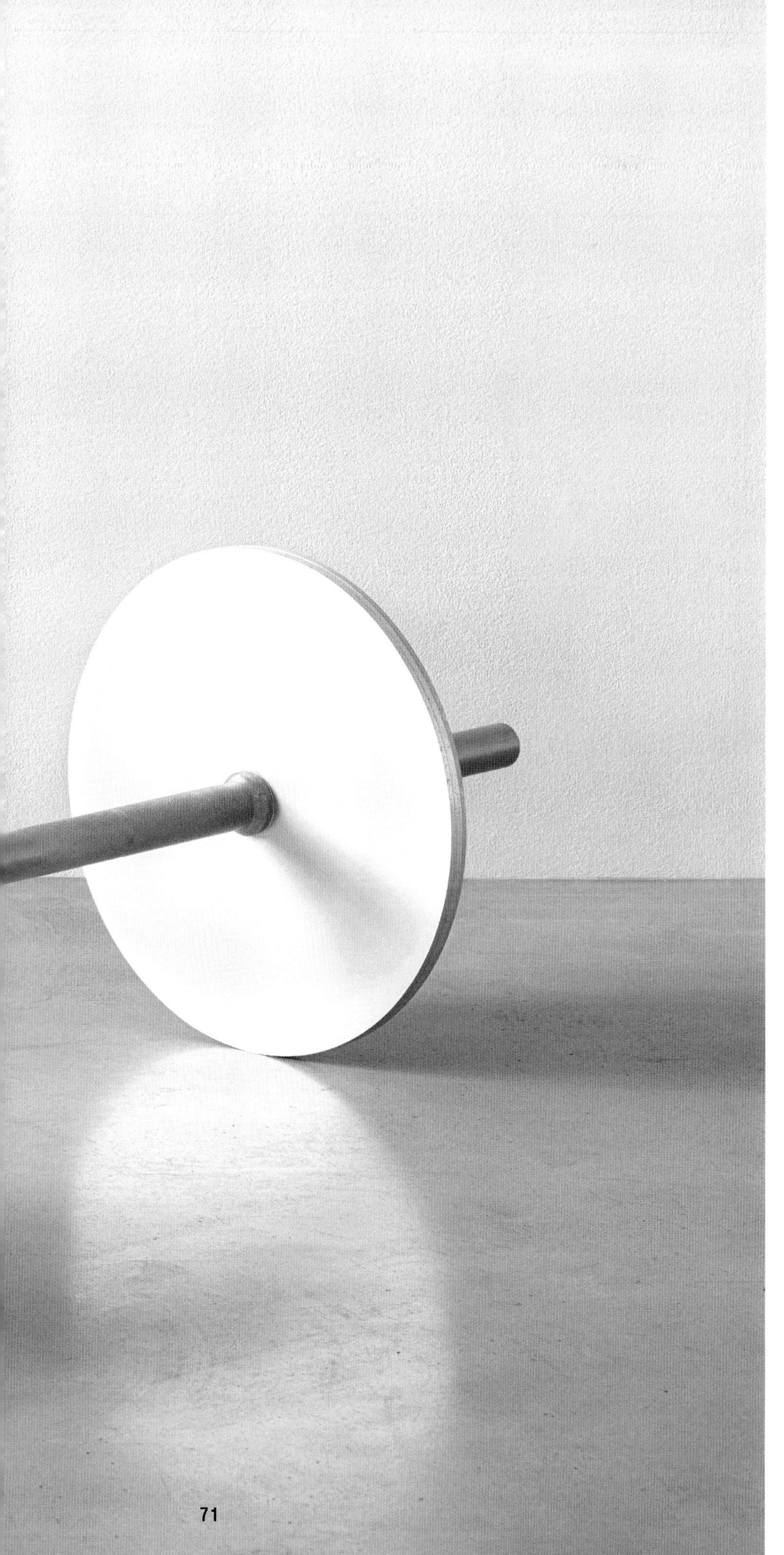

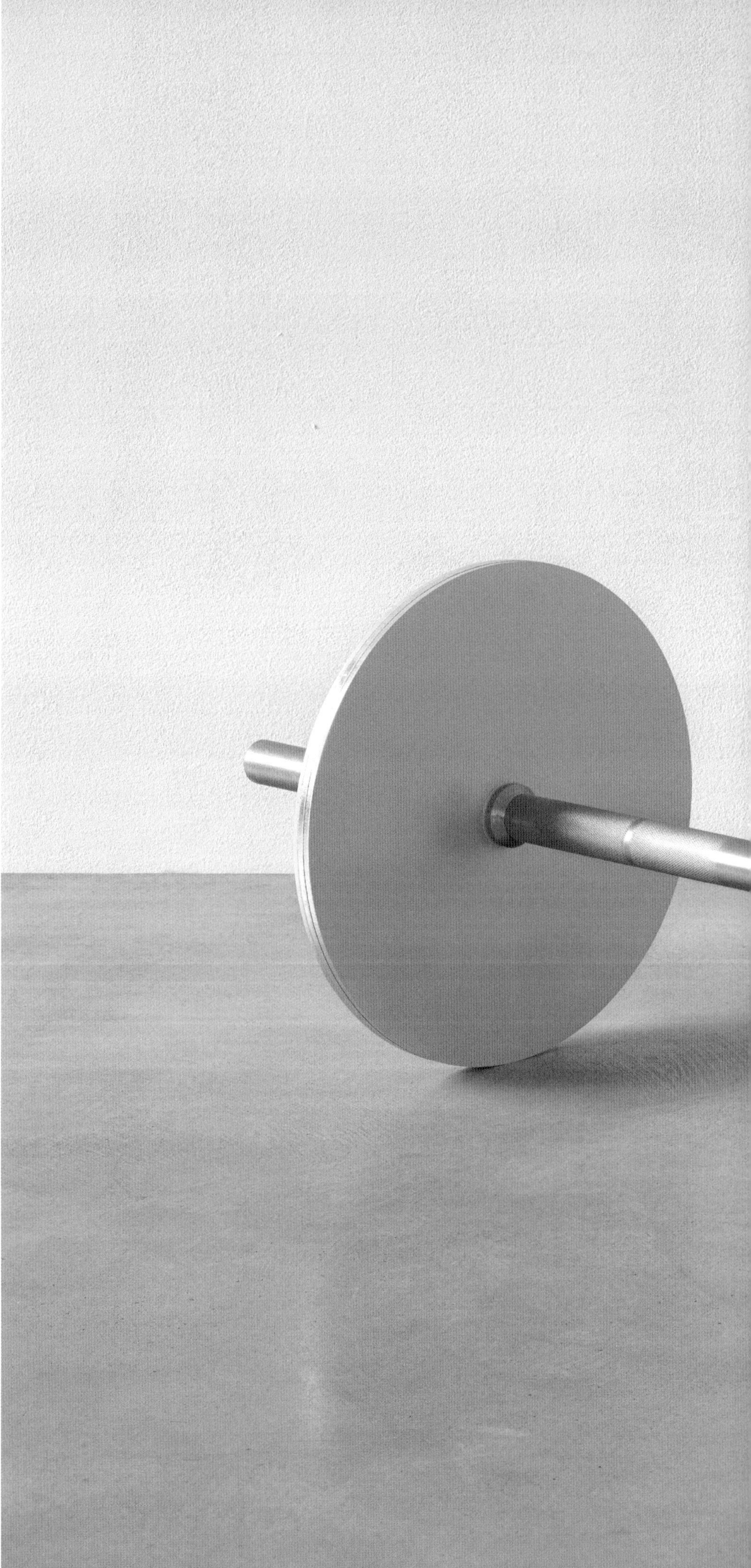

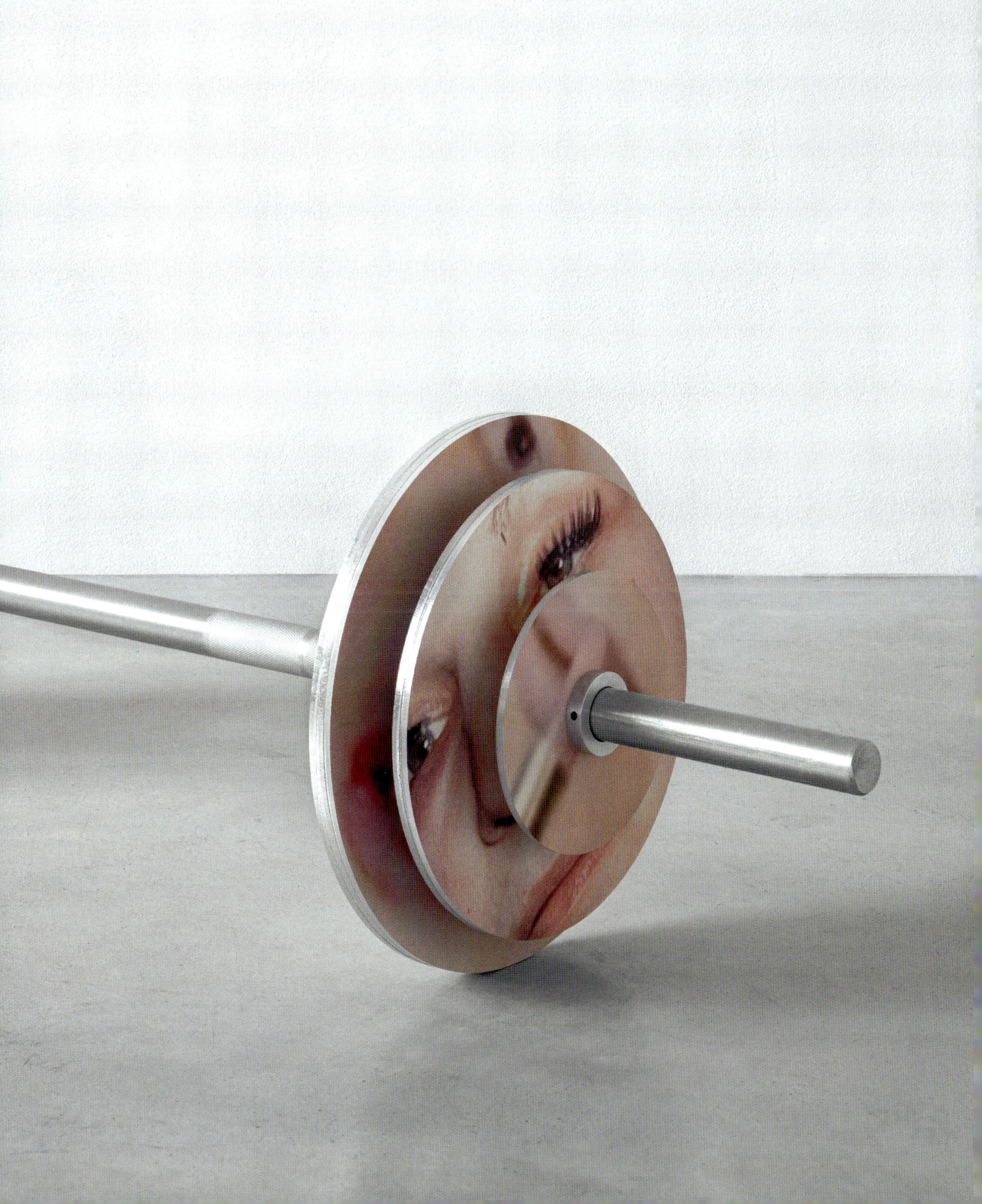

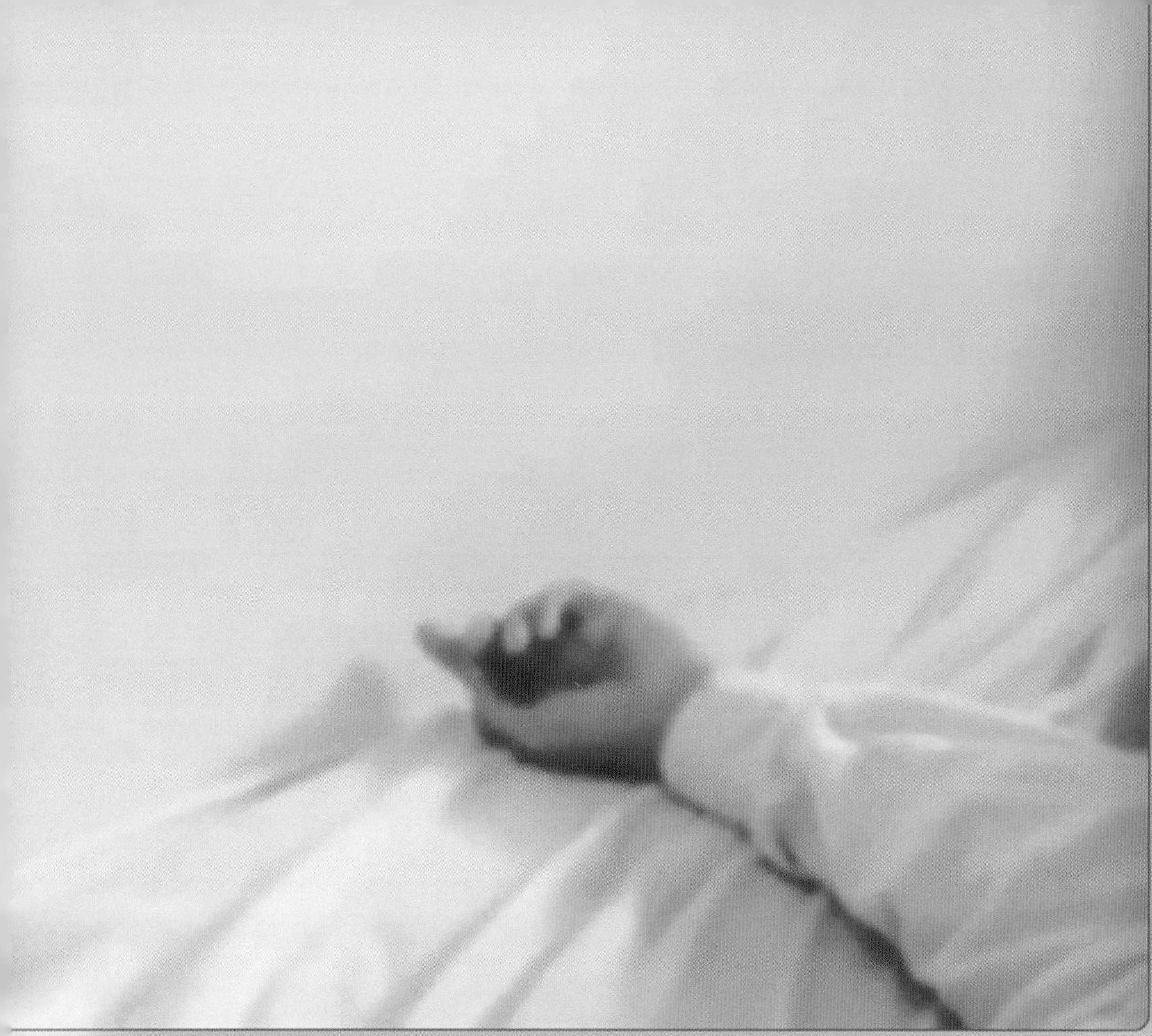

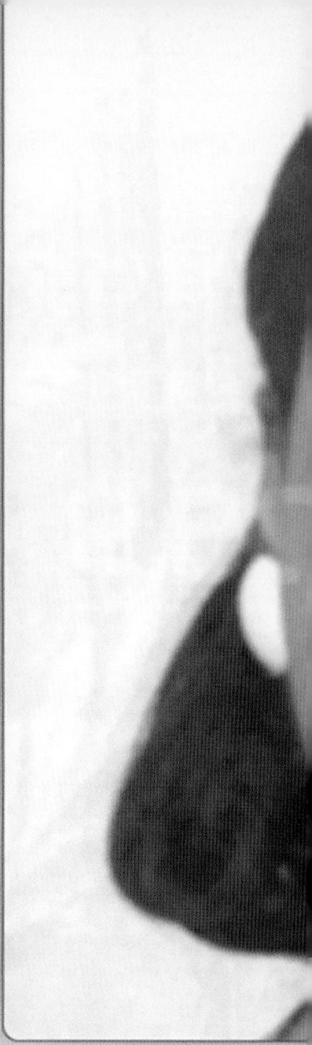

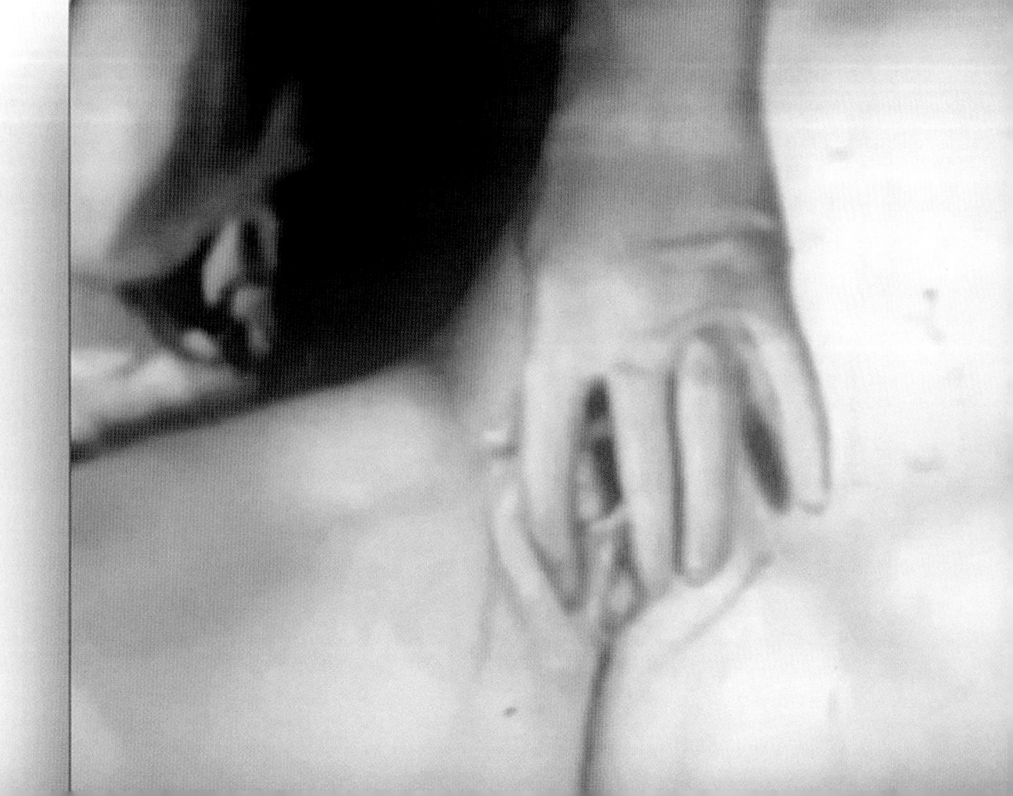

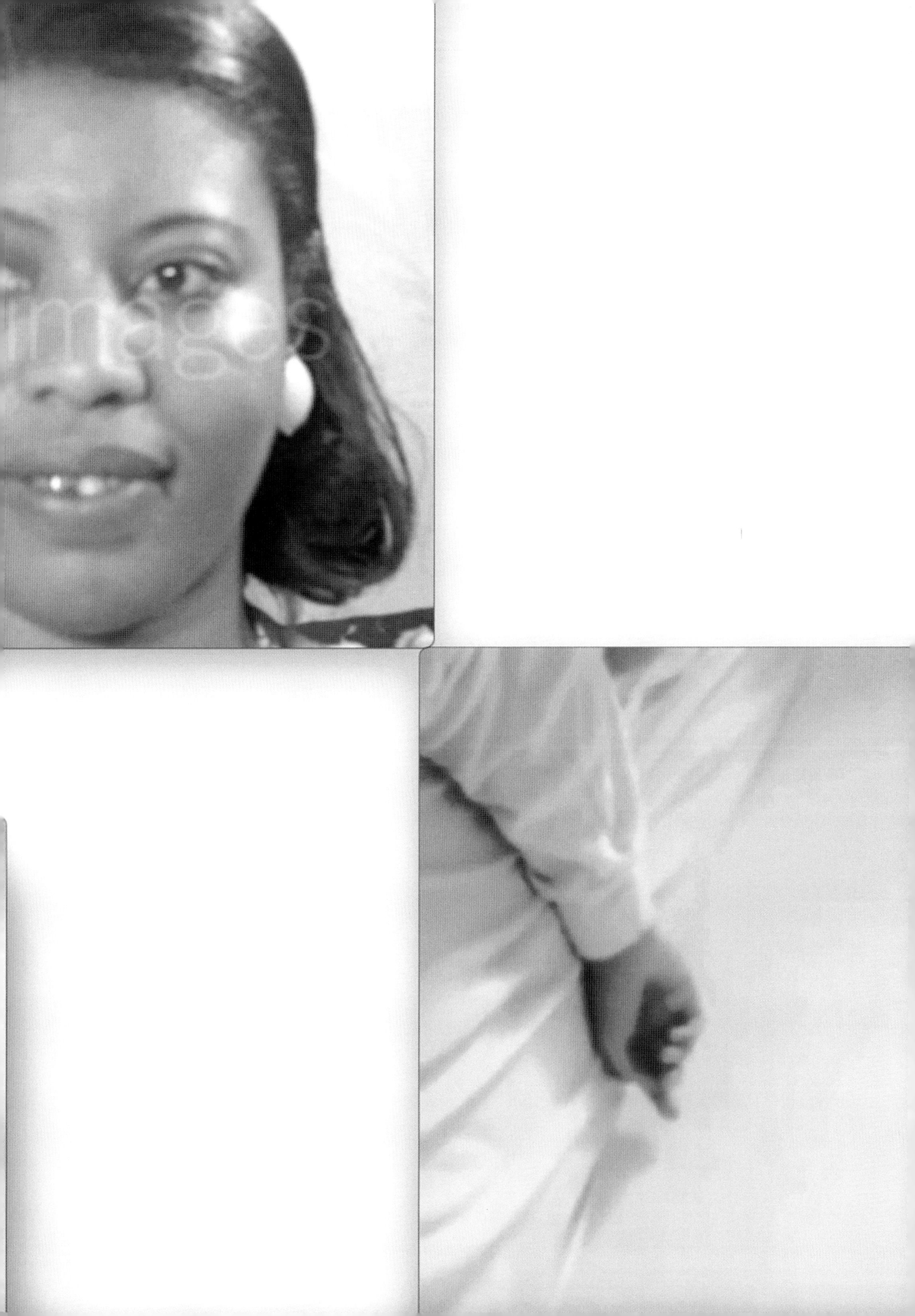

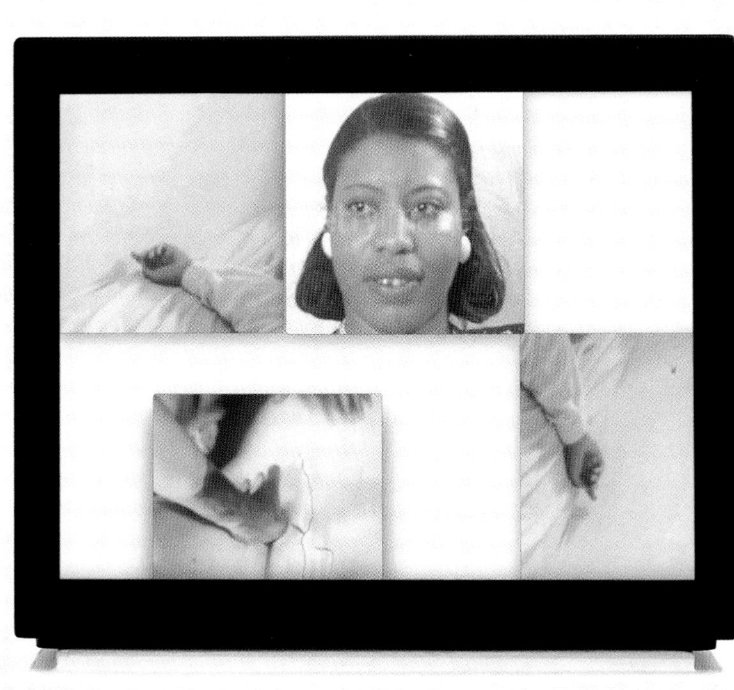

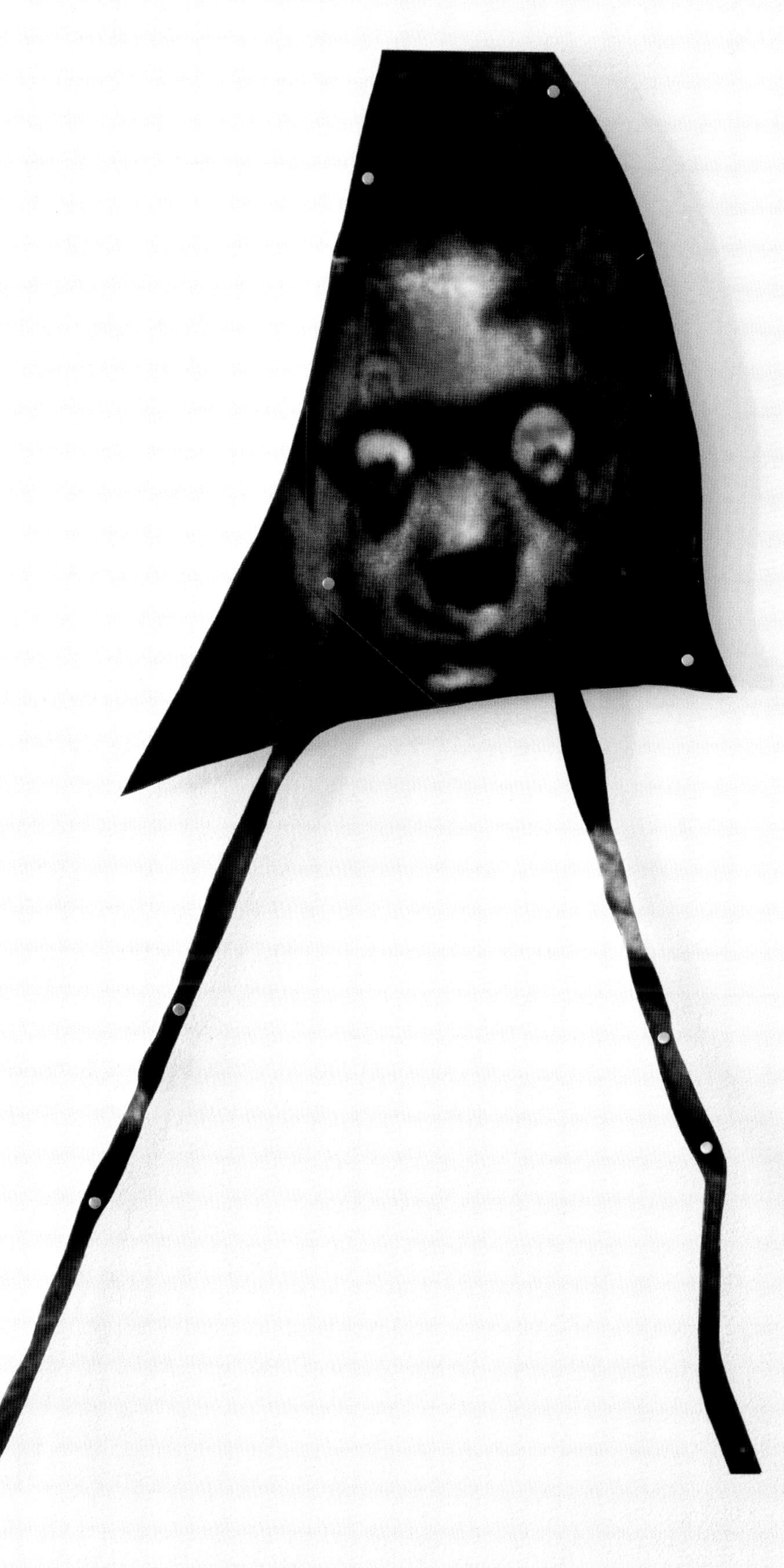

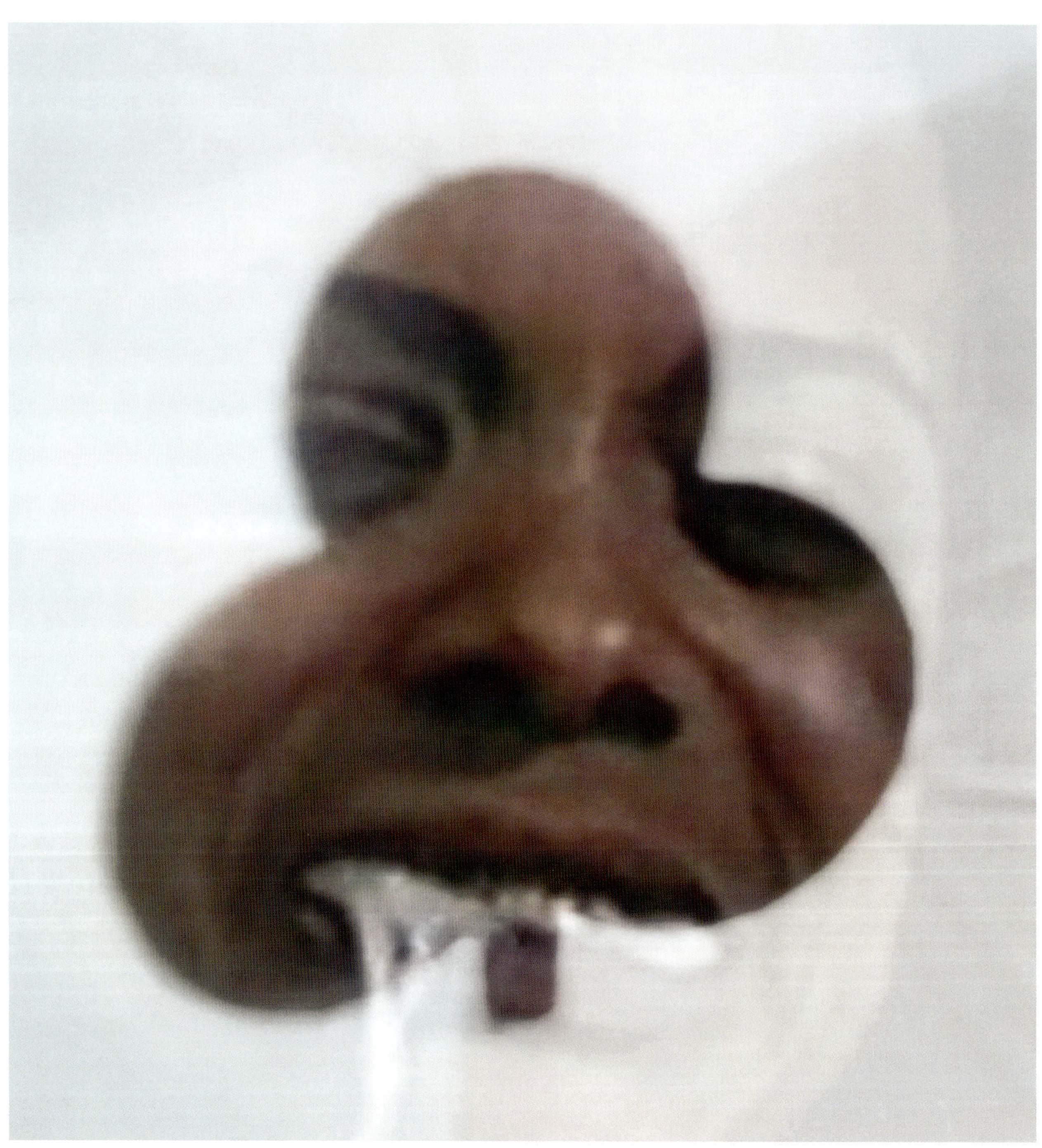

Clover I

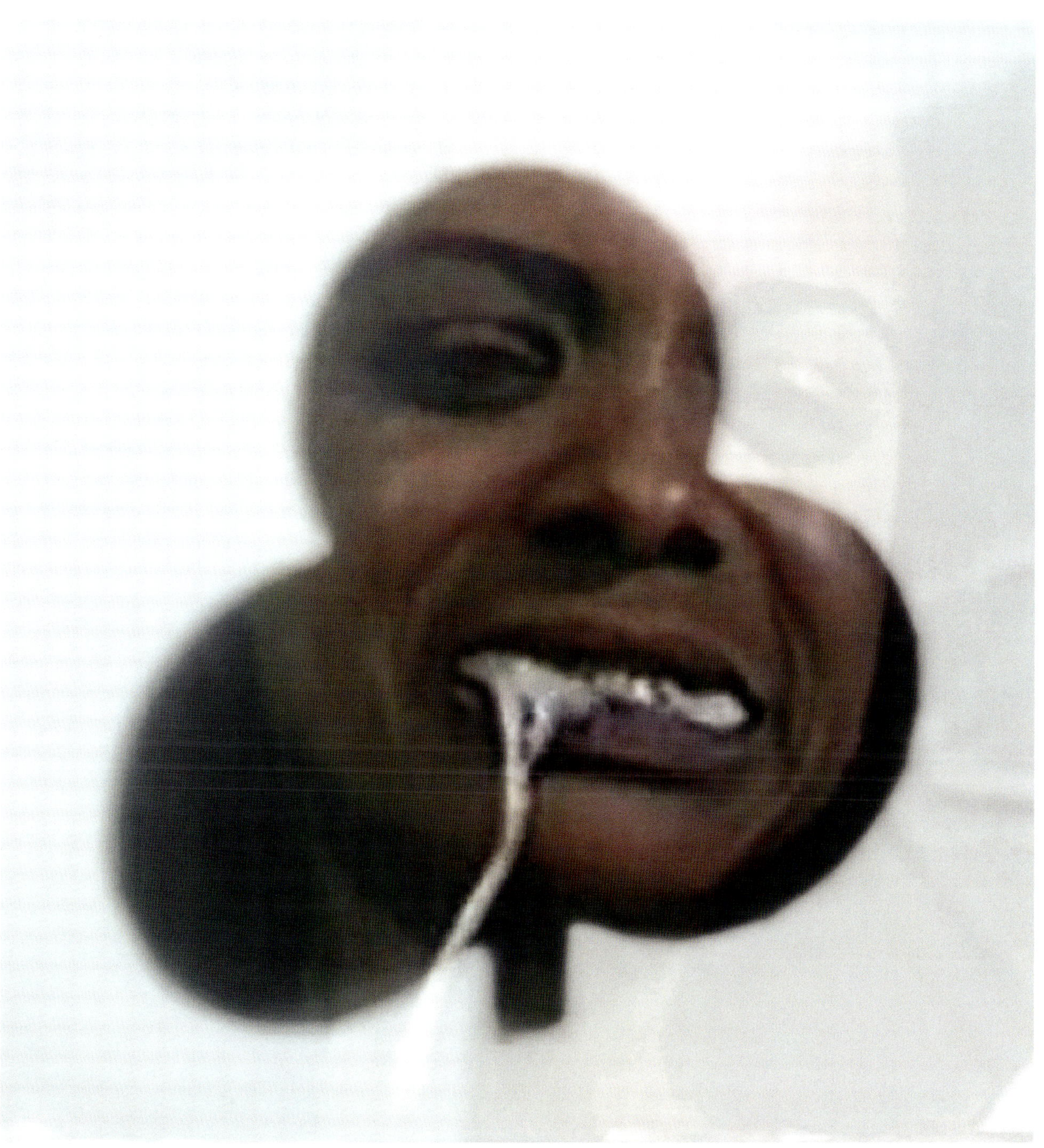

Clover II

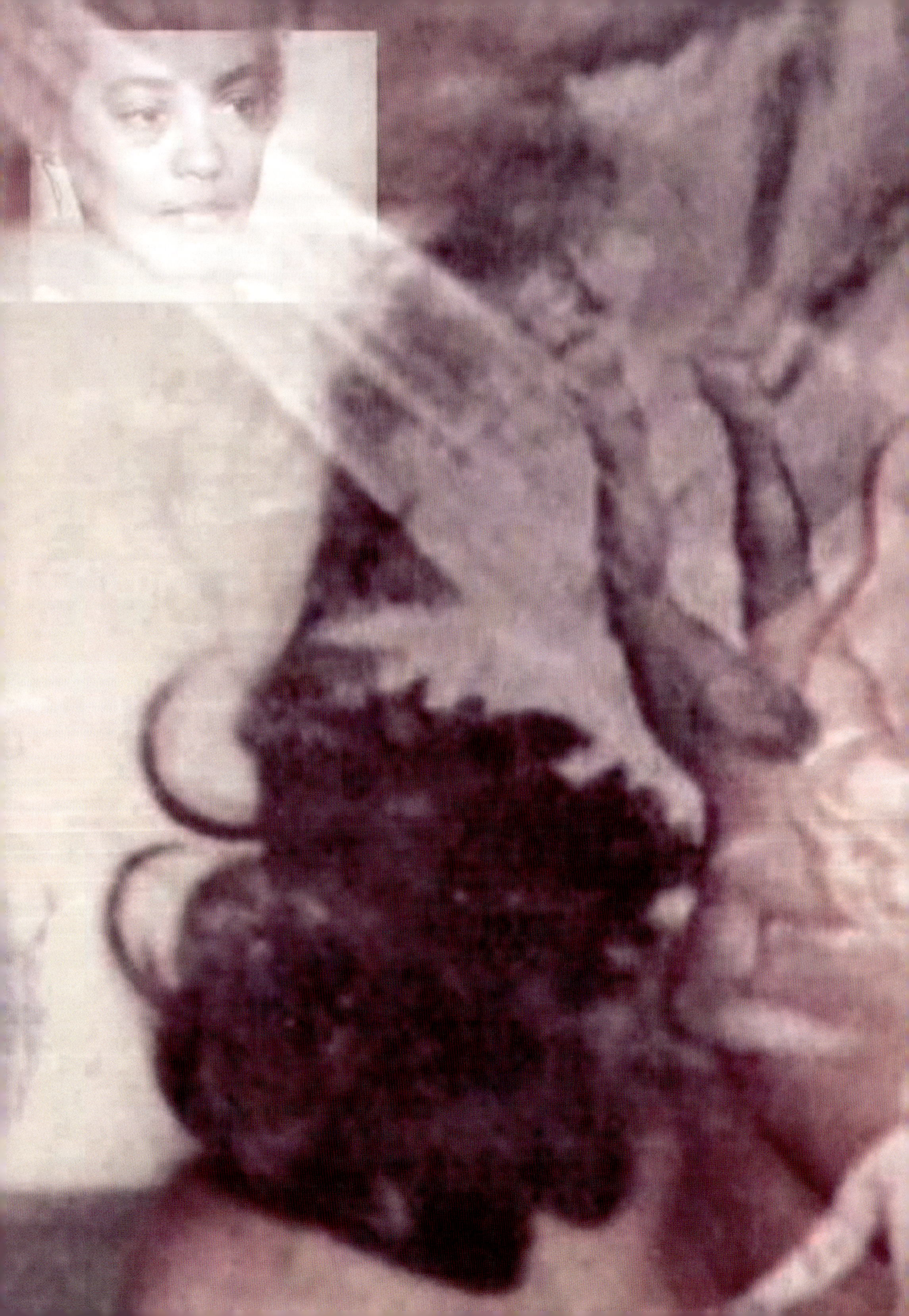

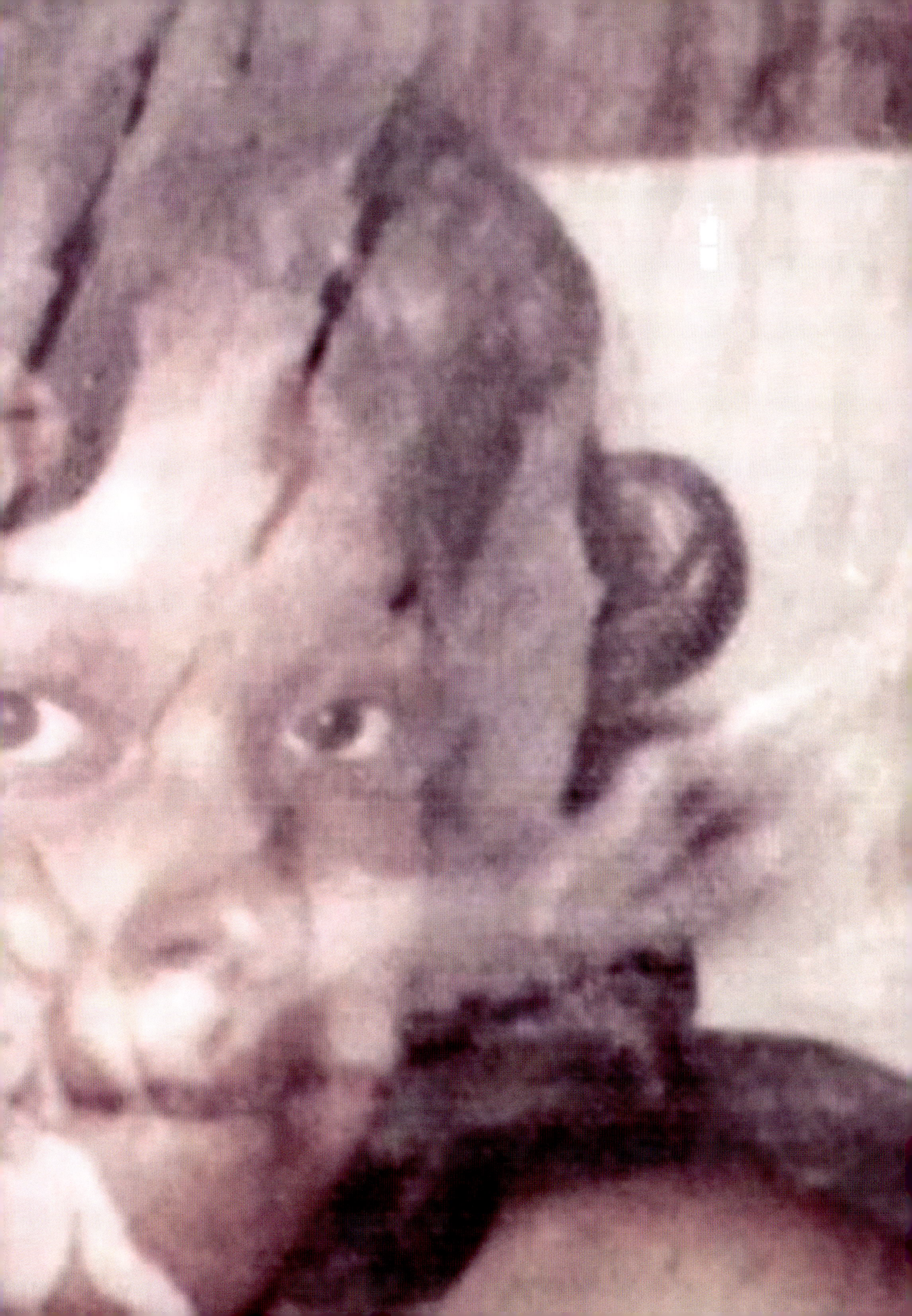

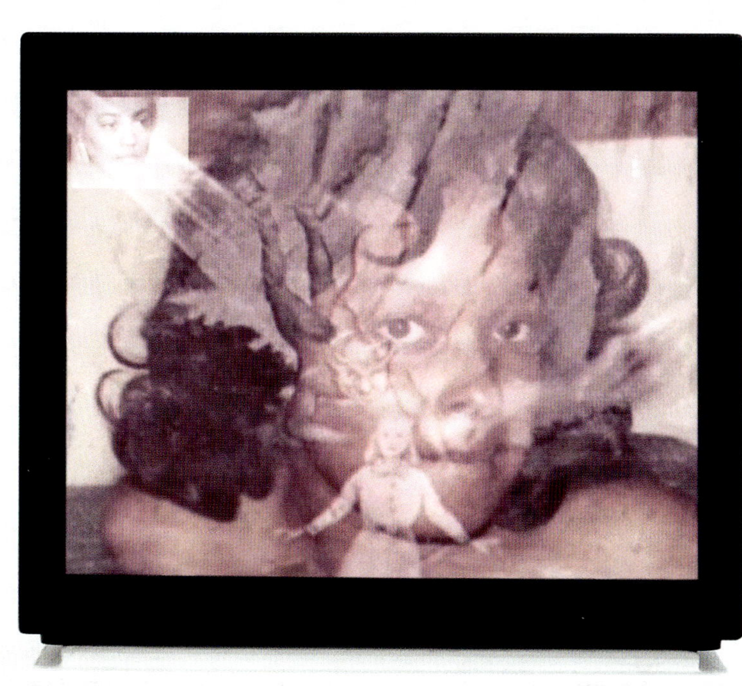

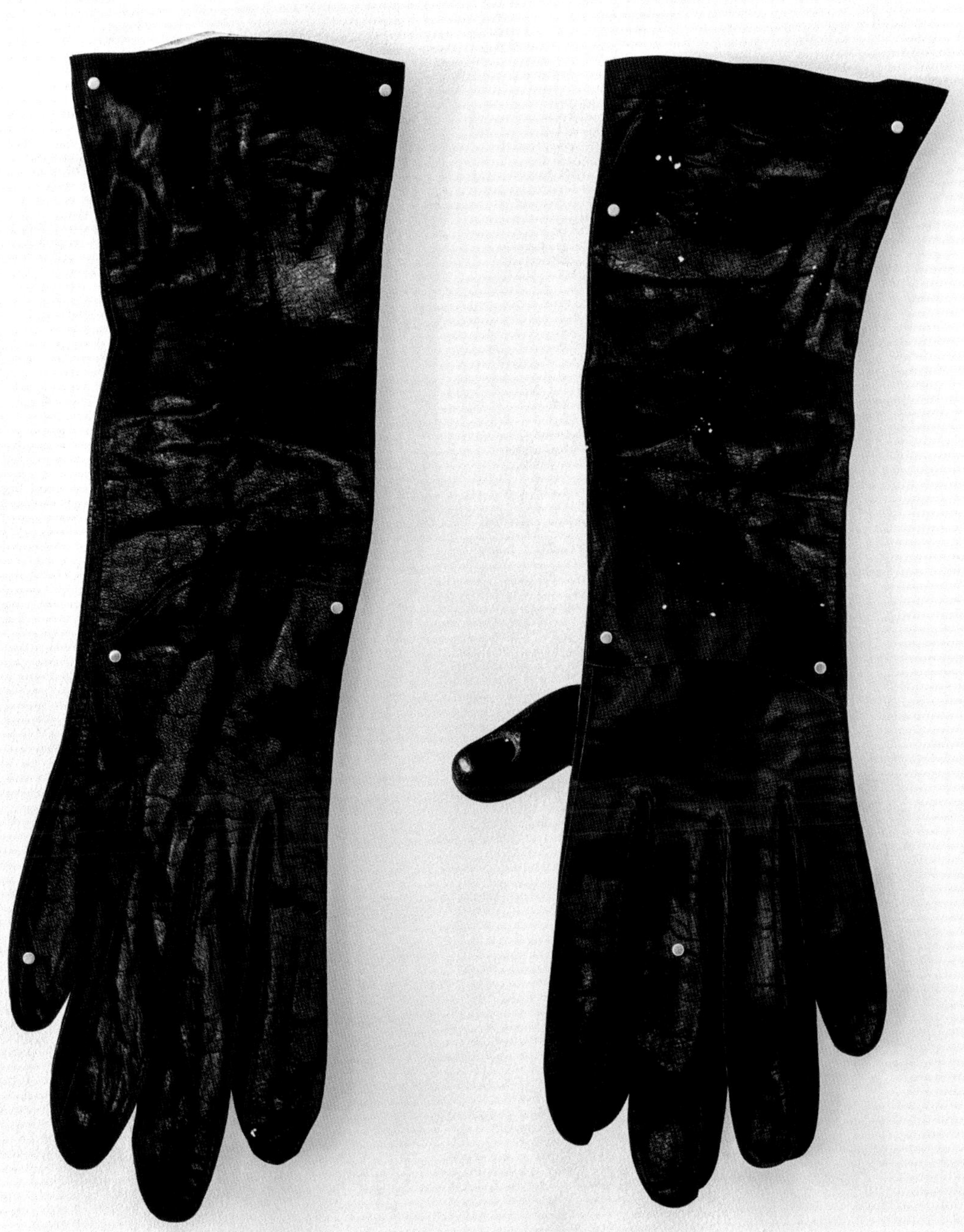

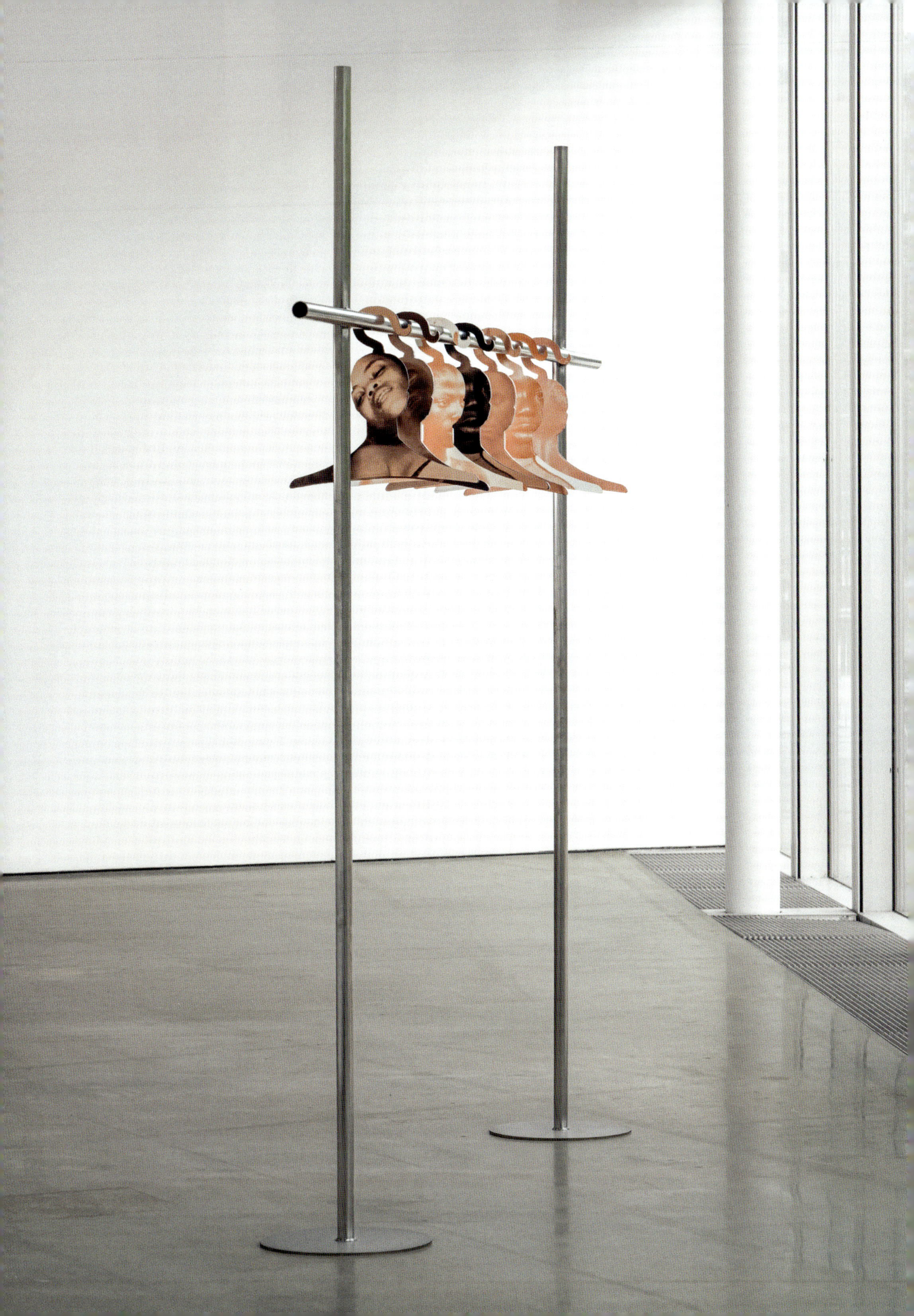

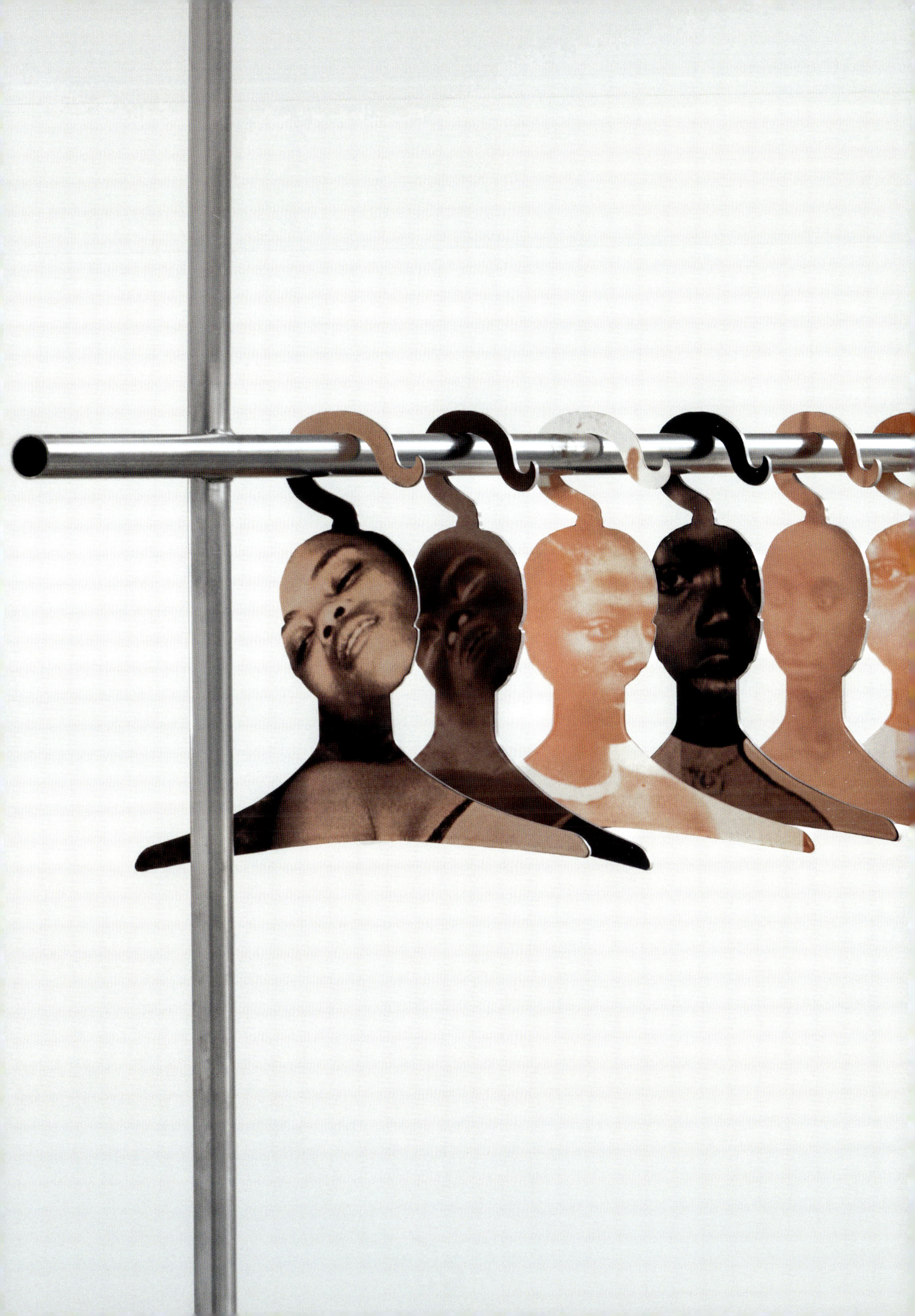

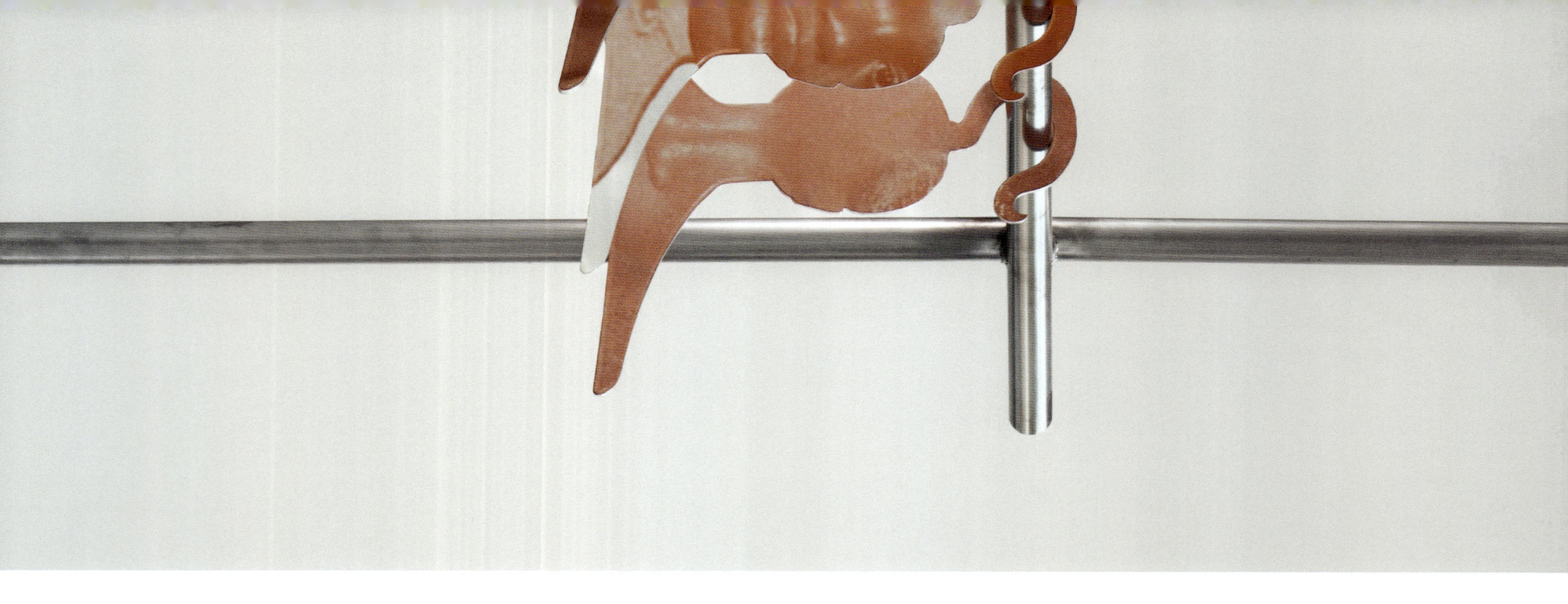

A Place Will Kill You

Leaving no one to blame
But the jokers pissing at the curb
A place will water hell
& pawn the blooms
Your father will think
What a good deal
Your mother will smirk
& set the table
You will prefer hard candy
New shoes or a slick penny
Something with a hard bottom

Whistle a machete into your back
Teach you salsa & jumpstyle
What is a block party without a girl
To lose something in the alley
What is a birthday without days
Of hunger to follow
A place will sharpen itself
Produce a fever that ricochets
A bridge to leave you bloody
The ribbon it chooses
Will restore or strangle
But never fade
A place will kill you
Jail your fitful becoming
Silence your unruliness
Be it the sweet grime
Or the hollow shaft of the plains
The lonely highway
Making enemies out of thunder
Each hungry bolt rending your dress
With a wolf’s wine
The wind a proper coffin
For the girl you toss aside
A place will kill you
Leaving nothing to sink
Your lovely teeth into
But the dying distance
& the wish to belong
Everywhere you’ve never been

C. LeClaire

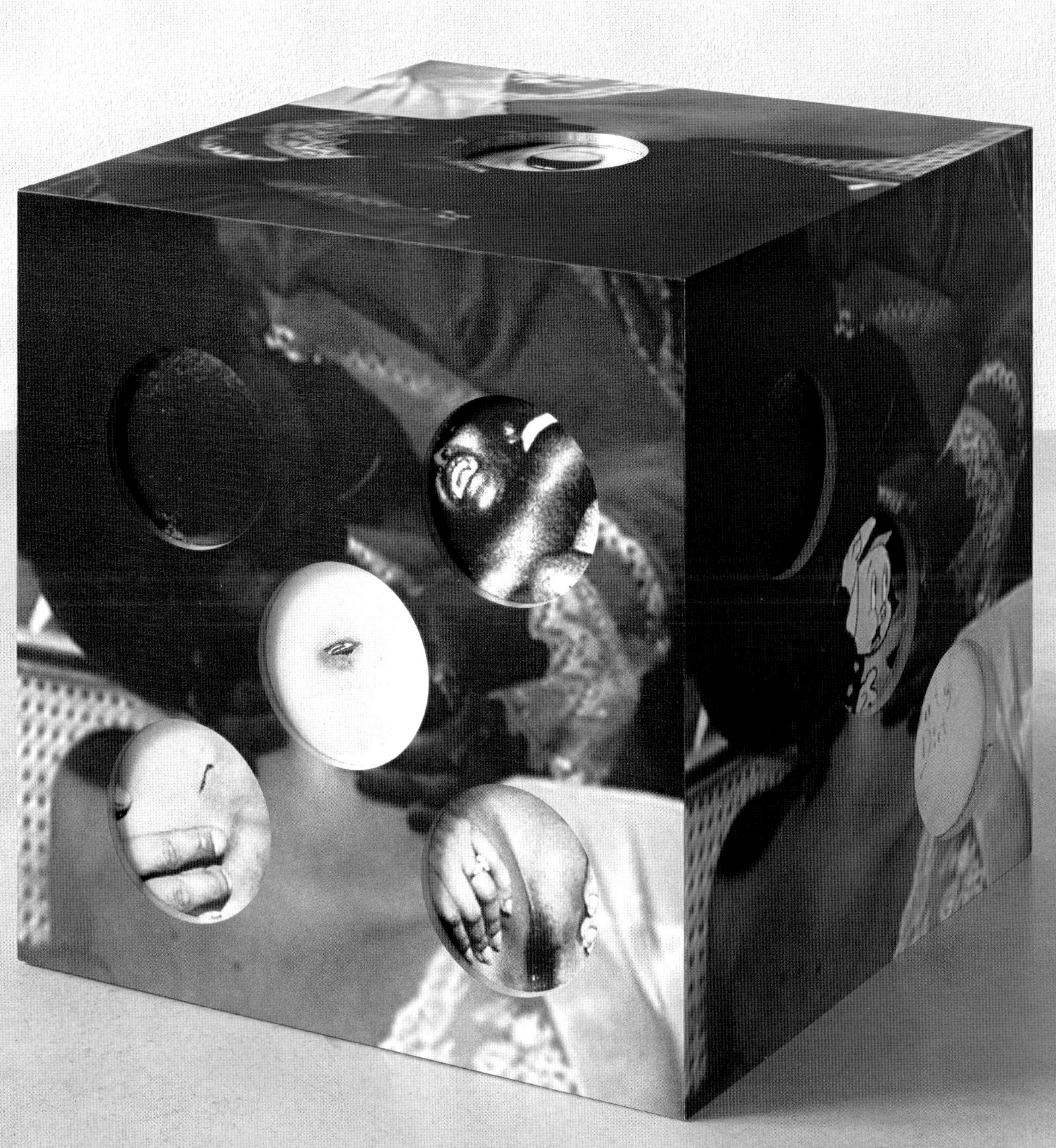

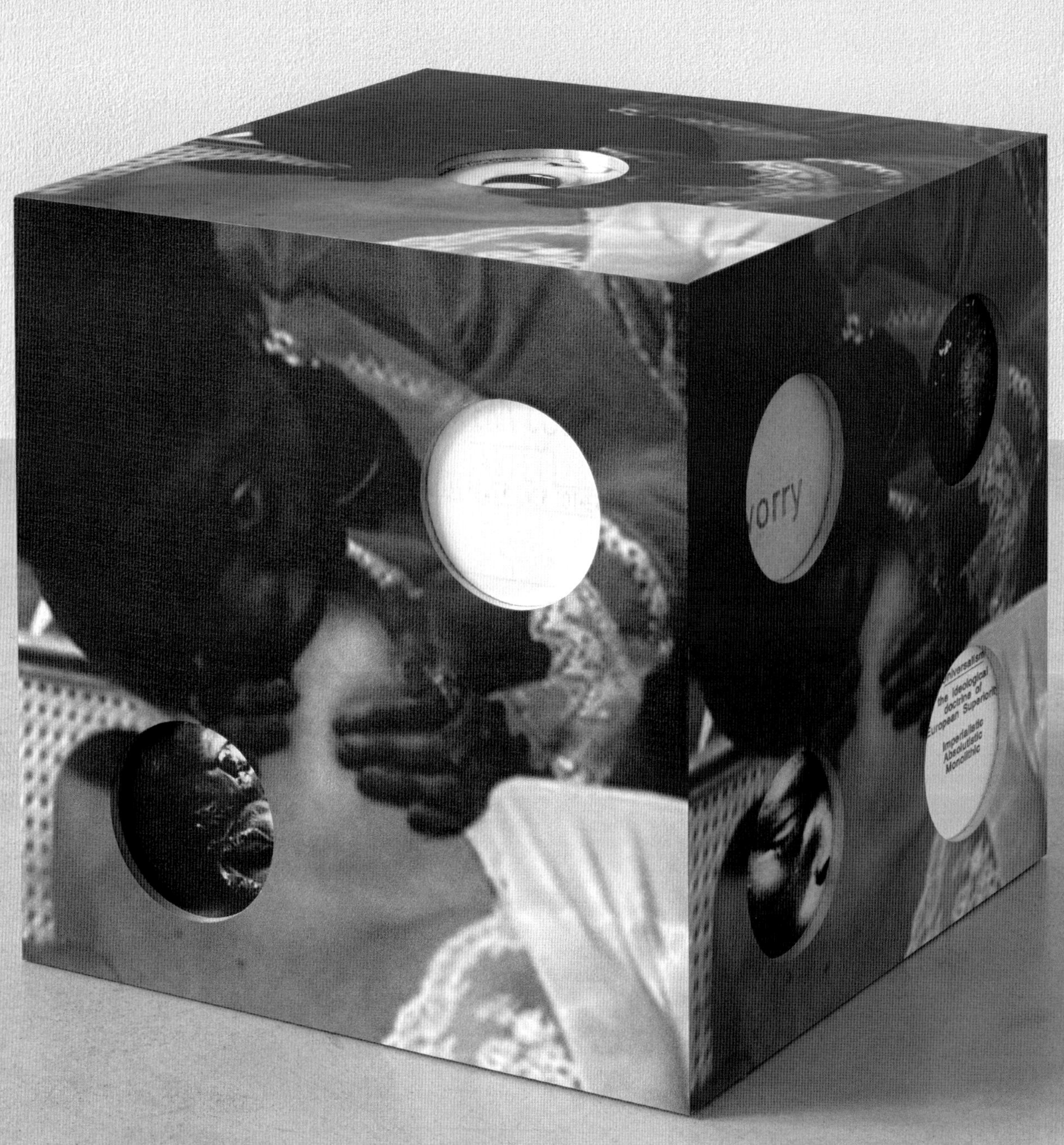
vorry
Universalism
the Ideological
doctrine of
European Superiorit
Imperialistic
Absolutistic
Monolithic

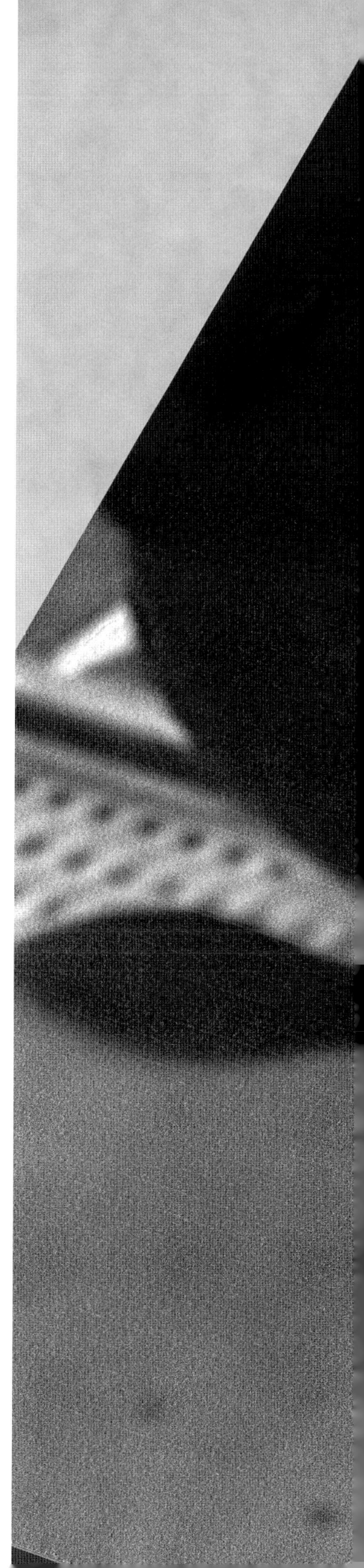

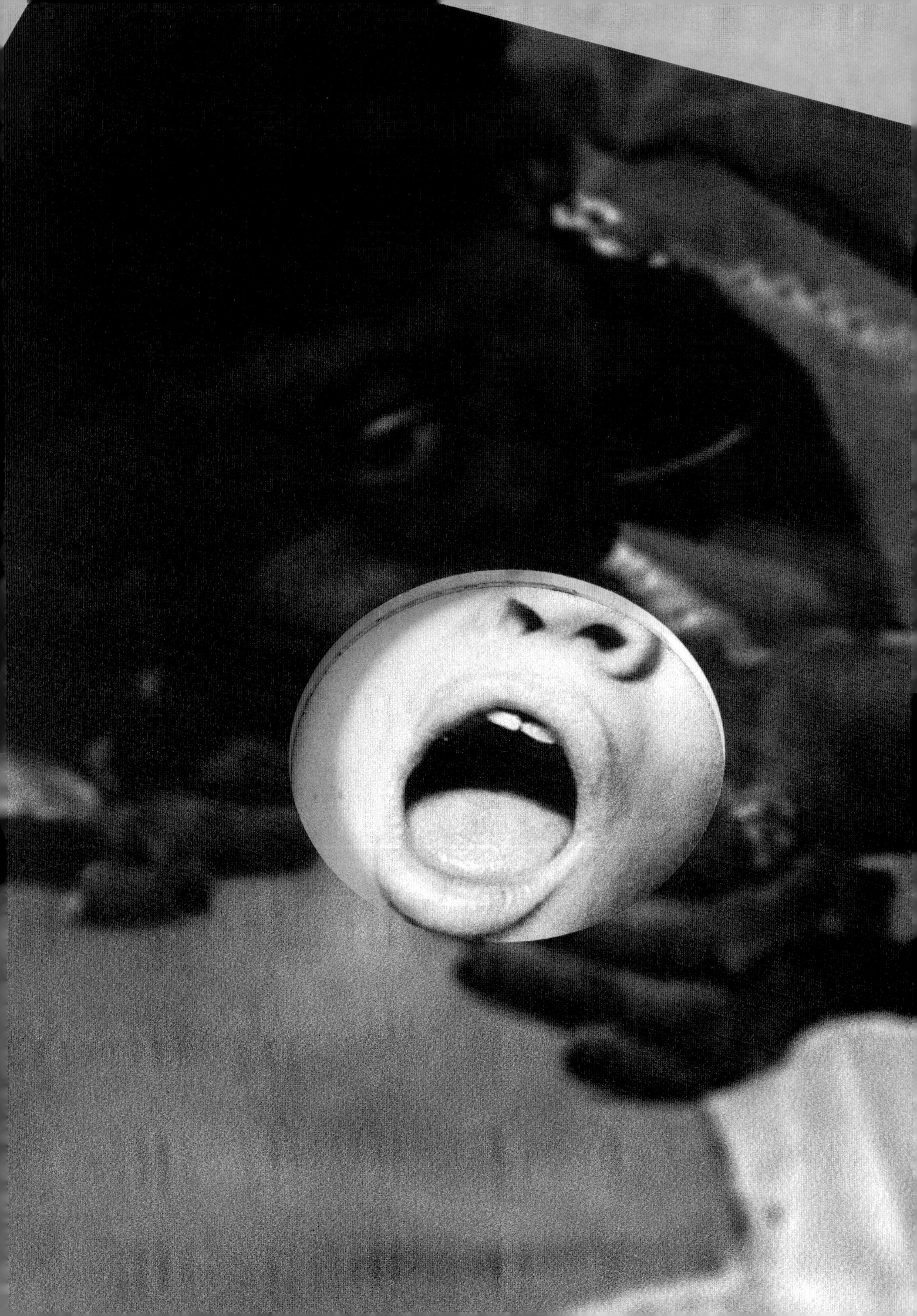

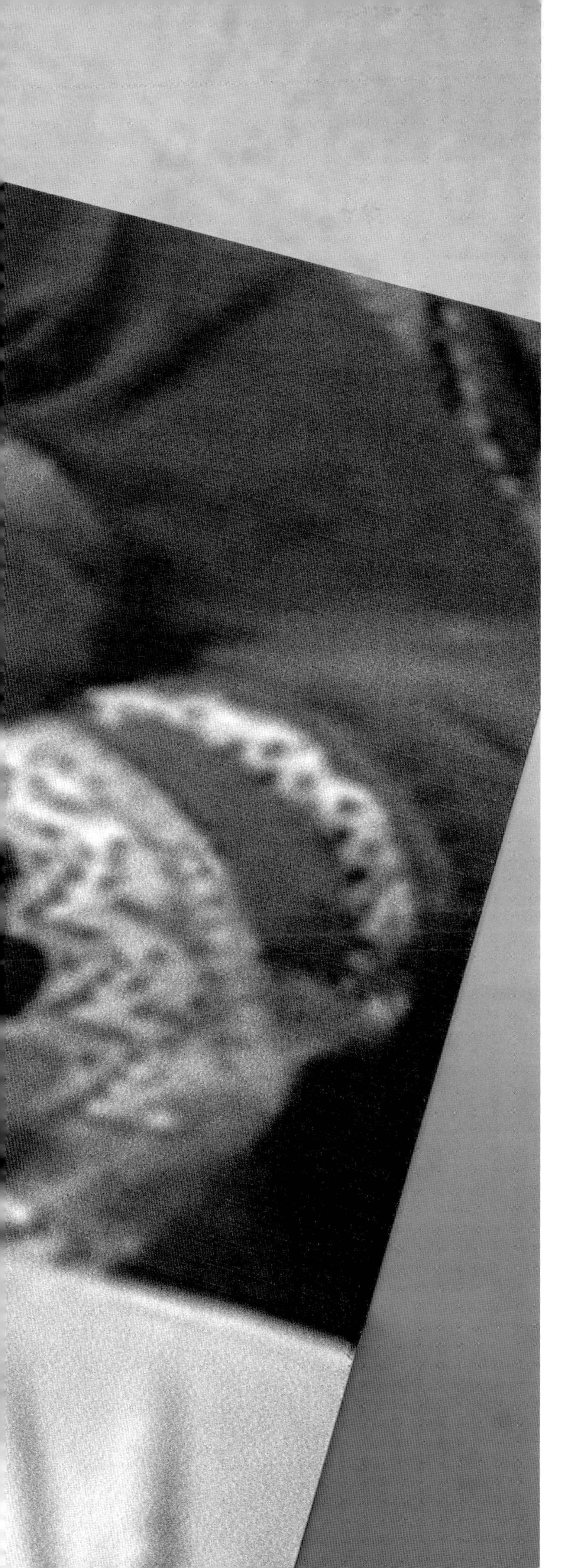

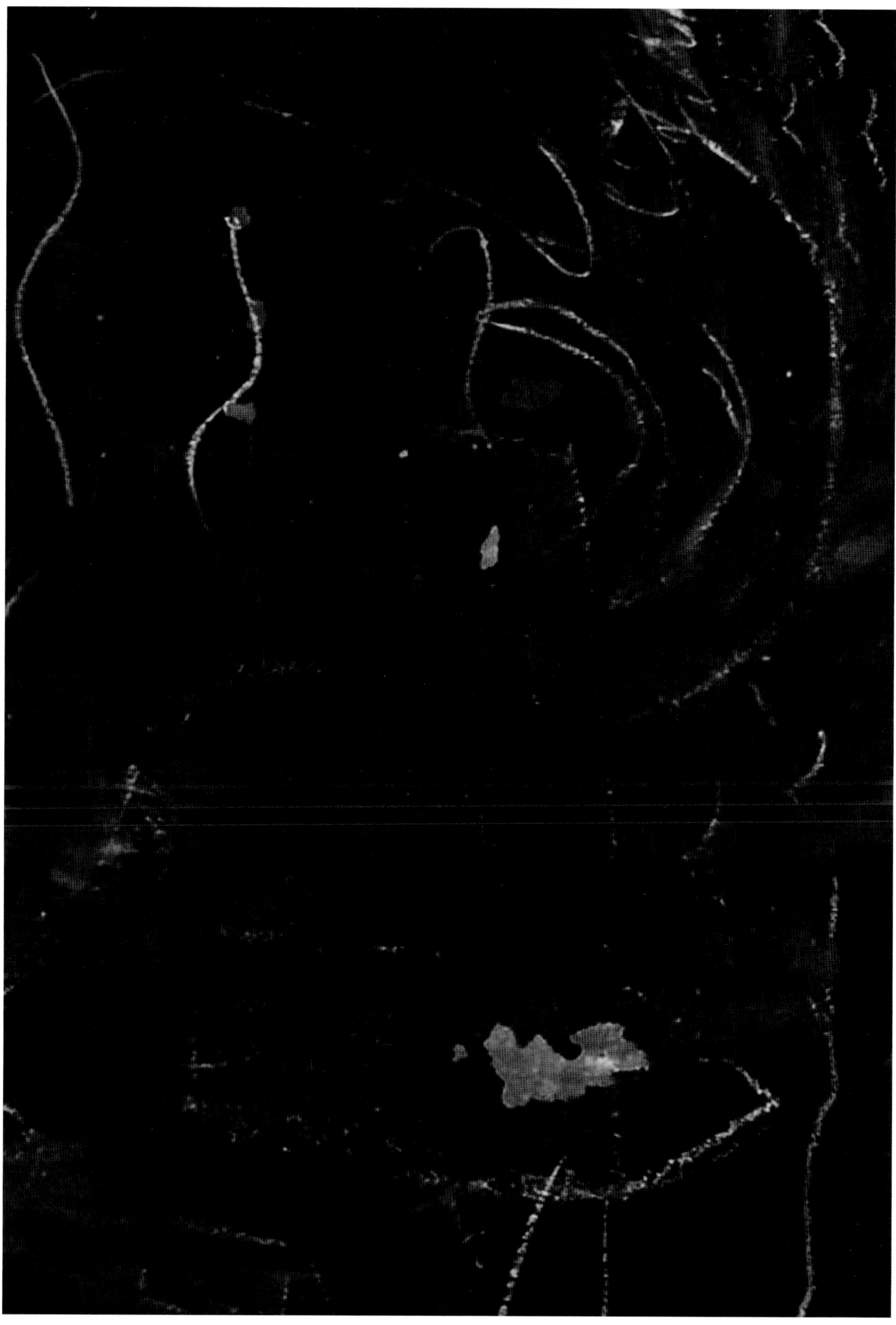

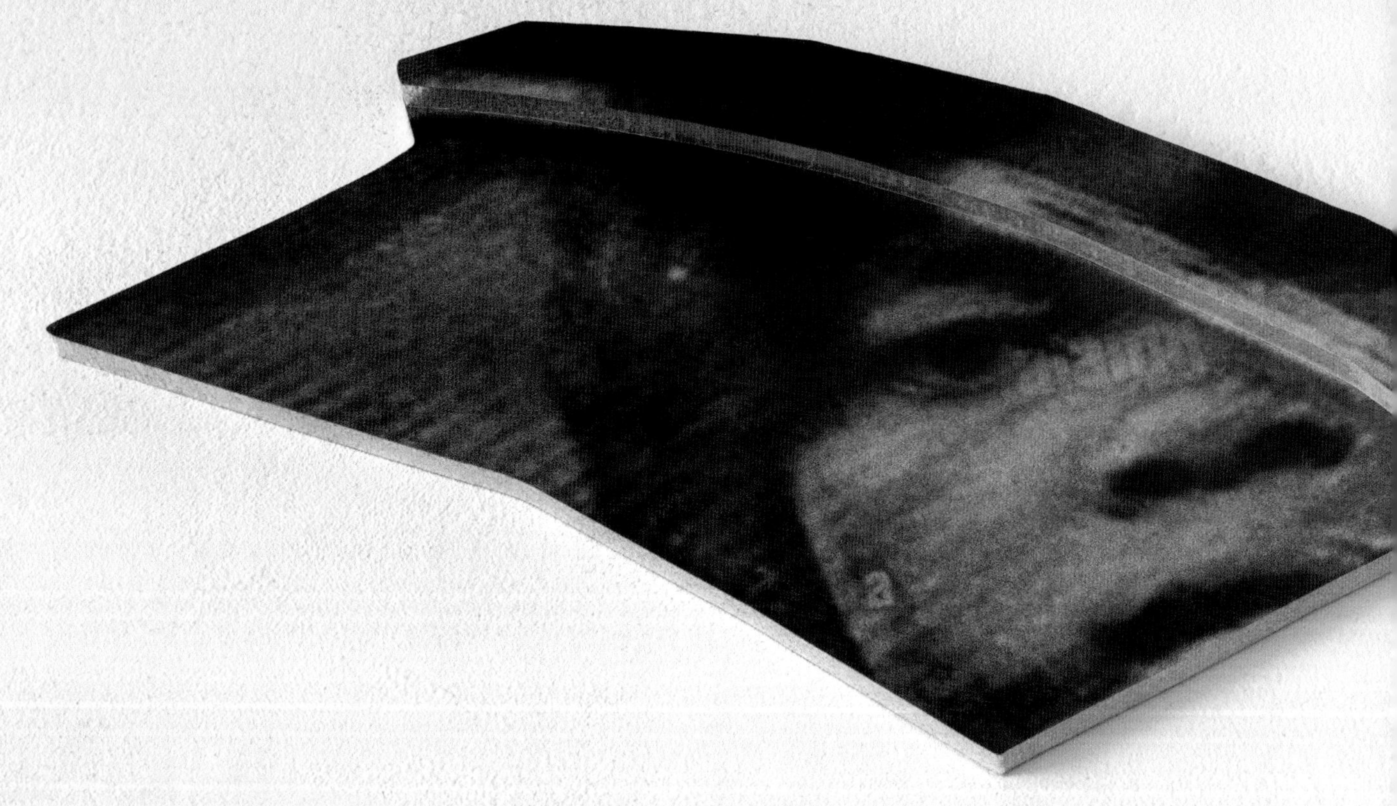

Comb

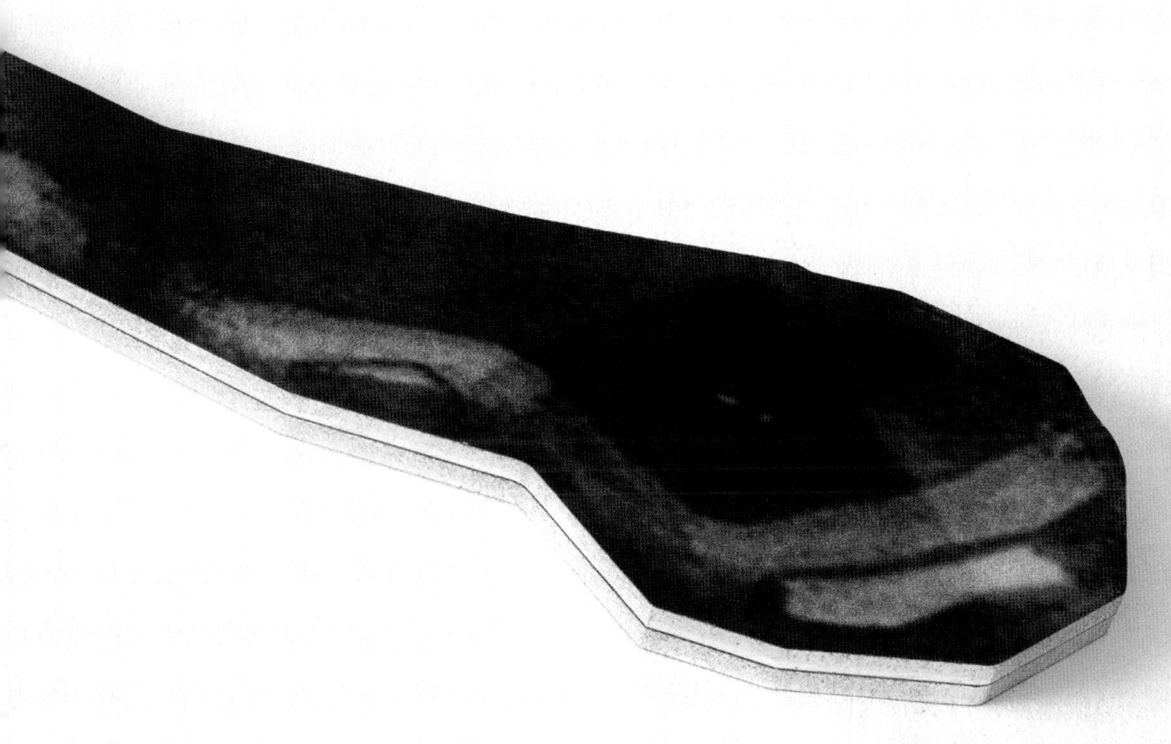

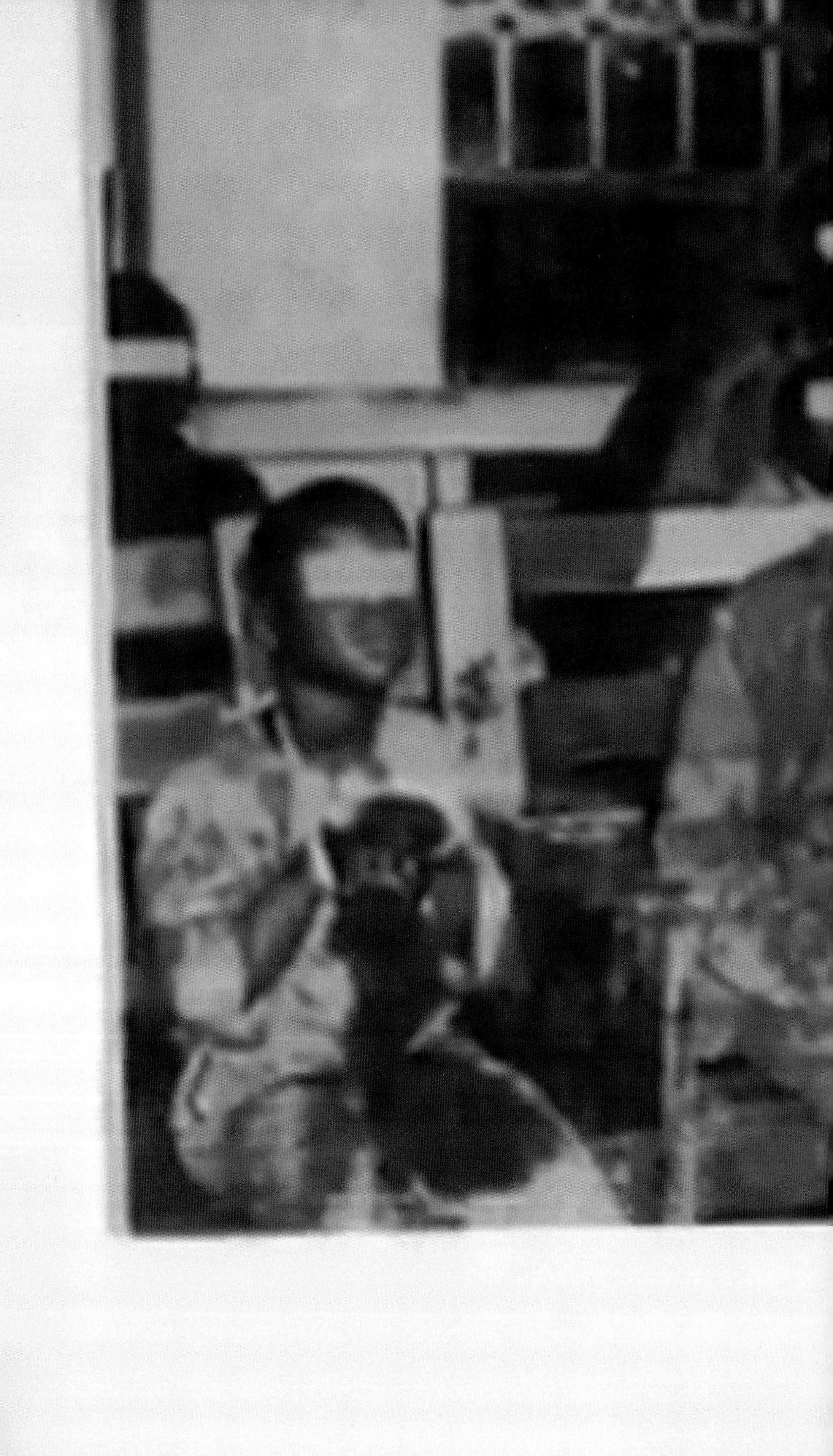

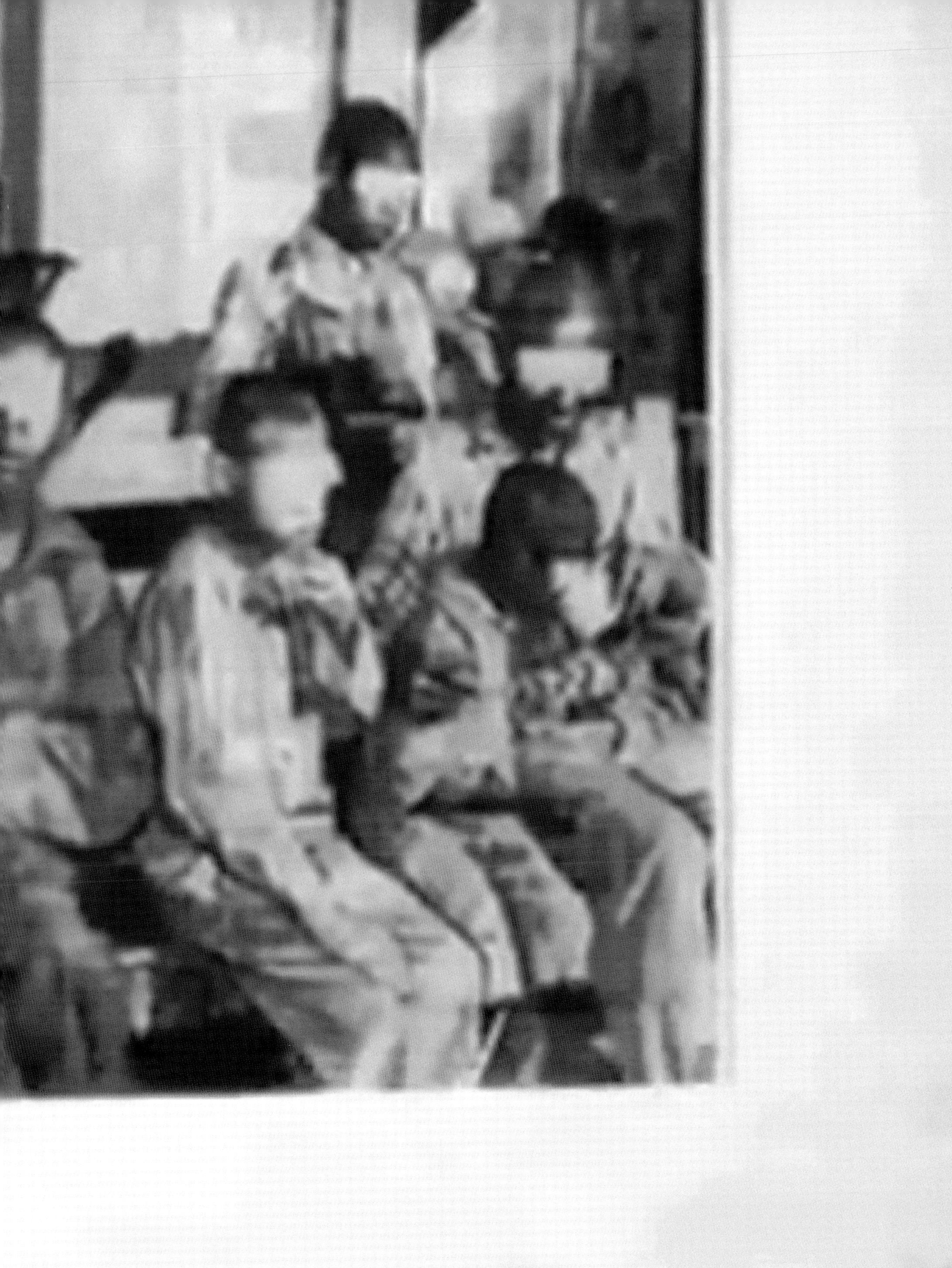

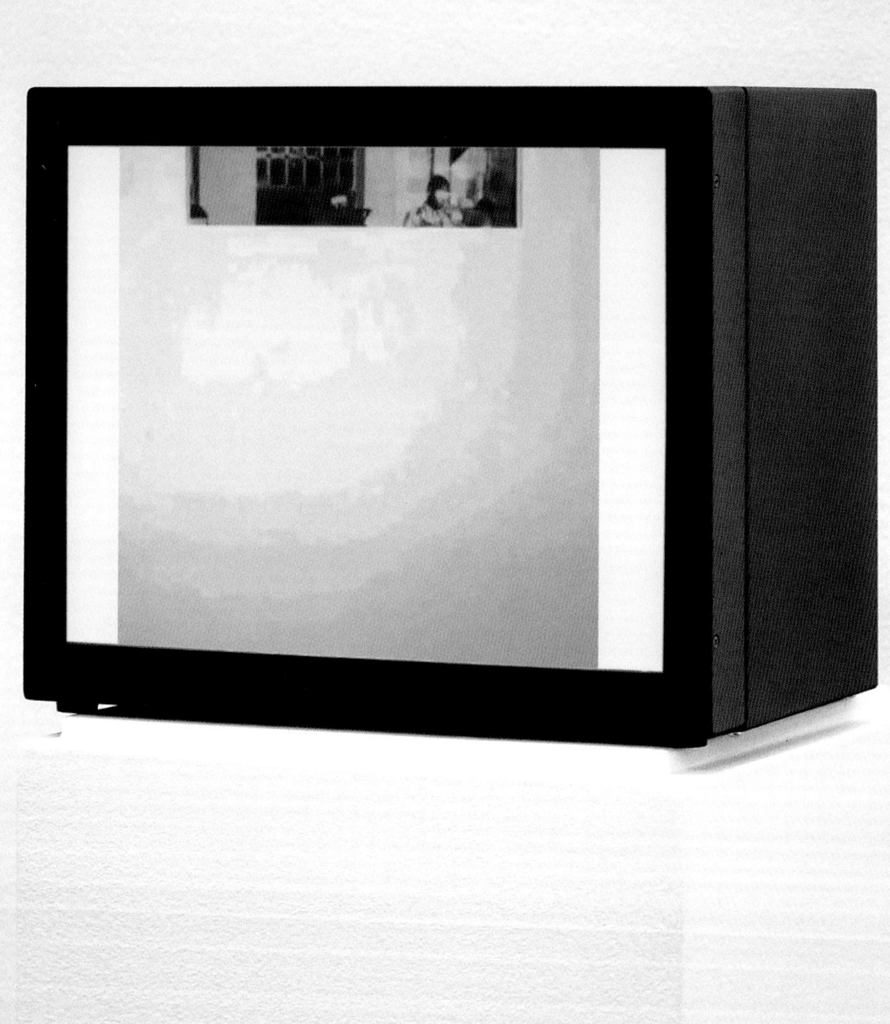

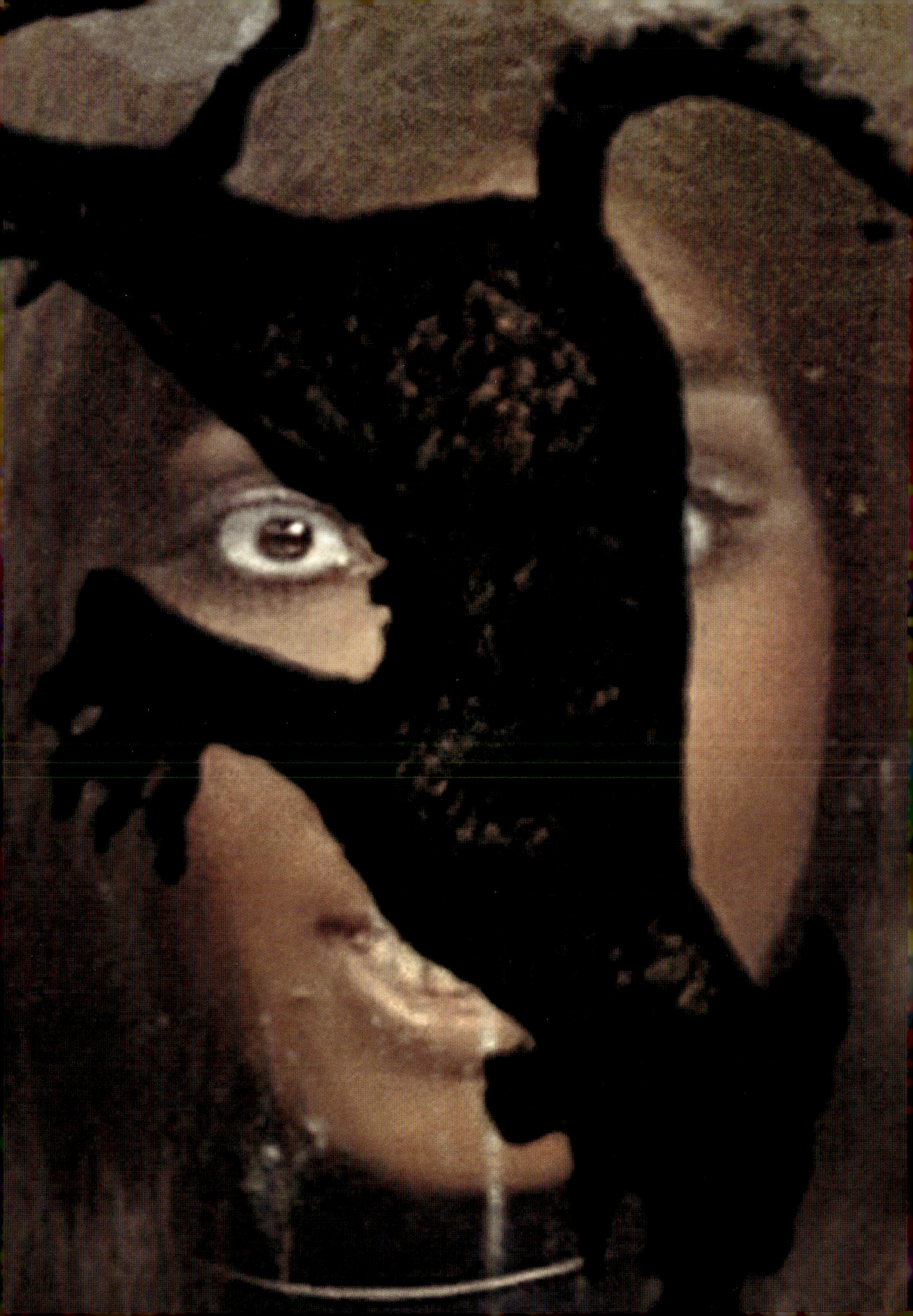

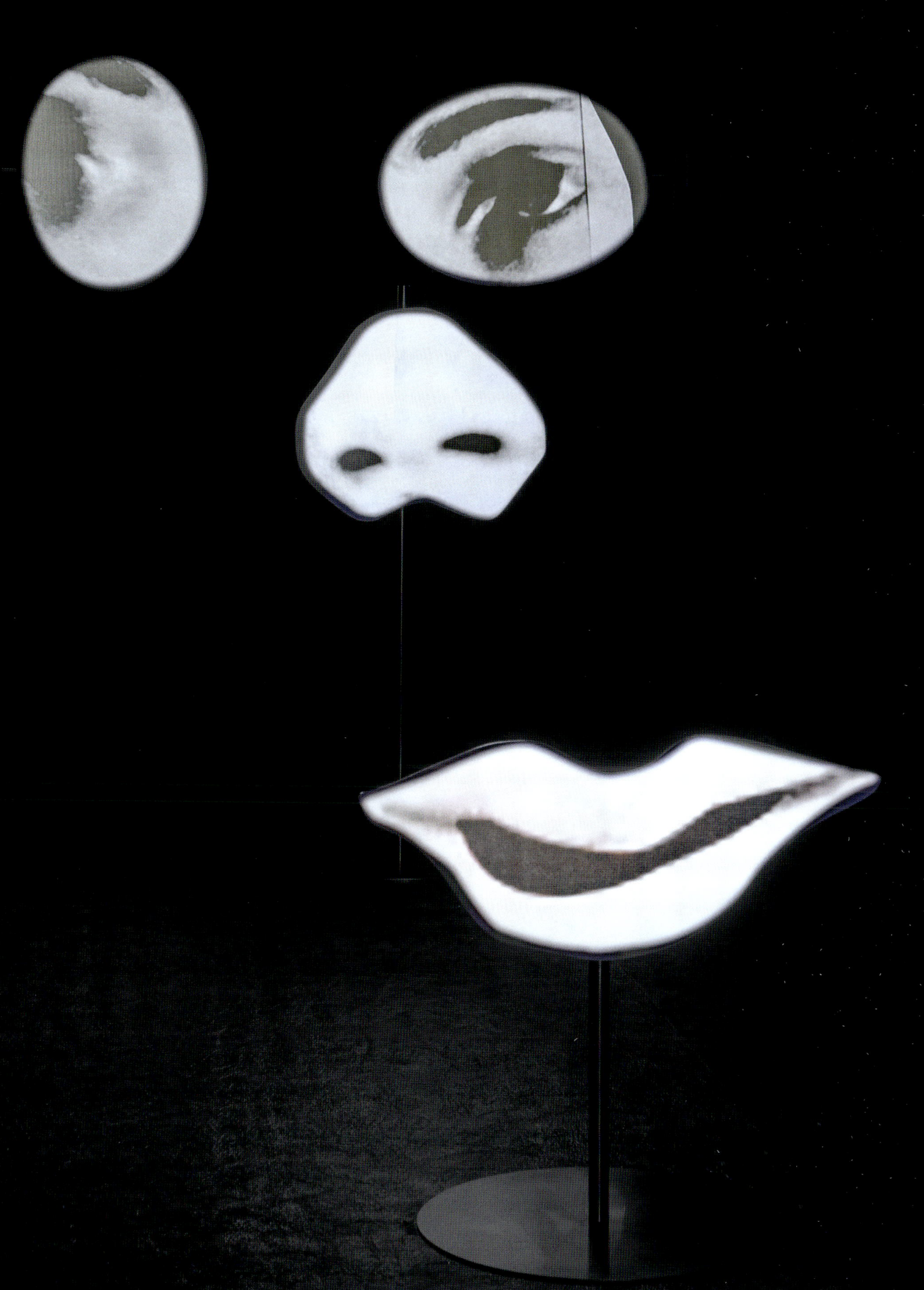

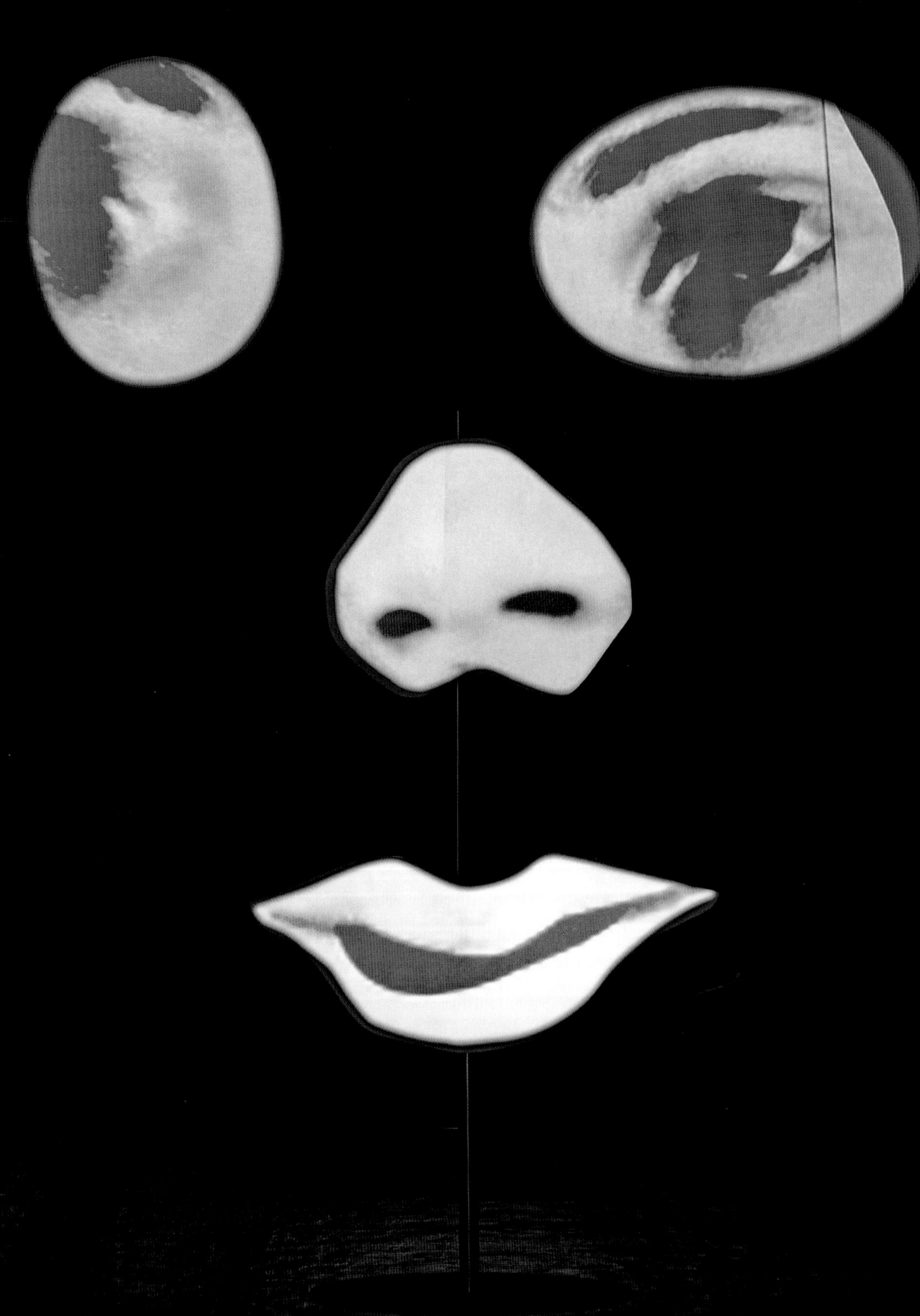

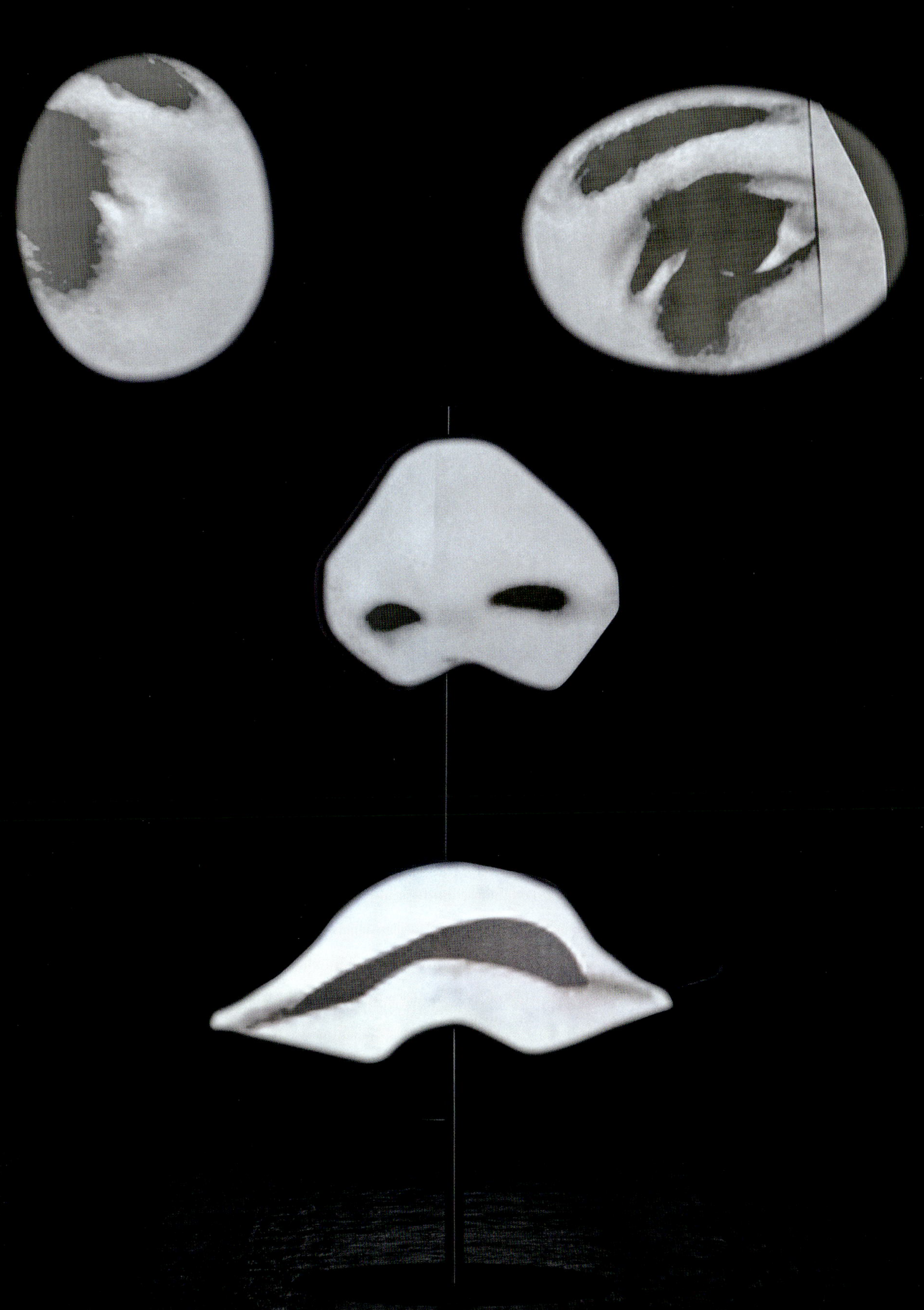

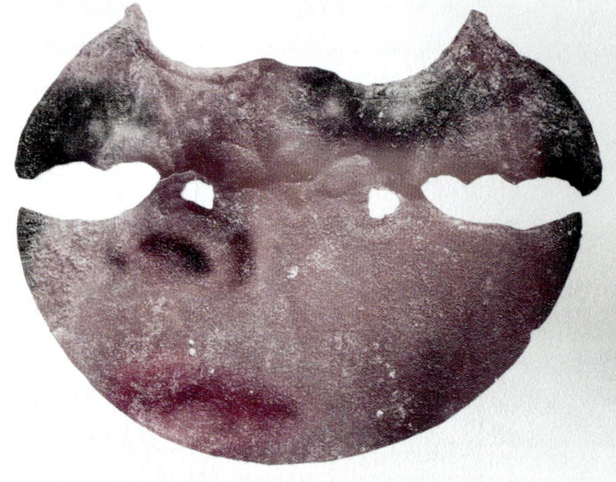

Dirty
Dirt

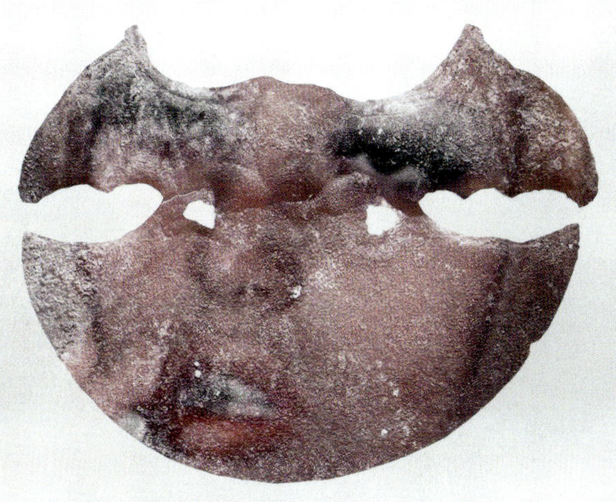

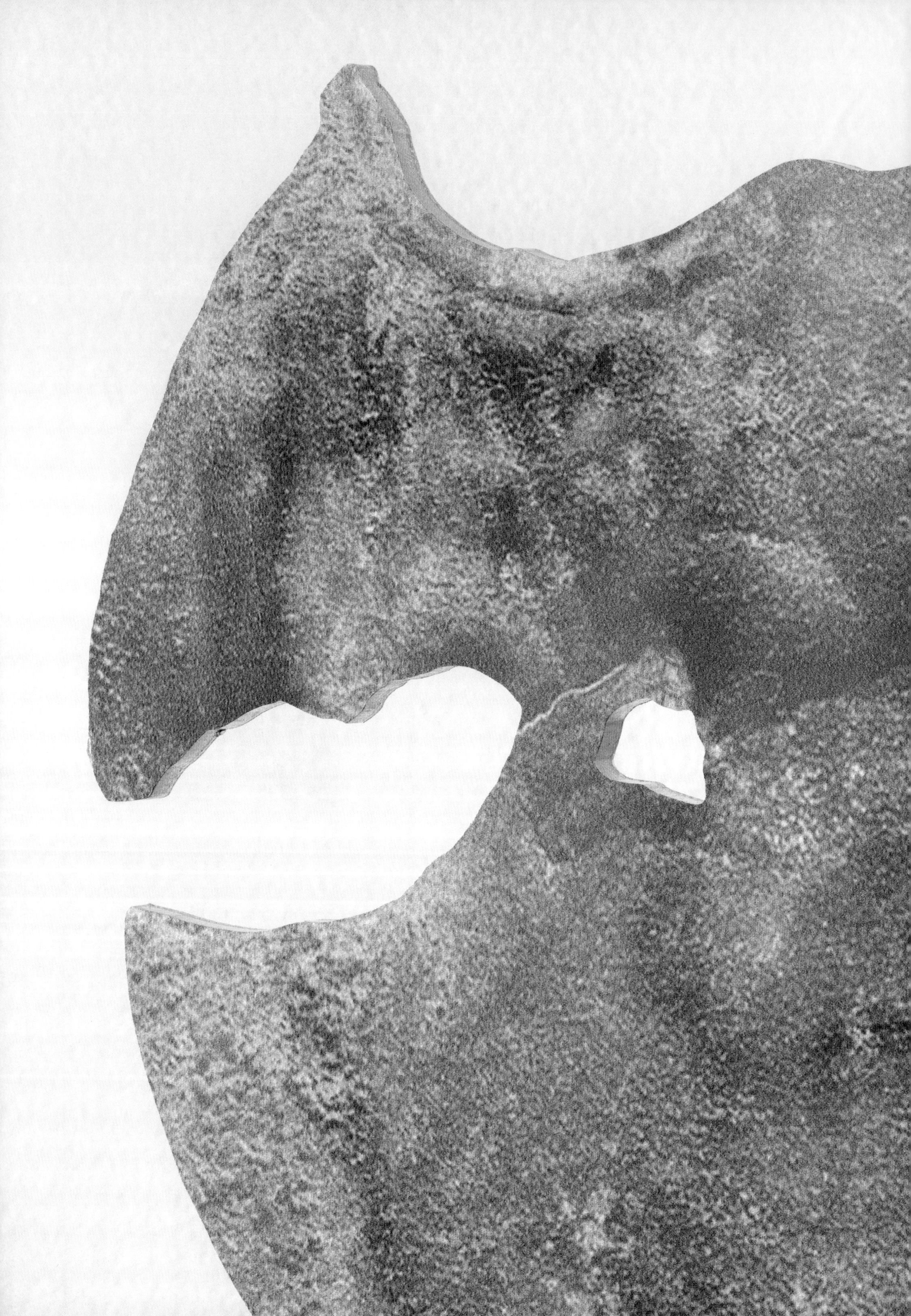

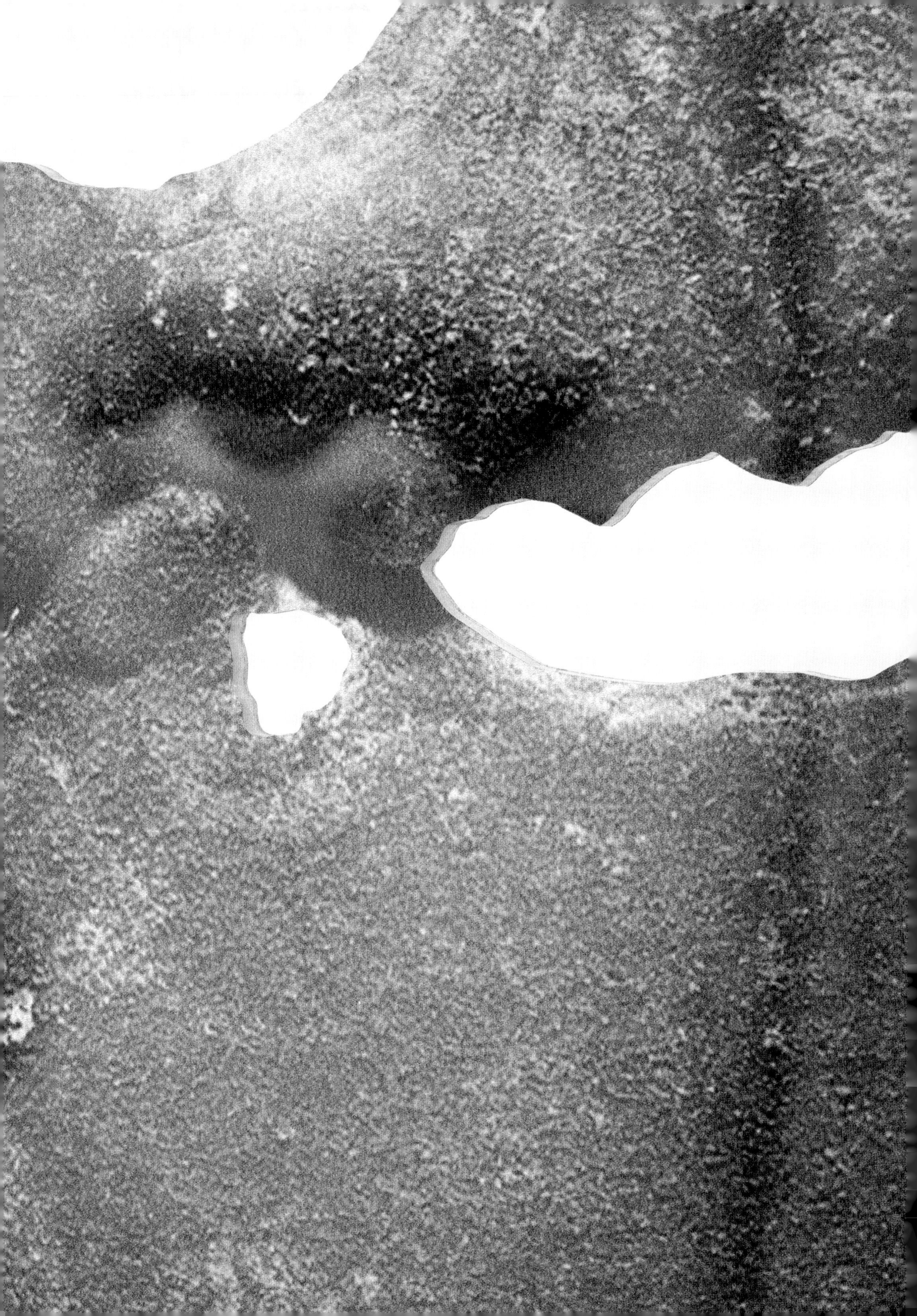

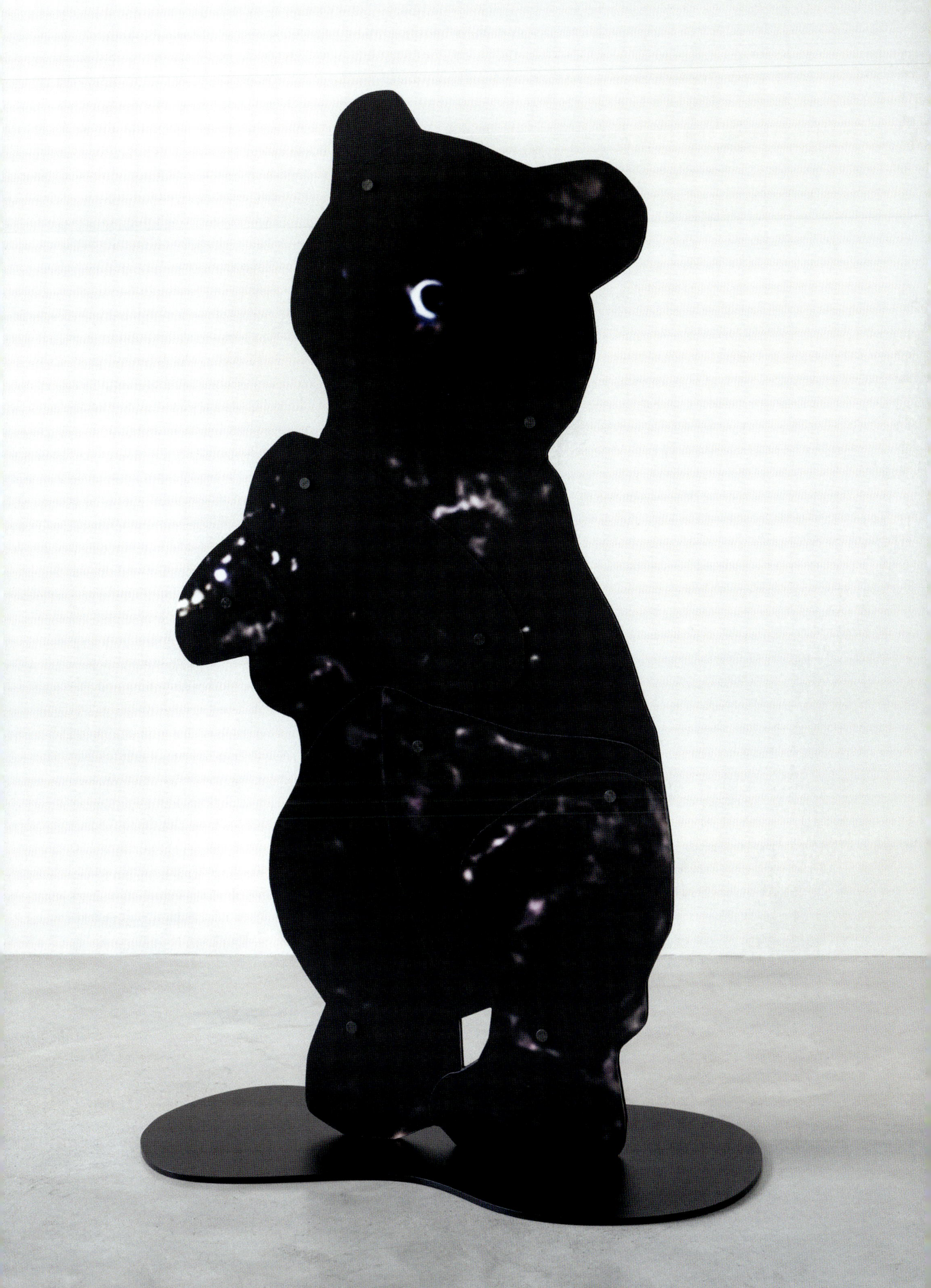

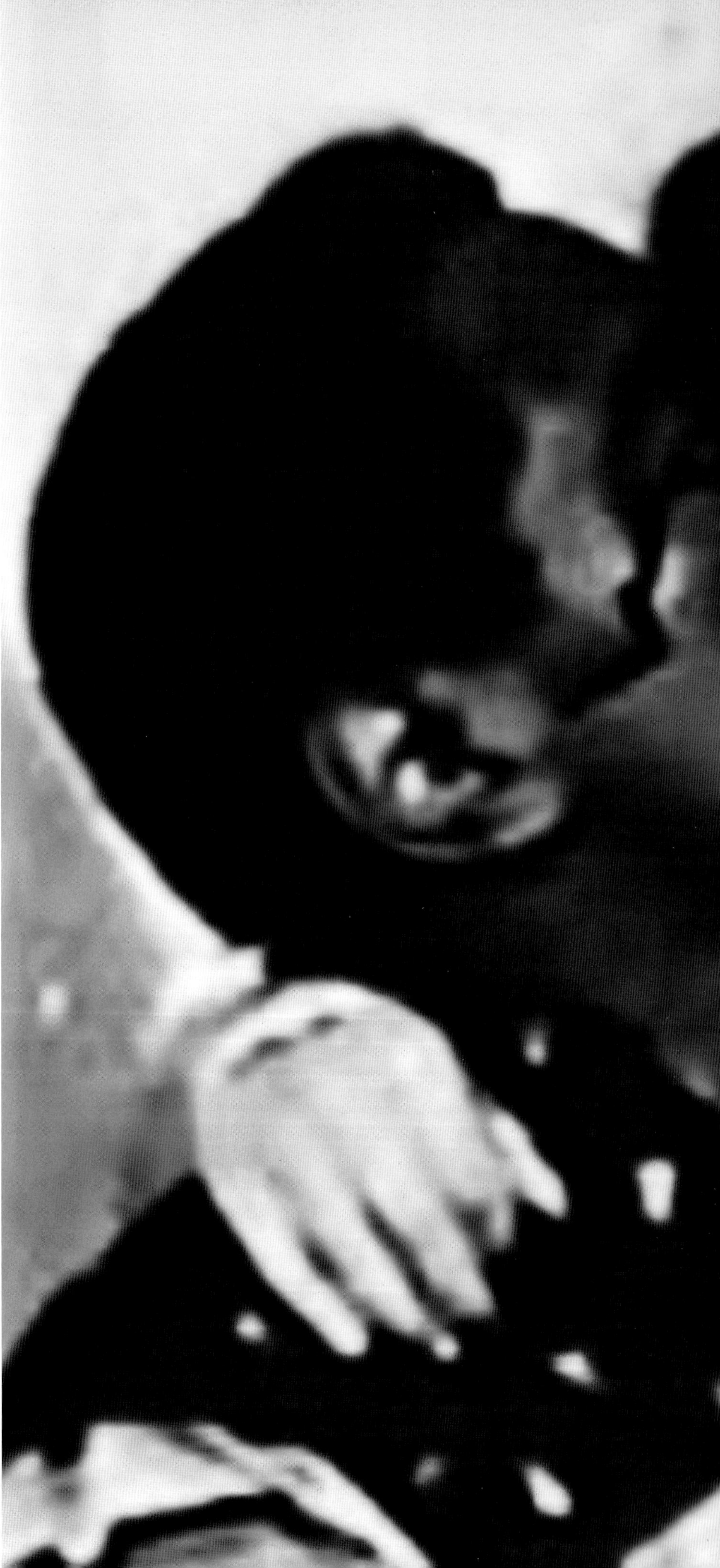

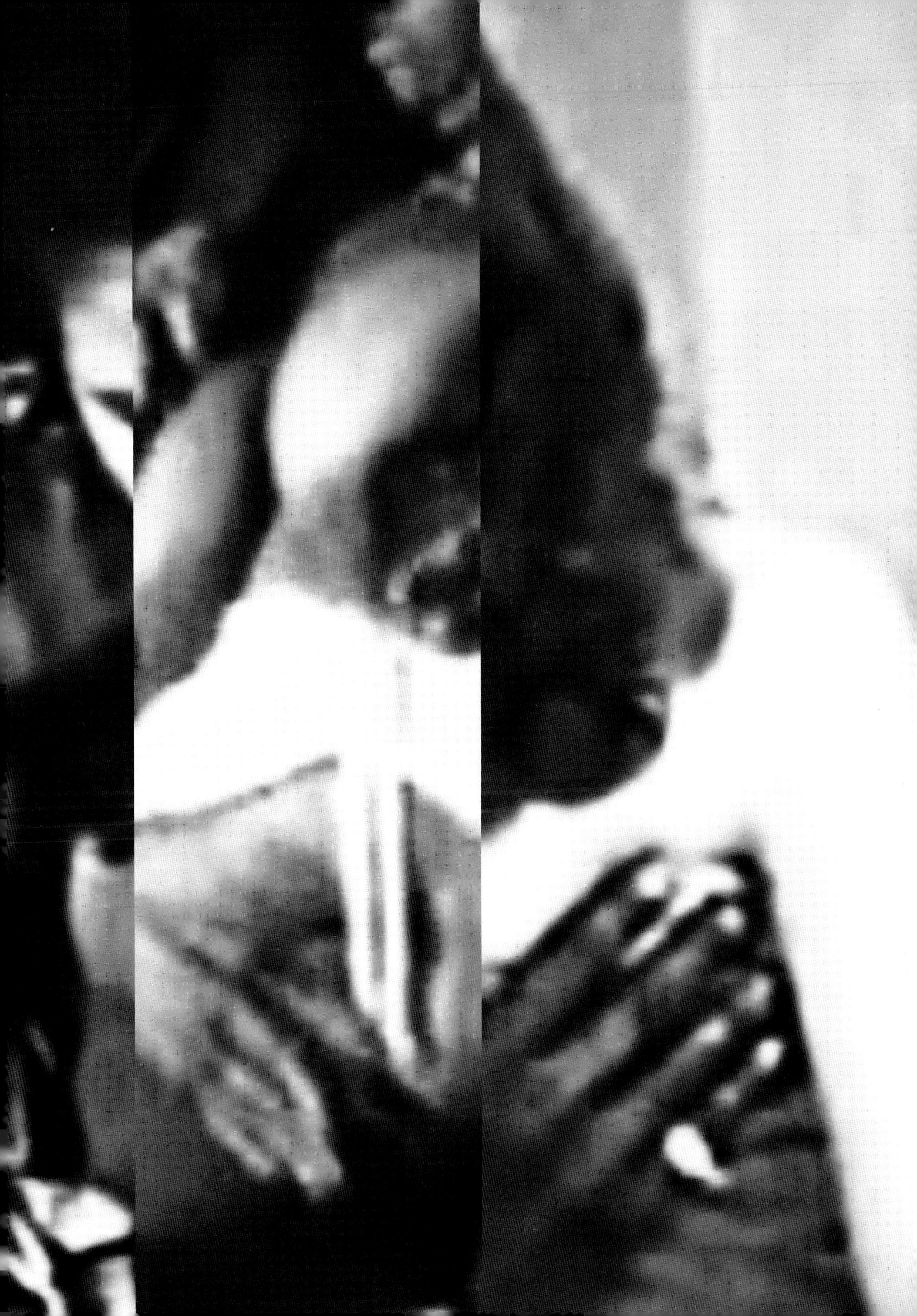

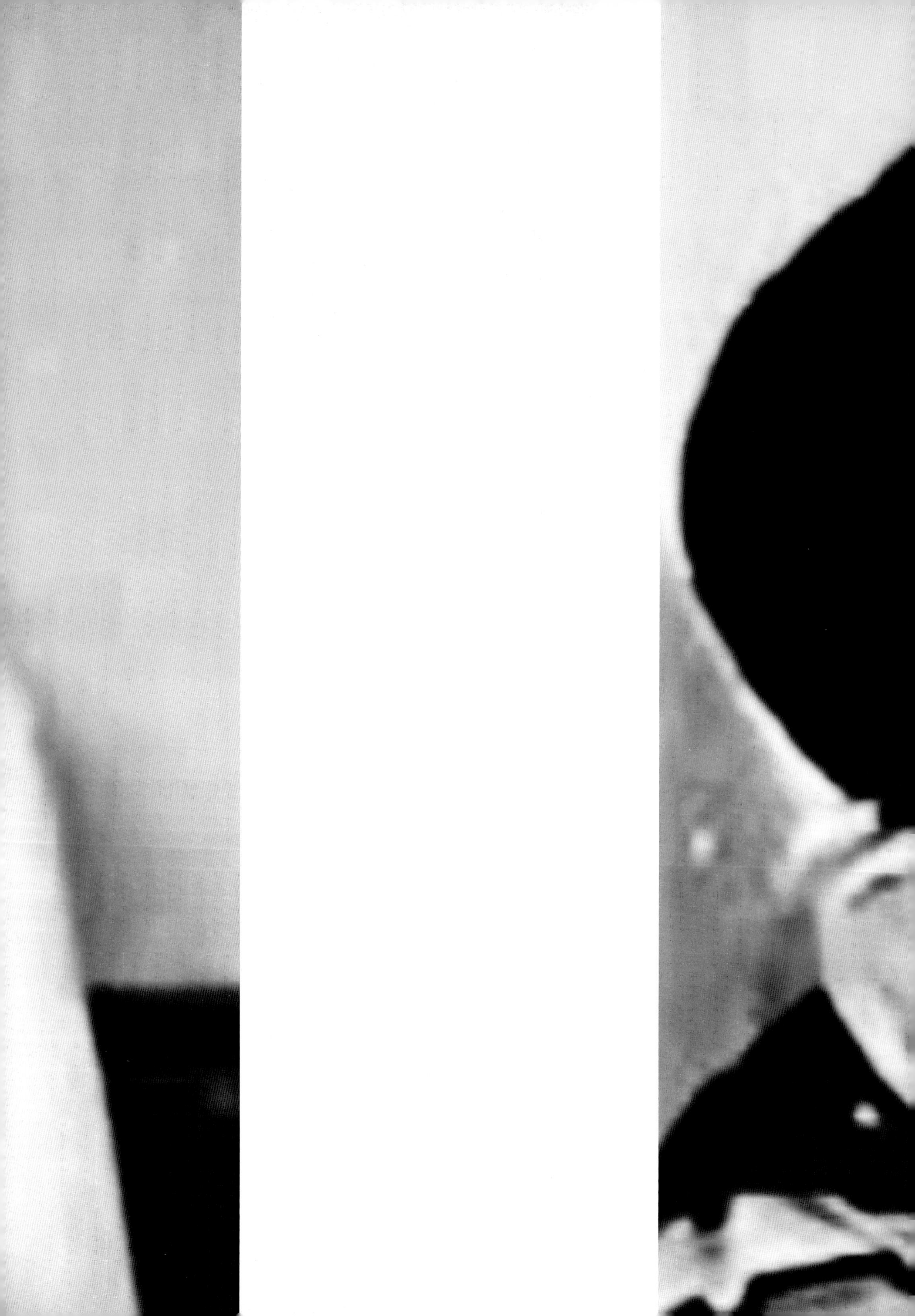

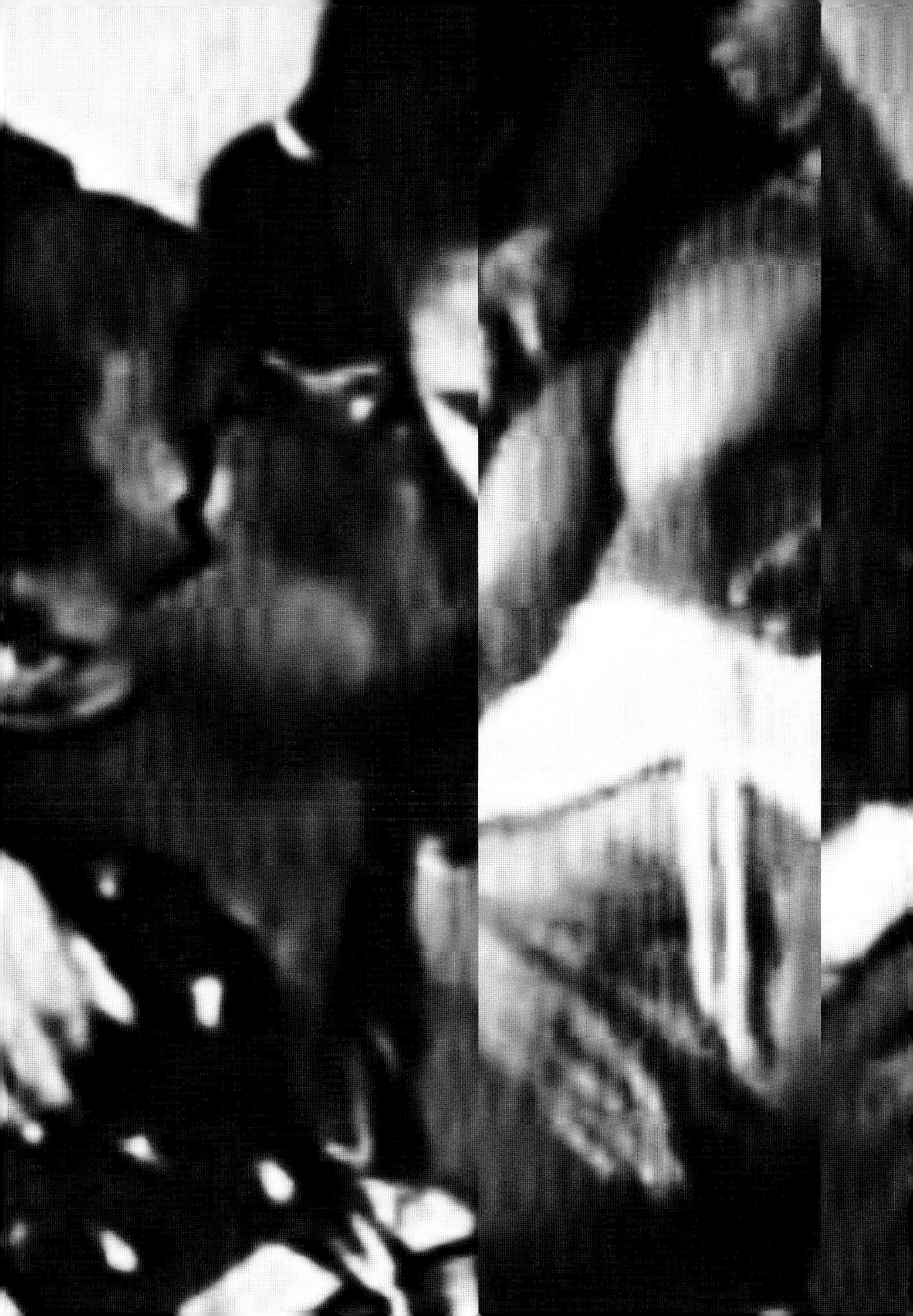

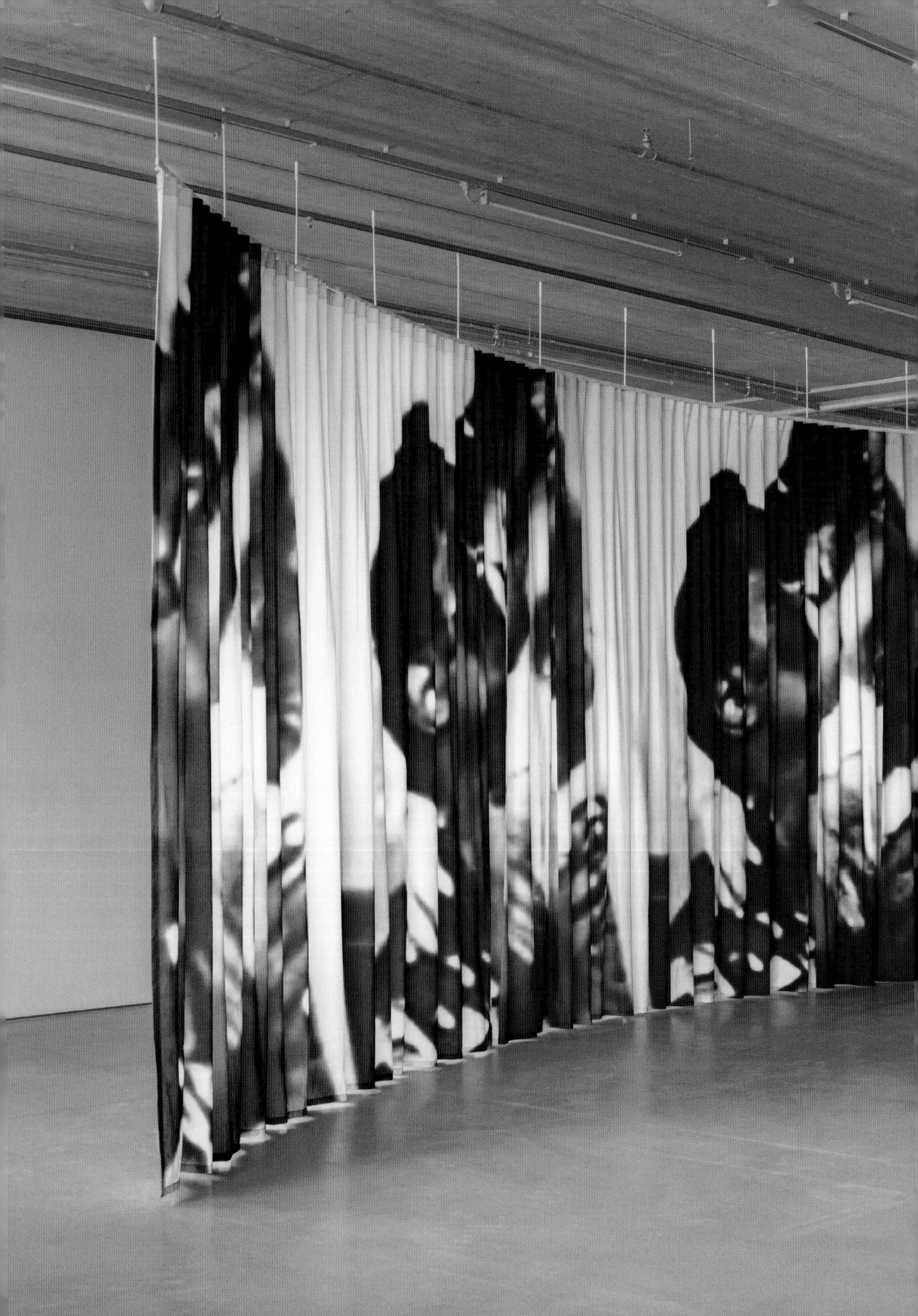

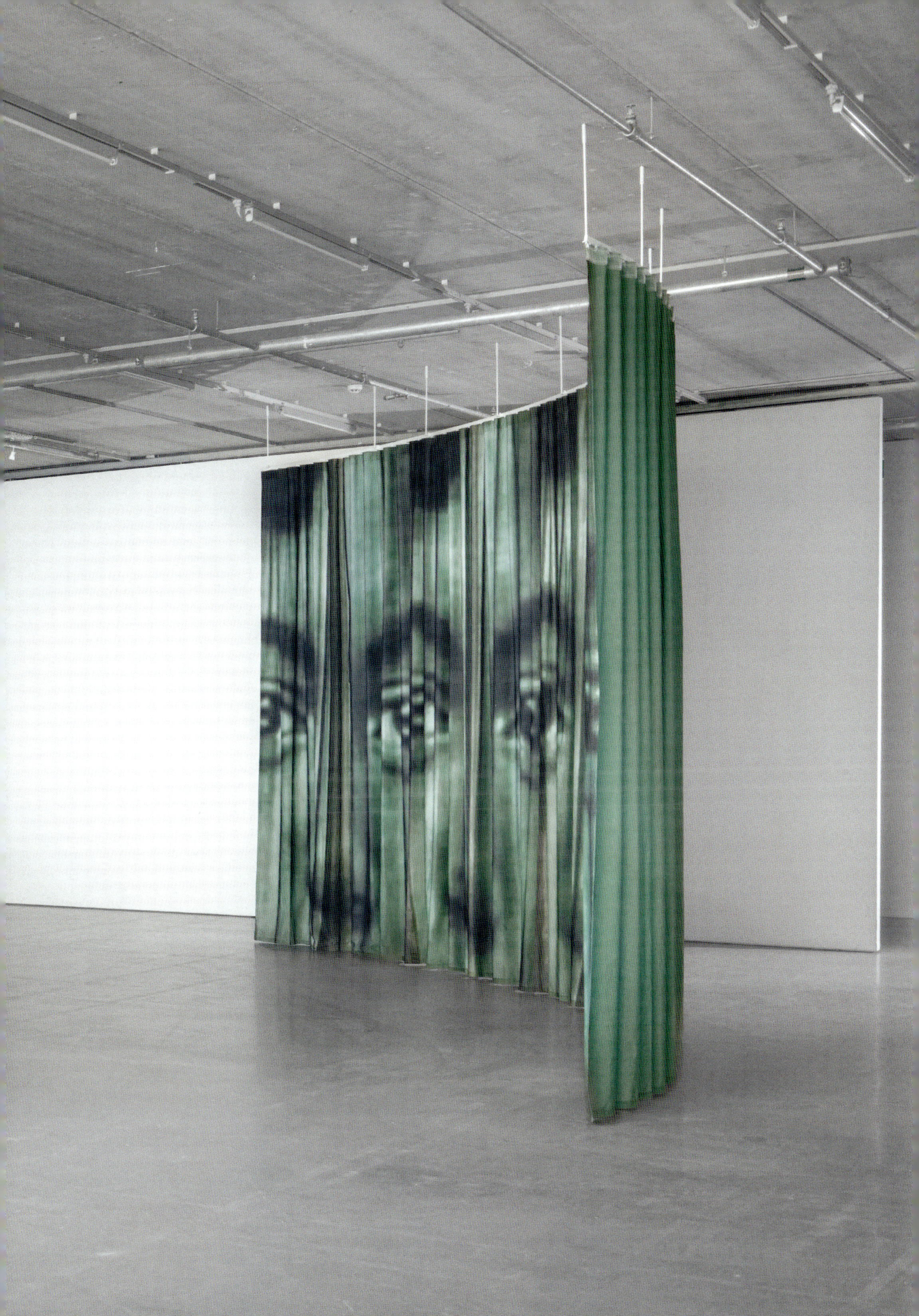

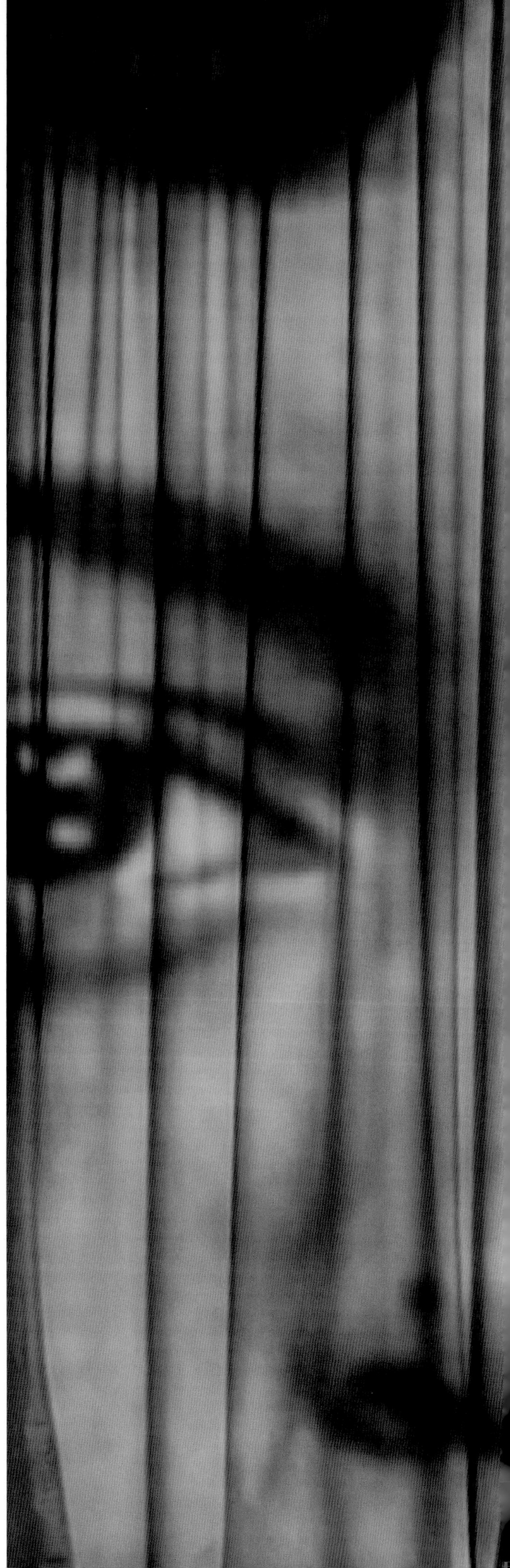

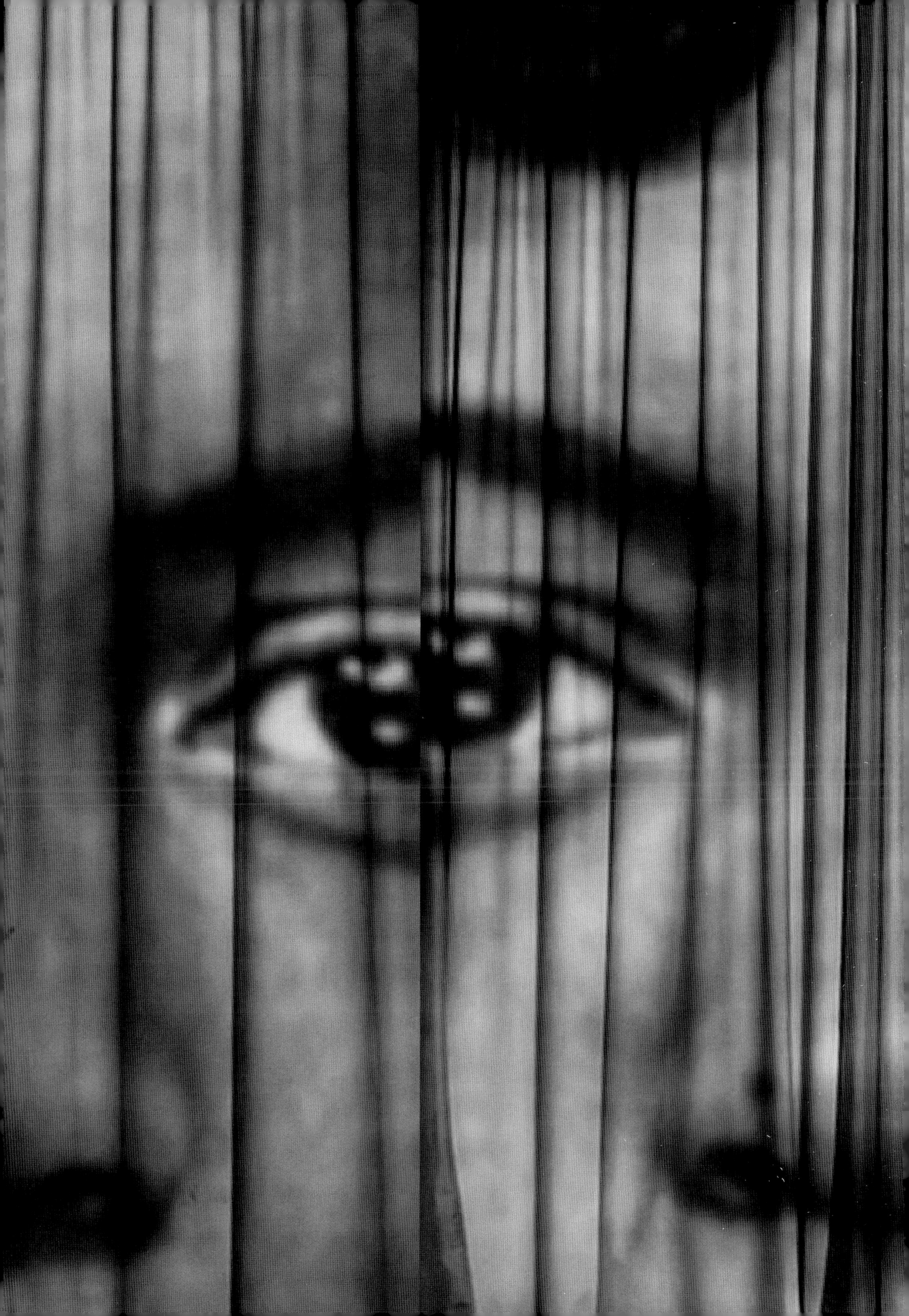

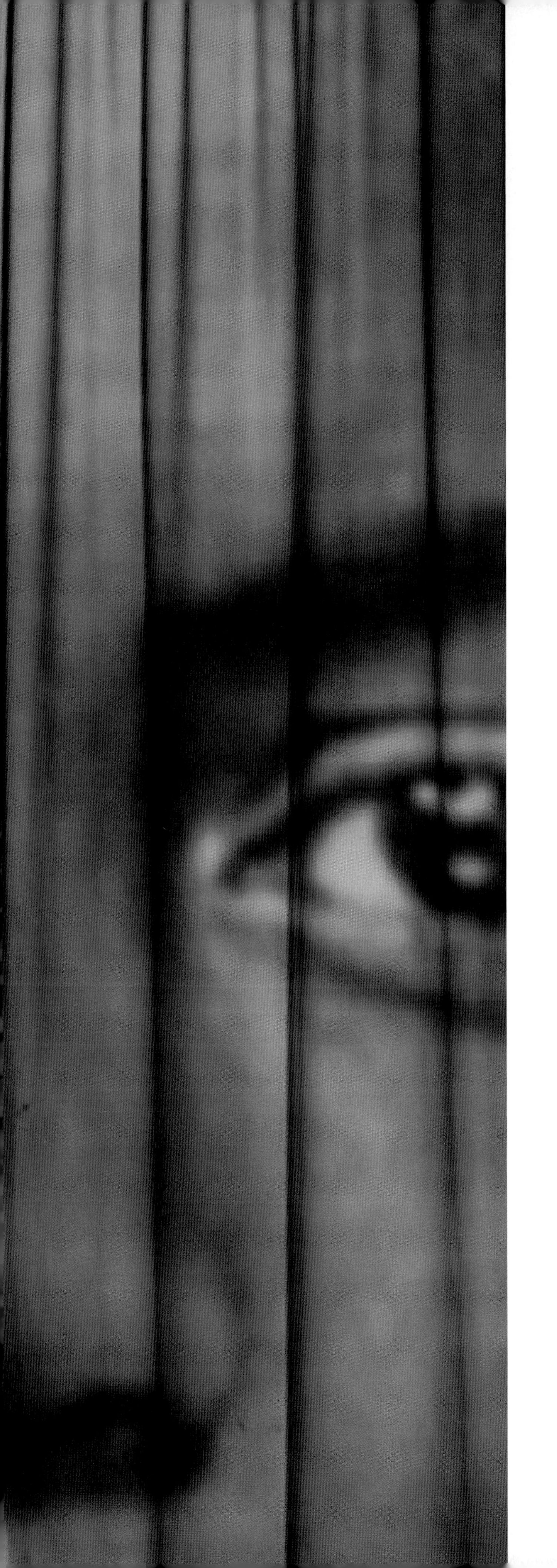

Just You, Just Me

Hilton Als

Some months ago—actually it's over a year now—I moved from one part of Manhattan to another. The distance wasn't tremendous, less than a mile, but the psychological shift was sizable: I was vacating a kind of way station that passed as a home for a room of my own. Even though I'd lived in the apartment I was leaving for over twenty years, I'd shared it with a number of friends, some gone now, and too many ideas about what constituted generosity and receptivity: if you had a roof over your head, then it behooved you to share it with others, no matter the financial and spiritual cost: giving might make someone else, anyone else, better.

That was my mother's ethos; she raised me and my five siblings in Brooklyn. My father did not live with us. He was more or less supported by his mother in her large house not too far way. He had a room in her house, at the very top of it, and it was sacrosanct: you didn't enter it uninvited. I never questioned my parents' arrangement; it was the way it was. But in the last years leading up to my leaving my first Manhattan apartment—which, by the way, I'd moved into the year my mother died, in 1989; I was born in 1960—I'd felt crowded in it or, more accurately, crowded out of it. Let me explain. Even though I ostensibly lived alone in that flat surrounded by piles—books, records, photographs, magazines—my body had been afflicted by emotional piles for a long time before I left all that junk behind. You see, everything I'd learned about hospitality from my mother—she who is every child's moral barometer, even if she's broken—had caved in on my soul; I could no longer sustain the Platonic soup kitchen I'd been raised to stock, and preside over; I could no longer maintain my mother's lessons of the heart.

By the end of my stay in my first New York place, all those sometimes excellent and sometimes not bodies that had crossed my threshold had impressed themselves on me no matter how the relationship was defined; it didn't matter if the day to day friendship had dissolved, or the person had died, or what have you: those former friends, bodies, were now a part of my body, and I could no longer bear their weight, or the weight of any of it. Then Love called, rather unexpectedly. Love didn't so much edge those bodies out as ask for a different place to house itself—a new home with less of everything that was not love. No *Pilgrim's Progress* burdens, or treating time as though it was valuable to others, but not myself. Love taught me that my time was my own. Mine. To say mine was evil if you came from the Ma school of things; it was a way of killing Ma and her brand of good will off, a way of being like all those others who hurt Ma and in hurting Ma hurt me. Love pushed against that. And how "mine" was forbidden when I was growing up.

Our Ma supported us in part with "help" from public assistance—welfare. Some images from those days: Caseworkers going through her cabinets to make sure she didn't have a crust of bread or a man or anything that would contribute to her wellbeing, let alone that of her children. If so, no more government "help." No more standing with my sister to get welfare food off a truck. No more social workers asking what your daily life is like as a way of finding out what your mother is up to personally, or whether or not she was mothering you at all. Love pushed against all that, and wanted something else, including the right to ask the questions I never thought of for myself, given that "I" had been trained by Ma's idea of love not to love. Another question Love asked: Why didn't Pa during all those years of lying and not lying about his absence give his family any nourishment, take his kids in before making at least one kid sick with tinned meat? Love pushed against all that, and this, too: The feeling that if I had my own place and a lock and a key, I would be no better than our Pa, wrapped up safe as can be and soft in his cocoon of a room nursing on the overly sweet milk of self-protection, a mother's indulgence, constant self-regard. Love assured me that having a space to work, one that wasn't entirely at the mercy of other people I had known, which is to say Ma's legacy of giving unto death, didn't have to be a thing.

In fact, it could be dismantled brick by brick so that out of the prison of Ma's days I could be a free man taught to praise.

Love was the principal architect of my new place and the principal dissembler of the past. The primary feature of my new apartment is light. There are windows on either end of a floor-through in a part of town that's notable for its proximity to the Hudson River while retaining vestiges of bohemian New York: trees, a square, crooked old streets with Dutch or Flemish names few if any of us know the story behind. History takes too much time. We are Manhattanites and preoccupied by our lives in Manhattan. Sometimes Love stays for the night and other nights Love cooks meals and in between these pleasures there's the fear of Love removing its presence. How will it go? Must it go? What is it doing now? What is it doing without me? Have I done enough for it to stay? Are you my mother? If you love me enough will I be my father and lock the door letting no one in? Love encourages me to get to the desk built in the room where I work and to even shut the door from his Love in order to get whatever it is I need to get done, done. Love can't always stay. Love weighs on me, not in the same way those other bodies did in the days when I followed Ma's ethos to a T. Love is not here sometimes—is out working or making a meal, or sitting in a room far off, on the other end of a joke. And yet there is love's presence in a disfiguring world. And then there is your disfigured body—the one that is misshapen by words and events Love cannot follow you into and you do not want Love to follow you into, shaped, as it is, by the once irrefutable loneliness I thought was the world.

The street leading to my house runs east to west, a trajectory that takes you from a once "bad" neighborhood to a very nice one. (In any case, it's difficult to find a "bad" neighborhood in lower Manhattan by now. Everything has been bought and made better here in the land of the plenty, the horn of the good.) I spend several mornings a week on the East side of my block dealing with personal stuff, including learning how to physically and mentally defend myself against those who do not feel my "I" should exist at all. Sometimes, this begins even before Love finds me for the day, or night. That ill wind follows me down my street the way thoughts followed Virginia Woolf down the road in her essay, "Street Haunting," written in 1930:

> How beautiful a street is in winter! It is at once revealed and obscured. Here vaguely one can trace symmetrical avenues of doors and windows; here under the lamps are floating islands of pale light through which pass quickly bright men and women, who, for all their poverty and shabbiness, wear a certain look of unreality, an air of triumph, as if they had given life the slip, so that life, deceived of her prey, blunders on without them. But, after all, we are only gliding smoothly on their surface. The eye is not a miner, not a diver, not a seeker after buried treasure. It floats us smoothly down a stream, resting, pausing, the brain sleeps perhaps as it looks.

But I am not gliding down the surface of my thoughts as I make my way from the east side of my street down to the west, in part because I am not Virginia Woolf, which is to say I do not go unobserved in the world of my street thus making me free to observe in relative safety and peace. In the world of my street I'm observed for a variety of reasons, and this individual and collective surveillance shapes my thoughts and my writing in ways that I resent, who wouldn't want to spend an evening having a walk in search of a pencil and coming back home without incident to think about it? The way I'm observed means my brain can't sleep as I look; that's a luxury I can't afford as I try to not kill the world that means to kill me. From the time I moved into my new home—the windows let in as much nature as is possible in Manhattan—but really several years before that, even, I felt something in Manhattan that even Love couldn't protect me from and what shall I call it? The *May I see your ID* syndrome?

On my block there's a big store, part of a chain that sells electronic devices. I've been in the shop exactly three times—once to get a device fixed, once to buy a Christmas gift with my white German goddaughter, and once to replace a missing something to fix another device. Each time I've gone into the store, done my business, and am about to pay, I've been asked for my ID. I am not asleep to the fact that none of the other customers—usually affluent Europeans, yuppie mothers and the like—are not asked for anything but their credit cards once they belly

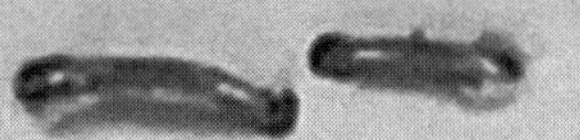

up to the electronic bar to make a purchase. For those of us who are not them, the exchange of capital for goods becomes a kind of sick room: *May I see your ID?* The sick room glows with blood, the blood that floods your face your neck your back as you hand over your ID instead of—what? A fuck you? And why not fuck you? Because the worker who asks you for your ID is black or Hispanic and male, too, and he needs to make a living, even if it's at someone's literal and figurative expense. He can't look at you. (A side note: This is always the point in the story when you become a third person figure; your body can't bear it and so becomes a different body, watching as things happen but trying not to feel, despite the rush of blood to the face, the neck, the back. In this situation and others like it your "I" recedes, running further and further back into the hidden world housed in the body the world hates.) He looked at you before, smiling, as you decided to purchase the shit you needed, but all of that changes when he asks: *May I see your ID*? The tone was the same as it was when he was showing you the junk you needed, friendly like, but now there's a threat: If you don't have ID who are you other than a thieving threat? There's a bright lift to his voice*: May I see your ID*? Surely someone trained him to say that just as my mother and father, respectively, showed me how important it was to despise racism and its various inevitable humiliations, and, on the other hand, to empathize with workers who were "oppressed" by a corporate system that puts their head in a yoke just so they know who's boss. Who is the slain, who is the victim? Speak! So wrote Sophocles in *Antigone* and maybe that's the start of the essay in my head that I can't write because of the blood pounding in it as the young man swipes my card and swipes my reason several blocks away from my home, away from Love. The transaction closed, the thing I needed now bagged, weighs heavy in my hand like evil, like shame: Why couldn't I forgo my mother's ethos and "read" that young man to filth? Because by not looking at me—*May I have your ID*?—he was, perhaps, frightened to discover what he would find on the other end of his learned question/inquisition: at the beginning or end of his own street rocky with the stones of compromise, smiling all the while, the better to survive.

The first time I experienced the *May I see your ID*? syndrome outside when I tried to enter Pa's room—*Whose child are you*?—I was fourteen or so and wearing white ballet slippers. I was a student at the School for the Performing Arts, which was then on West 46th Street. There, I majored in theater. To get to the school from my home in Brooklyn I took the IRT express—the 2 or 3 train—and got off at Times Square. I always wore ballet slippers then, and, frequently, tights. Sometimes I carried a bag—a kind of pouch—my mother made me. A queer costume for her queer child. One day, as I hurried through the filthy labyrinth that was and is the IRT subway system at Times Square, a cop stopped me. *Give me your ID*. I showed him my train pass. I didn't have any other ID. The blood was pounding behind my eyes. Something—instinct—told me not to show my real face—the face of my fear and hatred. I was no longer myself: I knew what it was like to be almost annihilated or have some part of your natural trust annihilated by men. Become "nothing" and maybe they won't kill you. When I was a kid, my boy cousins used to try to suffocate me with plastic bags. They wanted this faggot to die. Maybe that long-ago cop wanted this faggot to die. With no provocation at all, he walked me down some more filthy corridors and we ended up in his headquarters where I was booked as a truant. I said, once, that I was not a truant, that I was on my way to school, but that wasn't the story he wanted to hear or his buddies wanted to hear and something in me went silent. How could I contradict his idea of my body? With what? My ballet slippers? My mind? My love of art and theater and movie lovers in anguish? And let me just say that what I felt then is not so very different than what I feel as I walk towards my new home where Love waits. I'm adrift in a stop-and-frisk universe that has always been a stop-and-frisk universe. My silence is a form of protection: Do I want them to cut my tongue out, too? Or an equally effective private part of my anatomy? This feeling goes back for centuries, no doubt, and is in my DNA and has saved my life in the past, all the way back to the ships and the lash. But it has also stomped on my heart and given Love quite a job. Call it what you will—white backlash, Obama-era payback or whatever—but I find our present condition difficult to write about.

Even before I moved out of my old apartment with all those bodies, one could feel the need for blood to be spilled in the streets, an extension of all those shot bodies in North Carolina or mowed-down bodies in Lexington, Kentucky, not to mention other parts of the world, now and forever, somewhere, always. As I've said some folks call our present condition white backlash, but I call this wave of violence the tedium of having to give a shit. All those years in college reading *Beloved*, all those seminars on women's bodies, including reproductive rights, and Dad down at the office having to deal with having to hear about equal pay even if he never forked it over. All those years of talk of immigrant care and elder health care and social security this and fair that. Even entertainment wasn't safe. Tender movie and TV shit about lesbians and gays and trans people and will it never end? So, says the guy sitting in that classroom or in that movie theater, emboldened by the vile sliming that comes via the airwaves night after night, so says this guy as he watches TV reflecting the rich and his constantly rightly exasperated-by-all-this-difference President, Lock those immigrants up, says this guy following his Commander-in-Chief's example, sterilize them, separate them from their children like in the slaves days, and let me get mine, my *stuff*.

Once, in my old neighborhood, a guy with a BMW was looking lovingly at the stuff stored in the hood of his shiny car as his little son, a toddler, walked out into the street and was minding its own unsupervised baby business when the world stopped but reality didn't: as the baby toddled, taxi suddenly rounded the corner near where the baby was and I screamed, the car stopped, and the man stopped looking at his stuff for a moment to pick up his living stuff. Then, holding his neglected child, this Pa followed me home to make sure that I wasn't going to report him to the police. I should have. Ma's ethos interfered: Perhaps the man had "learned" something, Ma said, in my heart, while my body said: If I went to the police, who would believe us? Would I be the dude who pushed his baby into the road? while caring rich fathers looked on helplessly? Looking at his BMW stuff, that father—a version of my father?—was, perhaps, tired of giving a shit even when it came to his own child and its baby needs. Maybe he was tired of all those other baby needs over the past eight years or so, when he had to deal with imagining how someone else might feel. Maybe he was tired of living through some version of the civil rights era again, all those Obamas, it was exhausting to be made of the world's concerns, all the moral bullshit of the underprivileged and what not, including those guys in ballet slippers who scream when a baby may be harmed, who the fuck wants to deal. Now it's my turn, the same guy may think, My time, mine, and what I want to ask is how long will it be before even the most enlightened person starts calling me a nigger? This guy may say: If all those niggers and cunts out there can't take what we've had to swallow all these years—all those years of trying to empathize with crap that has nothing to do with us at all, that has nothing to do with power—surely it's all those niggers' and cunts' time to deal with us guys who have had to listen to what they've had to say, all that whining, ignoring the fact that America was never theirs and always ours ignoring the fact that America has always heard them first. And because these guys are American, they want me to hear them first.

Here's some stuff they've said that they are surprised you don't want to listen to as you listen because of Ma's ethos, the body that took it all because Ma considered it her job. At a memorial service where I eulogized a white woman I didn't like but her family asked me and what can you do? one of the bereaved came up to me and said, I've been reading you for years, I didn't know you were black. And so big. Then, at a party, out of nowhere: I really like *Dear White People*, as if you're in the cast. At a business meeting with a potential producer: Don't you miss that comedy troupe that used to say, "I'm black and I suck dick"? At a small theater, a small black female performer in a solo work. The show is over, and, retiring to the men's room for a moment, a gentleman in the opposite stall: You were so great in the show. Then there is the usual—mistaking me for another writer of color and when I said, No, I'm the other one, looking at me cockeyed: Was I sure? Then there's the guy you go out on a date with before you find Love who tells you that his relatives owned a plantation in Haiti years ago and the people who worked it looked like you. Sometimes, you try to convince others, these guys, that you are yourself—*Where's my ID?*— especially, hideously, if they are your friends. Remember the moment when the dying woman you were trying to help said: You see that black guy crossing the street, my grandfather would have called him a mook. Remember the former friend who loved to tell the story of how when her father thought someone was unattractive, he'd say, They're uglier than a bag of nigger rectums. Or the other dying friend who said, while bending over to kiss her, Whoa, this is just like the Tennessee Williams story, "Desire and the Black Masseur." This casual and not so casual hatred and aggression even in presumed love is as old as America, a country in part defined by people defining who they are least *not*. While America is happening to my mind and body, I try to make sense of it as I walk towards home and Love, but my mind can't make writing of it, somehow, because how can you tell a story that all the metaphors in the world can't enhance or help make it into art?

Love wants so many things, wants your story without metaphors if it comes to that. Love says, Tell it baby, tell about that walk from East to West, marred and marked by others, that which makes for a different kind of reflection. Tell it, because Love is interested.

All a writer has is his epoch and how it shapes him. In her very interesting introduction to the first volume of *The Best American Essays* series, Elizabeth Hardwick wrote that the essay was a "slithery form, wearisomely vague and as chancy as a fish in the open hand." In short, the essay, like love, like life, is indefinable but you know an essay when you see it and you know a great one when you feel it because it's concentrated life, whole and in bits. Indeed, the essays I'm attracted to are essays that have something unfinished about them, a circle that cannot be closed, filled with dread—even or especially when humorous—anxious that certain national politics, say, are generated by nothing more and nothing less than certain revenge fantasies vis-à-vis identity politics, say, all those bodies rising up out of the dust and grief of racism and sexism to say "I."

In "Why I Write," a 1976 talk about her early years as a writer, Joan Didion said that she borrowed the title of her essay from another—George Orwell's "Why I Write"—because, first off, she liked the sound of the words: *Why I Write*.

> There you have three short unambiguous words that share a sound, and the sound they share is this:
> *I*
> *I*
> *I*
> In many ways writing is the act of saying *I*, of imposing oneself upon other people, of saying *listen to me, see it my way, change your mind*. It's an aggressive, even hostile act. You can disguise its qualifiers and tentative subjunctives, with ellipses and evasions...but there's no getting around

> the fact that setting words on paper is the tactic of a secret bully, an invasion, an imposition of the writer's sensibility on the reader's most private space

And in her *Best American* introduction, Hardwick said, "The aggressiveness of the essay is the assumption of the author to speak in one's own voice."

Re-reading Didion and Hardwick, I wonder if, indirectly, these authors were telling us something about their experience as women, and that their description of aggression was the result of having been aggressed upon, told what to do, claimed, putting their "I" aside on more than one occasion to make a difficult situation work, to pacify a husband, to not be a target? Just as queer writers of yore, and writers of color who had to smile and twirl in between bitter descriptions about life in America in order to be read at all, often told the reader more about who they were in between the lines, saying "I" if you are a different person, can feel like a dangerous proposition, let alone reality: being a target hurts. And since writing is the author's deepest self, writing about one's "I," standing up for it, can feel like an aggressive act, I suppose, given how us targets are programmed not to. I wonder how many heteronormative men and some queer ones worry when asking for your ID, or saying, in so many words, stay out of my room, or worry about how aggressive their language is after they put a plastic bag over your head, trying to smother your faggot voice and concerns. How did we get here? That's the subject of many of the essays that we read and remember. How did we get here and are we stuck here as men and women and Other?

Living as we do in a broken world, writing—essays—are bound to become more broken, fractured, as power becomes insistent on showing its power further by breaking more backs, jailing the innocent, cracking Love in the knees. The majority of us are not whole individuals because there is no such thing as a whole society. Sometimes, on my walk home, in the short space between the rest of the world and my front door, sometimes I will have a moment to dream and reflect and I speculate on what the essays to come will look like, read like. Of course they'll be made up of many things, including questions and images and gestures, because we live in a world of too many things and half-understood selves. But these essays of the future will or should start with questions, generally political in nature and if you don't think so think again.

Here's one essay borne out of these times: The comedian Richard Pryor asking once why were targets on shooting and archery ranges always black? Add to that the sound of the woman crying, "Why are they shooting?" as she filmed Antwon Rose being gunned down in East Pittsburgh. Another essay: Looking at Jean-Michel Basquiat's 1983 painting *Defacement (The Death of Michael Stewart)*, which the artist produced after Michael Stewart, another graffiti artist, was beaten to death by policemen in the subway. I remember Michael Stewart, he was the guy my female friend went home with the night I told her we could not be lovers. We were in our early twenties, players in a club on lower Broadway, in Manhattan. After we parted for the night, my complicated companion didn't waste any time finding herself a guy, a thin man of color with dreads who seemed to be drowning in his overcoat. (Interestingly, she had been involved with Basquiat off and on for some time before and after he made that painting dedicated to her murdered friend.) Basquiat, on hearing of Stewart's death: That could have been me, that could have been me. I didn't have the presence of mind to say then: But it is.

Another essay: The music video "This Is America," starring the performer Donald Glover. Directed by Hiro Murai, who oversees many of the episodes of *Atlanta*, a history-making series about race, relationships, and place, also starring Glover. In "This is America," Glover performs under the name Childish Gambino. The look of the clip is airy and claustrophobic. Folks record acts of violence on their cell phones. A KKK figure rides in on a horse. Glover plays both sides of the racial coin. As a "white" man he blows away a chorus of black singers in a church, impersonating Dylann Roof murdering nine black people in a church in South Carolina. As himself, Glover critiques how blackness can become a pose, commodified, and how that commodification repeats itself, for bigger and bigger bags of cash. At one point, he stands on a pile of cars, just as Michael Jackson did in his 1987 "Bad" video, and just like Beyoncé did in her 2016 "Formation" video. This is black anger as entertainment. Is Glover doing the same thing by putting out a video at all? At the end of the piece Glover, black and naked with fear, is chased down a seemingly endless corridor by white people.

The terror in Glover's eyes and open mouth, gasping for breath, is familiar to me and now to Love as Love holds my body, not seeing it as the wrong one but as *the* one. And that's the thought and feeling that gets me down the stairs on most days when I leave my house to walk East to West. I have a little ritual when I close my apartment door and face my day, after checking to see if I have my ID, checking to see if I'm ready to make the journey once more. (Joan Didion: "Everyday is all there is.") I look across the street at the colored lobby guy sitting at his station. He's an essay unto himself. Every day I go out and he's at work in his glassed-off world, we wave to one another, quietly happy and satisfied to find that we're still here, each in the other's world.

A version of "Just You, Just Me" by Hilton Als first appeared as the introduction to *The Best American Essays 2018*, ed. Hilton Als and Robert Atwan.

List of Works

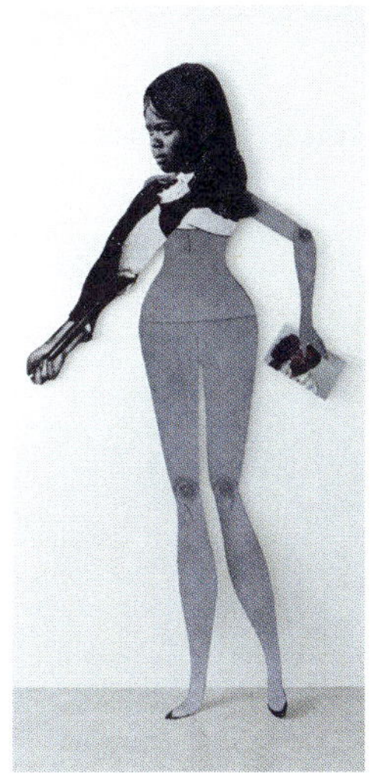

Big Girl I
2024
Collage, paper, paper clip, mounted on aluminum
257 × 150 cm

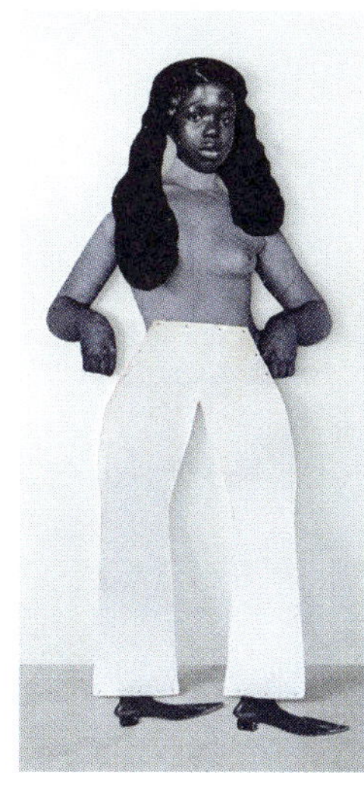

Big Girl II
2024
Collage, paper, paper clip, mounted on aluminum
273 × 126 cm

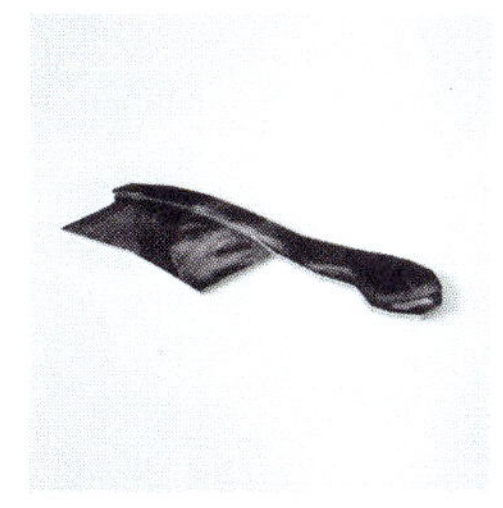

Comb
2024
Metal sculpture
H 1 × W 39.5 × D 12.5 cm

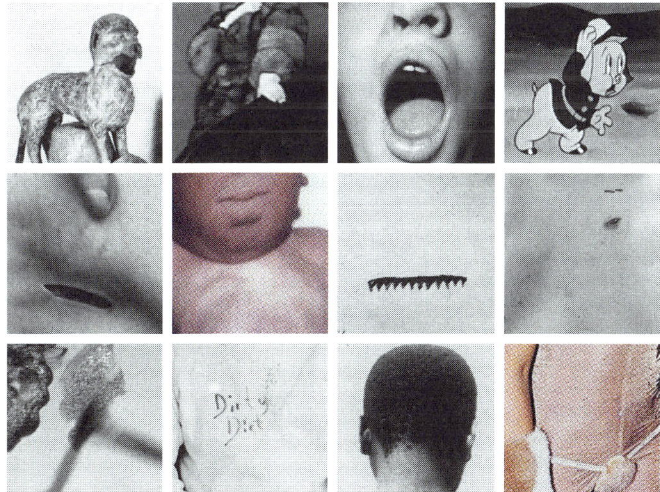

Cloud of Confusion
2024
12 prints on photo paper, mounted on aluminum plate
60 × 60 cm each

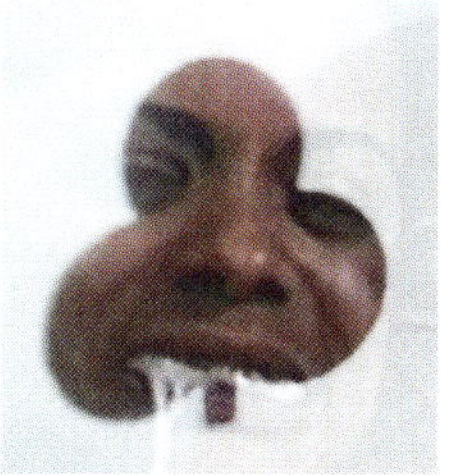

Clover I
2024
Photogravure with blind embossing, white ash frame, TC glass
Framed 86.5 × 82.5 cm

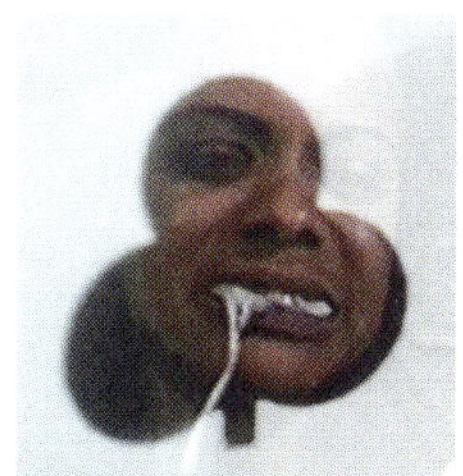

Clover II
2024
Photogravure with blind embossing, white ash frame, TC glass
Framed 86.5 × 82.5 cm

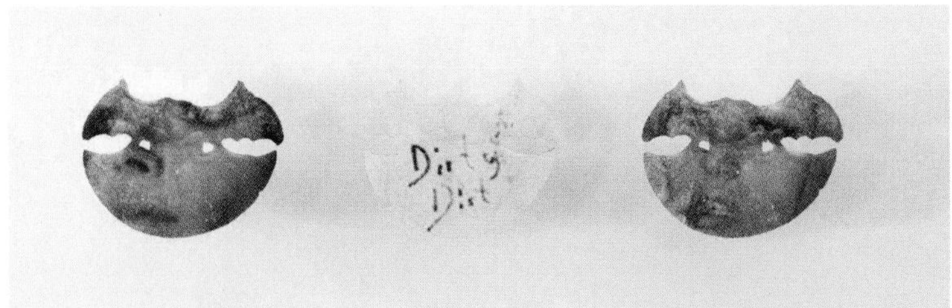

Complexities Plus Complexities
2024
Metal sculpture mounted on wall
H 29 × W 38 × D 16 cm each

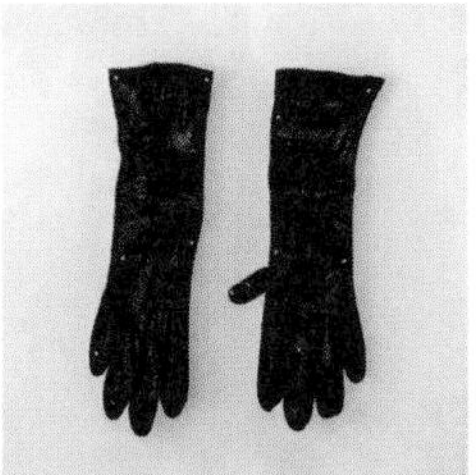

Gloves with Thumb
2024
Collage, paper, paper clip, mounted on aluminum
Left: 76 × 23 cm
Right: 74 × 31 cm

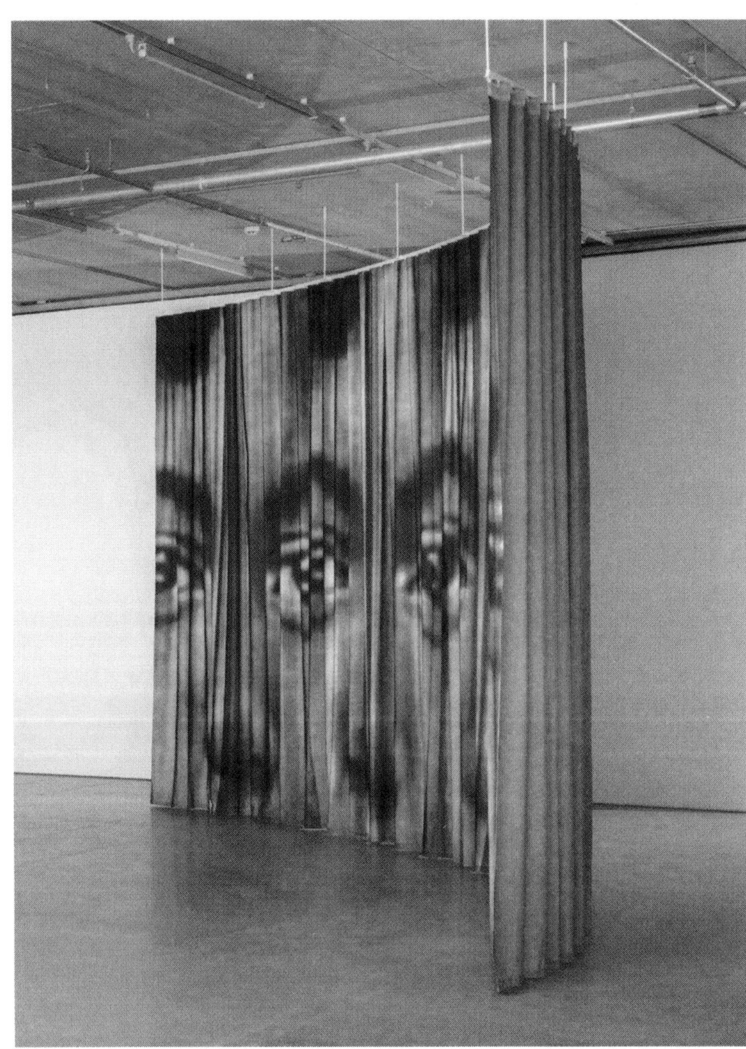

Her
2024
Printed fabric, metal curtain rod
3.7 × 12 m

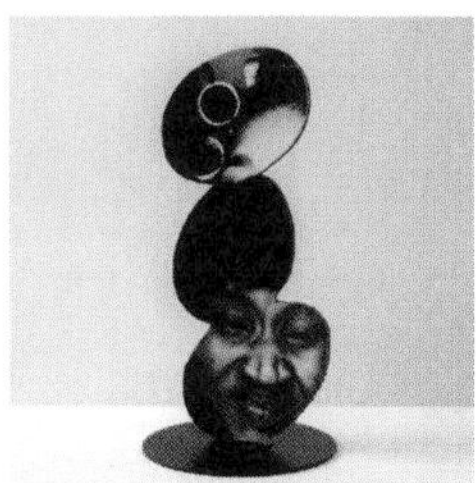

Giggles
2024
Metal sculpture
H 59.6 × W 30 × D 30 cm

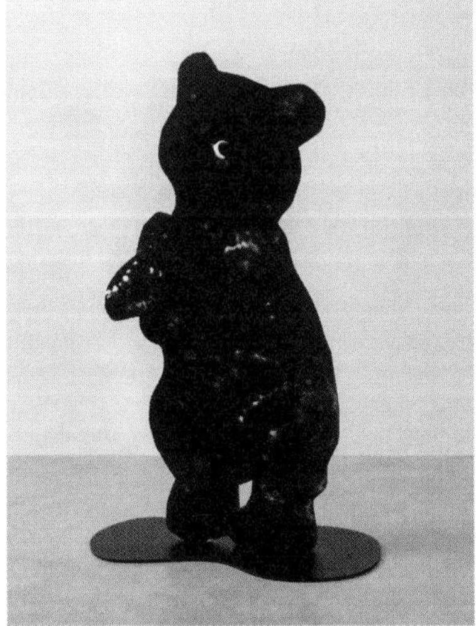

Jumpy Fits and Facial Tics
2024
Metal sculpture
H 108 × W 65.8 × D 38.7 cm

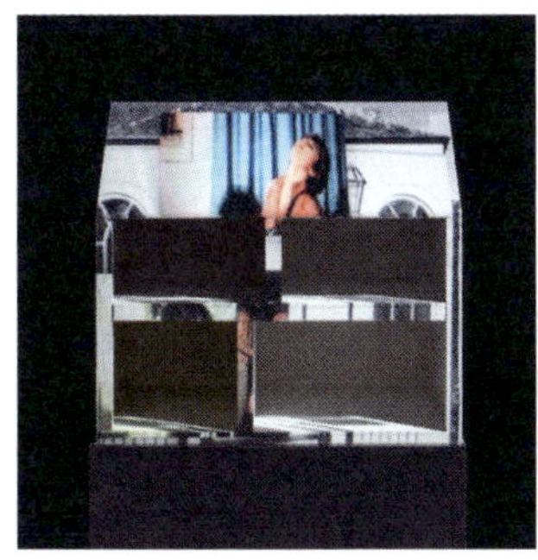

House Party
2024
Video installation, projected onto a doll's house, presented in a black box
13 sec. looped

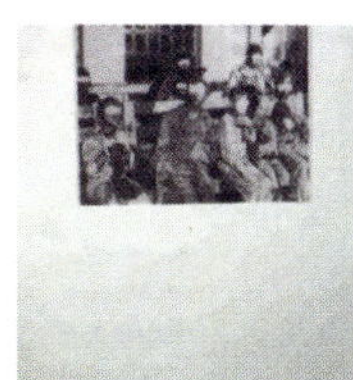

How We Got Over
2024
Video without audio
5 sec. looped

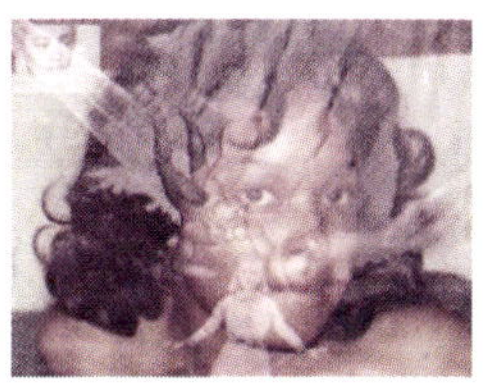

I'm Depressed
2024
Video
7 sec. looped

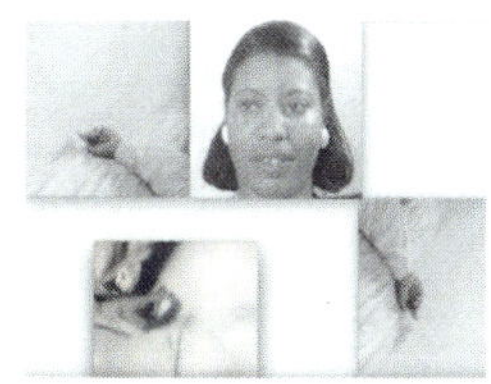

Over the Edge
2024
Video without audio
20 sec. looped

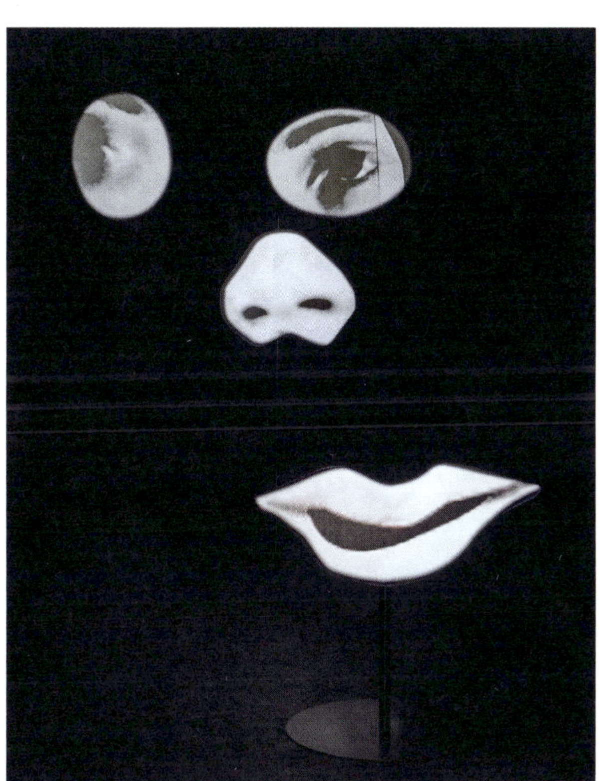

Of Course Everything Is Real
2024
Metal sculpture
Left eye: H 110 × W 91 × D 0.5 cm
Right eye: H 98 × W 136 × D 0.5 cm
Nose: H 70 × W 85 × D 0.5 cm
Mouth: H 41.5 × W 101 × D 0.5 cm

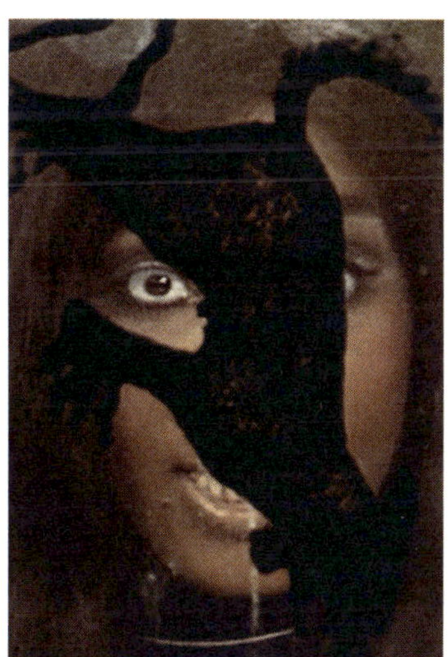

Love Is a Dog
2024
Wallpaper
4.2 × 3.35 m

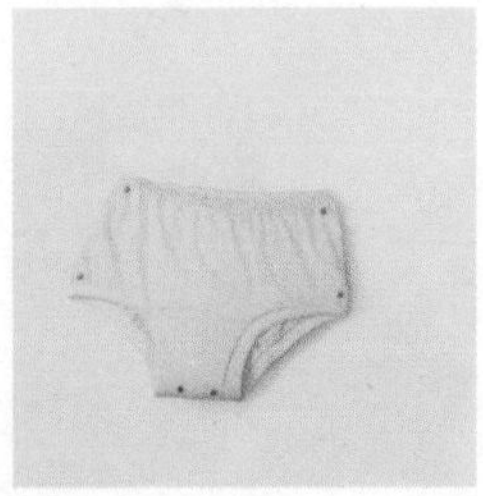

Object I
2024
Collage, paper, paper clip, mounted on aluminum
31 × 40 cm

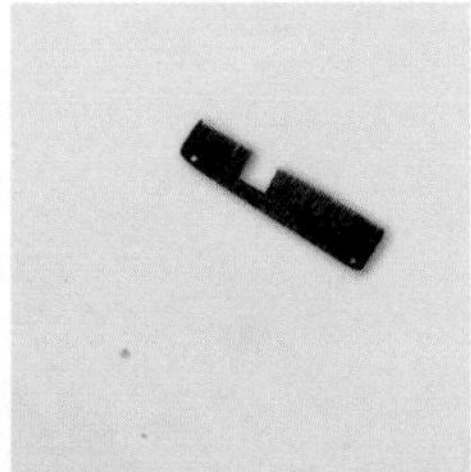

Object II
2024
Collage, paper, paper clip, mounted on aluminum
30 × 7 cm

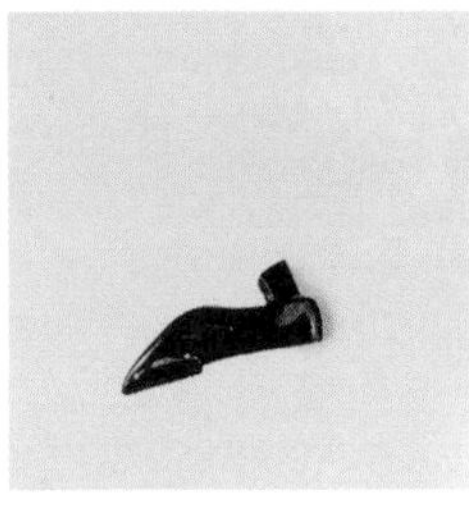

Object III
2024
Collage, paper, paper clip, mounted on aluminum
13 × 30 cm

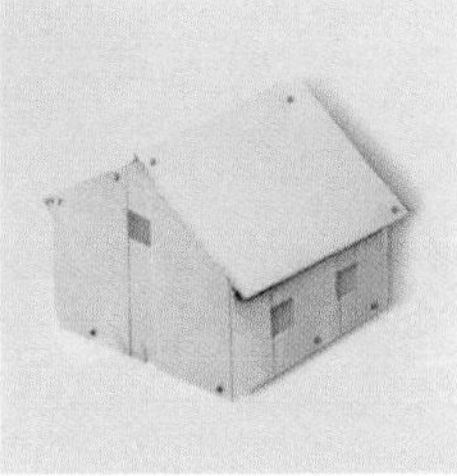

Object IV
2024
Collage, paper, paper clip, mounted on aluminum
44 × 51 cm

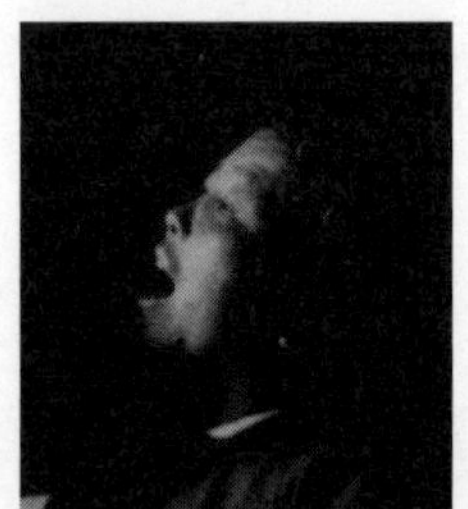

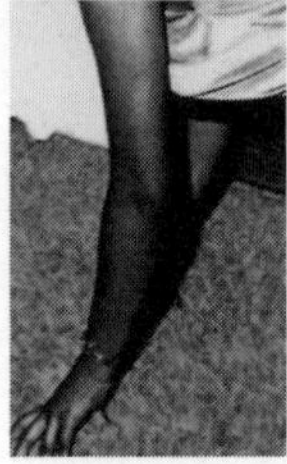

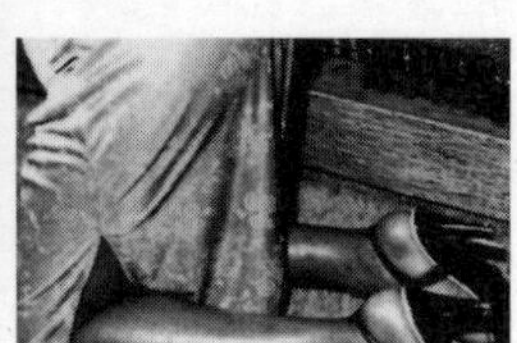

On My Hands and Knees II
2024
Prints on photo paper, mounted on aluminum plate
Face: 85.9 × 75.8 cm
Arms: 78.3 × 48.5 cm
Legs: 53.3 × 86 cm

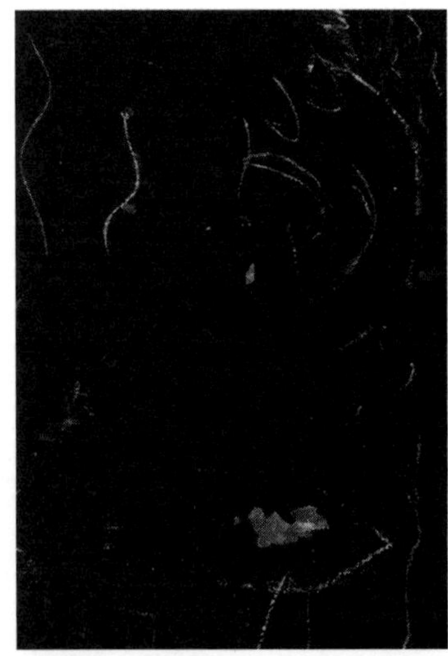

The Sound I Saw
2024
Print, paper mounted on aluminum plate
2 × 1.4 m

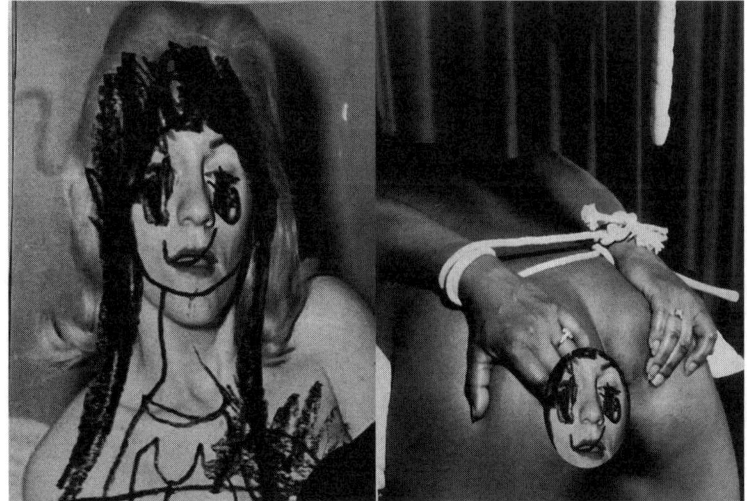

Lead by the Nose
2024
Wallpaper
399.5 × 565 cm

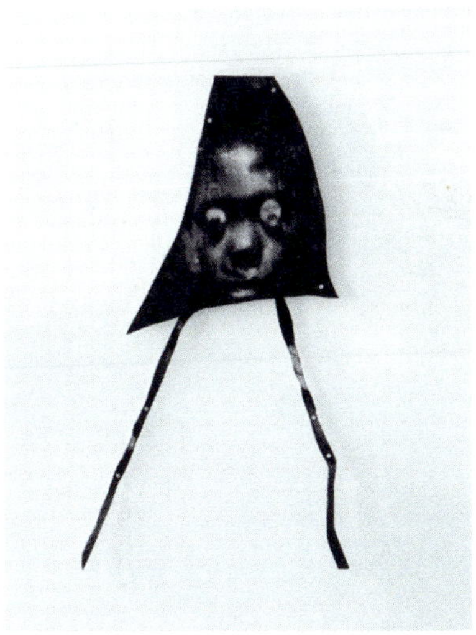

The Triangle That Could See
2024
Collage, paper, paper clip, mounted on aluminum
96 × 61 cm

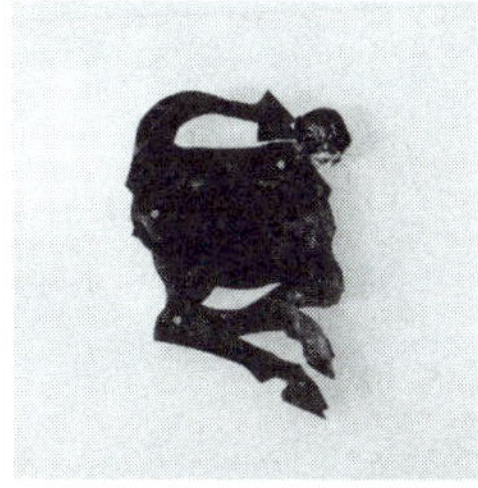

The Adventures of the Black Girl in Her Search for God
2024
Collage, paper, paper clip, mounted on aluminum
35 × 26 cm

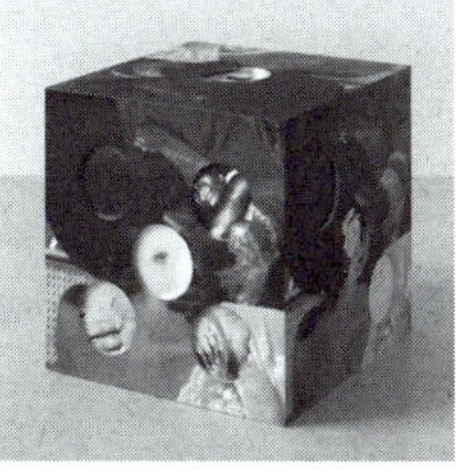

Trauma Catches Up
2024
Metal sculpture
H 29.5 × W 29.5 × D 29.5 cm

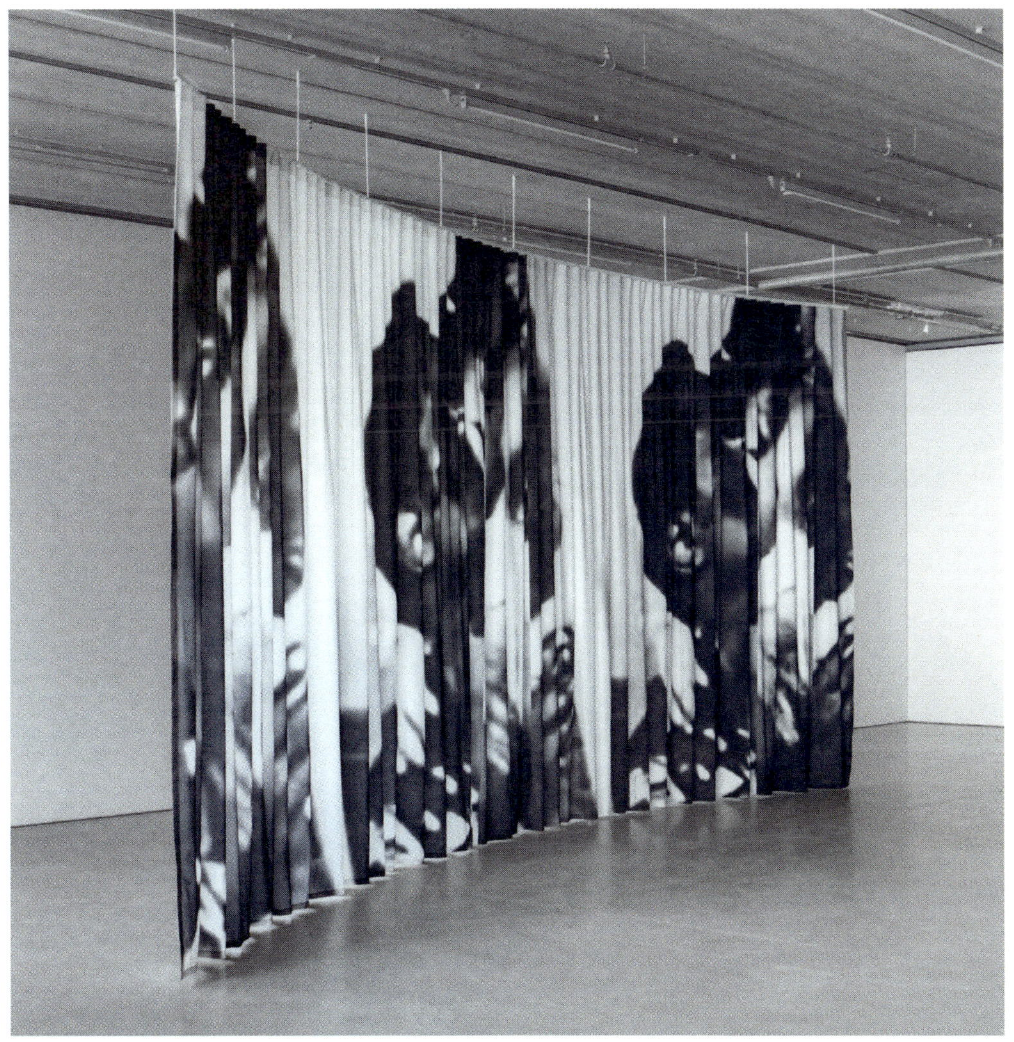

Them
2024
Printed fabric, metal curtain rod
3.7 × 12 m

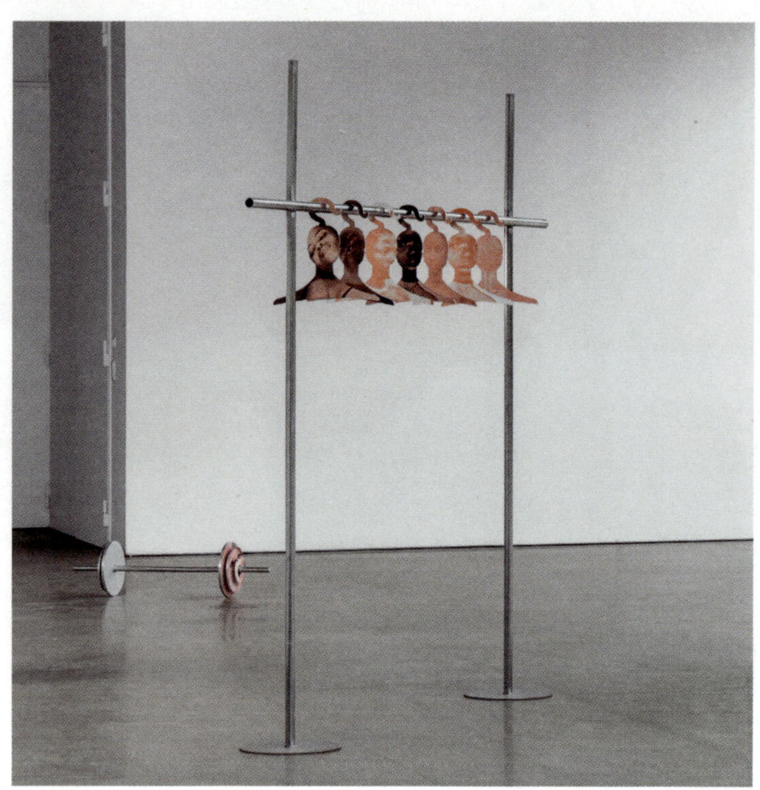

Unidentified Hangers
2024
Metal sculpture with print
Rack: H 230 × W 230 × D 40 cm
7 hangers, each:
H 37 × W 40 × D 0.5 cm

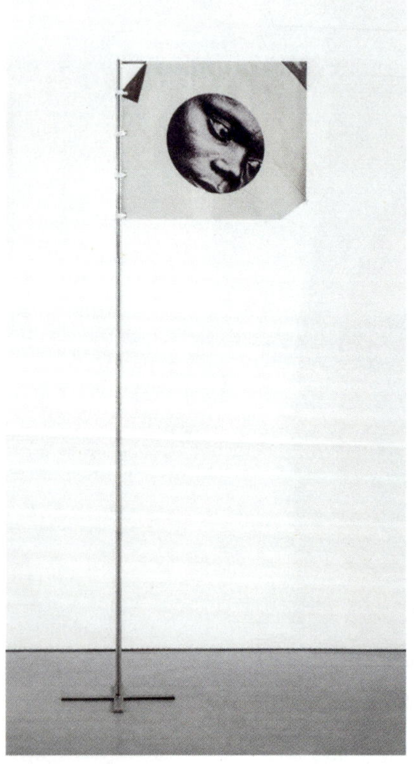

Two Eyes and a Pole
2024
Sculpture, printed fabric
and metal flagpole
Flagpole: H 350 cm
Flag: 86 × 100 cm

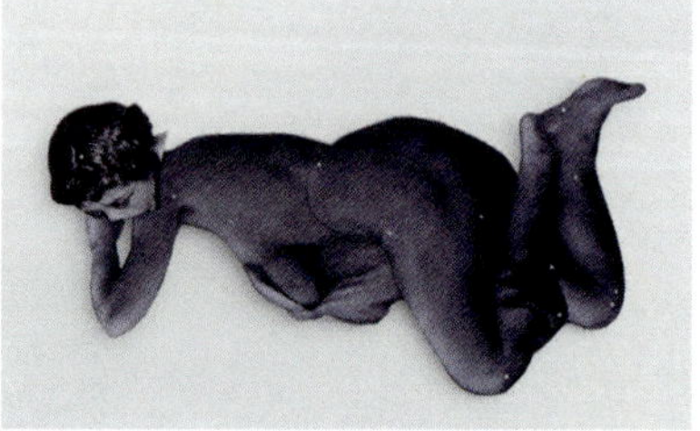

Woman with Hand
2024
Collage, paper, paper clip,
mounted on aluminum
67 × 122 cm

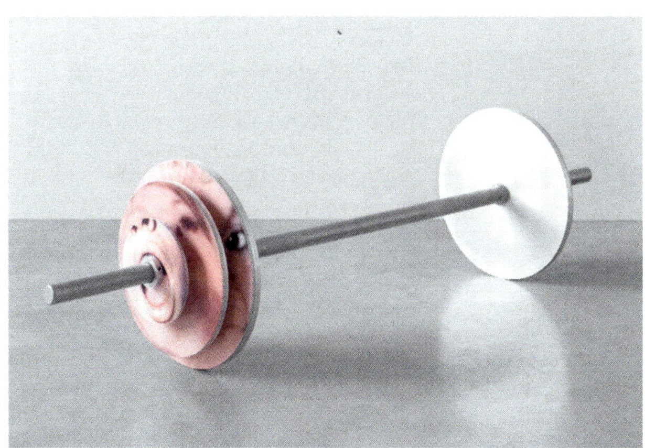

White Happiness
2024
Metal sculpture
H 30 × W 120 × D 30 cm

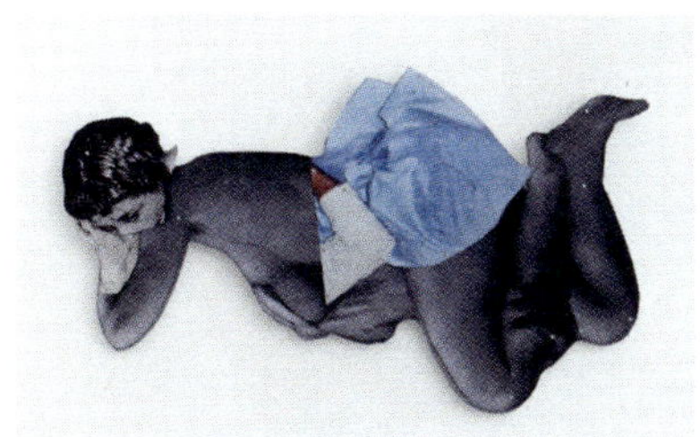

Woman with Dress
2024
Collage, paper, paper clip,
mounted on aluminum
70 × 123 cm

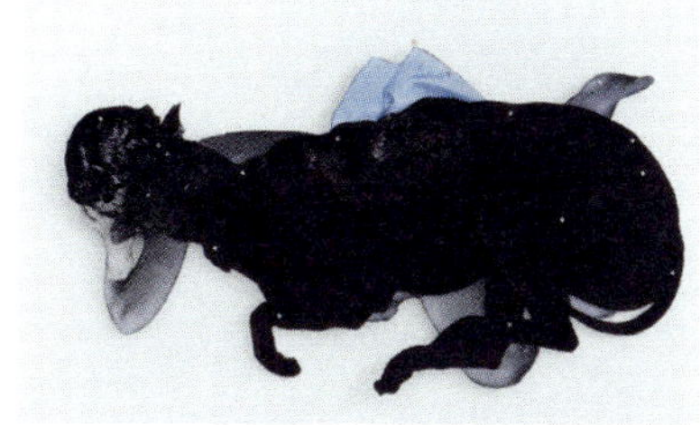

Woman with Dog II
2024
Collage, paper, paper clip,
mounted on aluminum
76 × 128 cm

Artist's Biography

Frida Orupabo lives and works in Oslo. She was born in Sarpsborg, Norway, in 1986 and obtained her Master's degree in Sociology from the University of Oslo in 2011.

Selected Solo Exhibitions

2025

SPECTRUM Internationaler Preis für Fotografie, Sprengel Museum, Hannover

2024

On Lies, Secrets and Silence, Bonniers Konsthall, Stockholm, Sweden; Astrup Fearnley Museet, Oslo, Norway (2025)

2023

Fear of Fear, Galerie Nordenhake, Mexico City, Mexico

Things I saw at night, Modern Art, Helmet Row, London, UK

2022

I've been here for days, Stevenson, Cape Town, South Africa

How Fast Shall We Sing, Mécanique Générale, Rencontres d'Arles, France

I have seen a million pictures of my face and still I have no idea, Fotomuseum Winterthur, Switzerland

2021

How did you feel when you come out of the wilderness, Kunsthall Trondheim, Trondheim, Norway

Frida Orupabo, 34th Bienal de São Paulo, Museu Afro Brasil, São Paulo, Brazil

2020

Hours After, Stevenson, Johannesburg, South Africa

12 Self Portraits, Gavin Brown's Enterprise, Rome, Italy

2019

A House is a House, Galerie Nordenhake, Berlin, Germany

the mouth and the truth, Portikus, Frankfurt, Germany

Medicine for a Nightmare, Kunstnernes Hus, Oslo, Norway

2018

Two-Thirds Pleasure, Galerie Nordenhake, Stockholm, Sweden

Cables to Rage, Gavin Brown's Enterprise, New York, USA

Selected Group Exhibitions

2024

The Verbund Collection, the Albertina Museum, Vienna, Austria

A requiem for humanity, La Casa Encendida, Madrid, Spain

Giants: Art from the Dean Collection of Swizz Beats and Alicia Keys, the Brooklyn Museum, New York, USA

2023

Deutsche Börse Photography Foundation Prize, the Photographer's Gallery, London, UK

Black Venus, Museum of the African Diaspora, San Francisco, USA

FLIGHT, Malmö Konsthall, Sweden

Chrysalis: The Butterfly Dream, Centre d'Art Contemporain Genève, Switzerland

2022

The Machine is Us, Munch Triennale, Munchmuseet, Norway

Customs, A4 Arts Foundation, Cape Town, South Africa

Afterimage, MAXXI L'Aquila, Italy

Currency, 8th Triennial of Photography, Hamburg, Germany

Living encounters, ARS22, Kiasma Finnish National Gallery, Finland

2021

Dear Truth, Hasselblad Foundation, Gothenburg, Sweden

Mother!, Louisiana Museum of Modern Art, Humlebæk, Denmark

How to Make a Country, FRAC Poitou-Charentes, Angoulême, France

Future Generation Art Prize 2021 Shortlisted Artists, PinchukArtCentre, Kyiv, Ukraine

Though it's dark, still I sing, 34th Bienal de São Paulo, Museu Afro Brasil, São Paulo, Brazil

Not Without Joy, Galerie Rudolfinum, Prague, Czech Republic

2020

We Fight to Build a Free World, Jewish Museum, New York, USA

Infinite Identities: Photography in the Age of Sharing, Huis Marseille, Amsterdam, The Netherlands

Summer Exhibition, Royal Academy of Arts, London, UK

Resistant Faces, Pinakothek der Moderne, Munich, Germany

What is the Present?, Museum für Gegenwartskunst Siegen, Germany

Dynamic Spaces, Museum Ludwig, Cologne, Germany

2019

May You Live in Interesting Times, 58th Venice Biennale, Italy

2018
Niepodległe: Women, Independence and National Discourse, Museum of Modern Art, Warsaw, Poland

2017
A Series of Utterly Improbable, Yet Extraordinary Renditions (with Arthur Jafa), Serpentine Gallery, London, UK; Julia Stoschek Collection, Berlin, Germany (2018); Moderna Museet, Stockholm, Sweden (2019); Galerie Rudolfinum, Prague, Czech Republic (2019)

Awards

SPECTRUM Internationaler Preis für Fotografie, 2025
The Royal Photographic Society Honorary Fellowship, 2023
Shortlist, Deutsche Börse Photography Foundation Prize, 2023
Shortlist, Future Generation Art Prize, 2021

Selected Publications

Appiah, Tawanda, Tina Campt, Kudzanai Chiurai, Eric Magassa, Santiago Mostyn, Frida Orupabo and Mats Stjernstedt. *Flight*. Exhibition catalog. Edited by Tawanda Appiah and Anna Granqvist. Malmö: Malmö Konsthall, 2023.

Etgar, Yuval, et al. *Vitamin C+: Collage in Contemporary Art*. Edited by Phaidon. London: Phaidon, 2023.

Sinazo Chiya, Rahima Gambo, Aziz Hazara, Monilola Ilupeju Olayemi, Sispho Ngodwana, Léonard Pongo, and Ajamu X. *my whole body changed into something else*. Exhibition catalog. Edited by Stevenson. Cape Town: Stevenson, 2021.

Hessler, Stefanie, Lola Olufemi, and Legacy Russell. *Frida Orupabo*. Exhibition catalog. Edited by Stephanie Hessler. London and Trondheim: Sternberg Press and Kunsthall Trondheim, 2021.

Fonds régional d'art contemporain Poitou-Charentes. *How to make a country*. Exhibition catalog. Edited by Lerato Bereng. Angoulême: Frac Poitou-Charentes, 2021.

Orupabo, Frida and Elvira Dyangani Ose. *Frida Orupabo: Hours After*. Exhibition catalog. Edited by Stevenson. Cape Town: Stevenson, 2021.

Akomfrah, John, Hilton Als, Paolo Bacigalupi, Amiri Baraka, Jean Baudrillard, Leo Bersani, Dionne Brand, Cm Burroughs, Judith Butler, Tina M. Campt, Samuel R. Delany, Gilles Felix, Deleuze Guattari, Henry Dumas, Akwaeke Emezi, Jerzy Grotowski, Ernest Hardy, Saidiya Hartman, Dave Hickey, Arthur Jafa, John Keene, Nathaniel Mackey, Greil Marcus, Fred Moten, Hans Ulrich Obrist and Yana Peel, NourbeSe Philip, Lucius Shepard, Hortense J. Spillers, Greg Tate, Cecil Taylor, James Tiptree Jr., Sylvia Wynter, and Denise da Silva Ferreira. *Arthur Jaffa: A Series of Utterly Improbably, Yet Extraordinary Renditions*. Exhibition catalog. Edited by Joseph Constable and Amira Gad. London: Serpentine Galleries and Koenig Books, 2018.

Contributor Biographies

Owen Martin is Curator at Astrup Fearnley Museet in Oslo, a position he has held since 2023. In addition to curating *Frida Orupabo: On Lies, Secrets and Silence* (2025, with Yuvinka Medina), he has organized the group exhibition *Between Rivers* (2024) and *Before Tomorrow* (2023, with Solveig Øvstebø), a new display of the Astrup Fearnley Collection across the institution's galleries. He leads the live program with Øvstebø and is overseeing a major new commission by Silje Figenschou Thoresen (2024). He was the founding Chief Curator of Norval Foundation in Cape Town from 2017 to 2023, where he organized projects with Michael Armitage, William Kentridge (with Karel Nel), Ibrahim Mahama, Zanele Muholi (with Khanya Mashabela), Lisa Reihana, and Yinka Shonibare (with Dr. Portia Malatjie), among others. He has edited several publications, among them *Before Tomorrow: Reflecting on the Astrup Fearnley Collection* (2023) and *Why Should I Hesitate: Sculpture* (2020), a 360-page catalogue raisonné of William Kentridge's sculptural practice; and also contributed to several catalogs. Previously, he held curatorial roles at Zeitz MOCAA in Cape Town and the Zeitz Collection. Martin holds an MA in Art History from McGill University (Montréal).

Yuvinka Medina has been the Senior Curator at Bonniers Konsthall in Stockholm since 2021. Besides curating *Frida Orupabo: On Lies, Secrets and Silence* (2024, with Owen Martin), Medina has spearheaded numerous acclaimed exhibitions featuring prominent contemporary artists such as *Tarik Kiswanson / Becoming* (2023), *Ayesha Hameed and Guests / Radio Brown Atlantis* (2022), *Lap-See Lam / Dreamers' Quay, Dreamers' Key* (2022), *Outi Pieski / Rematriation of a Ládjogahpir—Return to Máttaráhkká* (2022), *Victoria Verseau / Approaching a Ghost* (2021), and *Jacqueline Hoàng* Nguyễn *Untitled (Entitled)* (2021), among others. She has curated exhibitions for the Maria Bonnier Dahlin Foundation Grant Recipients from 2022 to 2024. Additionally, she led the institution's collaboration with Artists' Film International from 2018 to 2021. Medina has edited several publications, including the artist's book *Tarik Kiswanson / Becoming* in collaboration with Éditions Dilecta (2023), the monograph *Lap-See Lam / Dreamers' Quay, Dreamers' Key* in collaboration with Lenz Press, *Éva Mag / There is a Plan for This* (2020), *Peter Liversidge / Notes on Protesting* in collaboration with Art & Theory (2019), and has contributed to various other publications. Before her current role, Medina worked as a curator and programming curator at Bonniers Konsthall, where she organized many high-profile art projects. Her academic background includes studies at the London University of Arts (Central Saint Martins College of Art and Design) and Konstfack—University of Arts, Crafts, and Design in Stockholm, where she currently serves as an external representative in the Subject Council Craft.

Dr. Portia Malatjie is a Cape Town-based curator and Senior Lecturer in Visual Cultures at the University of Cape Town's Michaelis School of Fine Art. She is Adjunct Curator of Africa and African Diaspora at the Hyundai Tate Research Centre: Transnational at Tate Modern (London) and holds a PhD in Visual Cultures from Goldsmiths University of London (2020). She has published widely in peer-reviewed journals and exhibition catalogs, received multiple awards for her research and has curated several major exhibitions, most recently the South African Pavilion at the 2024 Venice Biennale. Her visual cultural and curatorial research explores African conceptions of Blackness through the intersection of sound, spirituality, and Black Feminist Thought.

Mai Takawira is an independent curator and researcher. She holds an MA in Modern Culture from the University of Copenhagen. Often her work centers on experiences of Blackness in the Nordics, from the precarious to the politically potent, as well as African-Diasporic dialogues across time and space and the translation work it produces. She has given lectures and workshops throughout Denmark and has been involved in various projects initiated by many of the leading museums and art institutions in the country. In 2017 Takawira became a member of the collective Marronage, which has used a multitude of strategies to critique the ongoing effects of Danish coloniality. Together with Nina Cramer she initiated the curatorial platform G/HOSTING in 2024, which activates critical and reparative approaches to colonial histories through curatorial and editorial projects. G/HOSTING is based in Copenhagen, but works in extension of transnational decolonial and black feminist movements.

Nina Cramer is a PhD candidate at the University of Copenhagen's Department of Arts and Cultural Studies. Her research examines contemporary artistic practices and discourses of the African Diaspora in Denmark, drawing on frameworks from Black Studies and queer feminist art history. Her PhD project is part of the research network the Art of Nordic Colonialism. In 2017 Cramer became a member of the collective Marronage, which has used a multitude of strategies to critique the ongoing effects of Danish coloniality. Together with Mai Takawira she initiated the curatorial platform G/HOSTING in 2024, which activates critical and reparative approaches to colonial histories through curatorial and editorial projects. G/HOSTING is based in Copenhagen, but works in extension of transnational decolonial and black feminist movements.

G/HOSTING is a platform that uses curatorial, editorial, educational and dissemination projects to activate critical and reparative approaches to ongoing colonial histories. Emphasis is on perspectives from the global majority. In collaborations with artists, writers, and cultural institutions, G/HOSTING facilitates interventions into exhibitions, collections, public spaces, and professional discourses. The name G/HOSTING describes the platform's two core concepts. Firstly, hosting as a means to create dialogue among Danish-based racialized cultural workers and with colleagues in other geographies (hosting). Secondly, attending to repressed colonial histories that haunt the present, the challenge of representation and the liberation of disappearing (ghosting). The platform is based in Denmark, but works in extension of transnational decolonial and black feminist movements.

C. LeClaire, a poet and writer based in Chicago, USA, is a Gwendolyn Brooks Open Mic finalist, an alumna of VONA (Voices of Our Nations Arts Foundation), and a participant in Winter Tangerine's creative writing workshop. Her poems have been featured in the film *Dear Nina*, the anthology *Chorus: A Literary Mixtape*, *Inside The Bell Jar*, *Linden Avenue Literary Journal* and *Rigorous*.

Hilton Als is an award-winning journalist, critic and curator. He has been a staff writer at *the New Yorker* since 1994. Prior to *the New Yorker*, Als was a staff writer for the *Village Voice* and an editor-at-large at *Vibe*. He has received numerous awards for his work, including the Pulitzer Prize for Criticism (2017), Yale's Windham-Campbell Literature Prize (2016), the George Jean Nathan Award for Dramatic Criticism (2002-03), and a Guggenheim Fellowship (2000). His first book, *The Women*, was published in 1996. His next book, *White Girls*, was a finalist for the National Book Critics Circle Award and the winner of the Lambda Literary Award in 2014. His most recent book, *My Pinup*, a meditation on love and of loss, of Prince and of desire, was published in November 2022. He is currently a teaching professor at the University of California, Berkeley, and has also taught at Columbia University's School of the Arts, Princeton University, Wesleyan University, and the Yale School of Drama.

BONNIERS KONSTHALL

About Bonniers Konsthall

Bonniers Konsthall is a venue for Swedish and international contemporary art, rooted in the Maria Bonnier Dahlin Foundation, which was established in 1985 by Jeanette Bonnier in memory of her daughter Maria. The foundation annually awards grants to young Swedish artists. As an extension of this initiative, Jeanette Bonnier founded Bonniers Konsthall as a physical representation of the Bonnier family's dedication to contemporary art. As a non-collecting institution, Bonniers Konsthall works closely with artists to realize their visions and engages diverse audiences through various programs and publications.

The Konsthall's distinctive triangular glass building, designed by Johan Celsing, is located in central Stockholm. Since opening in 2006, Bonniers Konsthall has commissioned and exhibited works by numerous Swedish and international artists, including Lap-See Lam, Tarik Kiswanson, Lawrence Abu Hamdan, Outi Pieski, Tomás Saraceno, Monica Bonvincini, Sharon Lockhart, Susan Philipsz, and Cooking Sections.

Acknowledgments

Bonniers Konsthall wishes to wholeheartedly thank Frida Orupabo for her immense contribution to both the exhibition and the catalog. We also want to thank our dedicated staff and board of directors. We deeply appreciate the support from everyone involved in the creation of this exhibition and catalog—especially the writers, Gabrielle Guy, Bettina Schultz, Costanza de Bellegarde de Saint Lary at Skira editore, Ben Loveless, and Ulrika Pilo at Galerie Nordenhake Stockholm, Claudia Sorhage at Galerie Nordenhake Berlin, Viola Eickmeier at Studio Violet, Svante Larsson at Kornskarpt, Lone Weigelt at Borch Editions, Förstoringsateljén, Fine Art Service, Big Image, Billes, Karin Drake, Linus Hillborg Hangmen, and Elvira Wikman.

Bonniers Konsthall Staff

Executive Director: **Ellen Wettmark**
Artistic Director: **Joanna Nordin**
HR Director: **Li Erlandsson**
Senior Curator: **Yuvinka Medina**
Producer: **Maria Elena Guerra Aredal**
Communications Manager: **Kajsa Pontén**
Communication: **Ida Sjödin**
Financial Manager: **Christina Tönnesen**
Host Manager: **Sara Dahlström**
Event Coordinator: **Sibel Norman**
Program and Shop Manager: **Carolina Andreasson**
Restaurant Manager: **Cecilia Carreon**

Gallery Hosts: **Jesper O.T. Andersson, Veronika Bedecs, Channa Bianca, Simon Blanck, Rebecca Digby, Anton Elfving, Hugo Hedberg, Olga Krüssenberg, Viktor Landström, Theo Lundgren, Nadia Maghder, Evelina Mohei, Emina Pacavar, Otto Ruin, Martina Skyttberg, Monica Swedberg, Johanna Tham, Linnea Wästfelt**

Note: correct at the time of publishing

Astrup Fearnley Museet

About Astrup Fearnley Museet

Founded in 1993, Astrup Fearnley Museet is one of Scandinavia's most notable museums for contemporary art. The museum holds the extensive Astrup Fearnley Collection, and presents changing exhibitions that draw on the collection as well as debut new commissions by artists from all over the world. The museum, designed by Renzo Piano, spans two buildings bisected by a canal, and is situated on the Oslofjord in the Tjuvholmen neighborhood of central Oslo, next to Tjuvholmen Sculpture Park.

The Astrup Fearnley Collection dates to the 1960s, and is one of Europe's most comprehensive collections of international contemporary art. The collection does not concentrate on specific eras, styles, or groups, but pays close attention to the work of a wide variety of artists. The museum maintains the vibrancy of the collection by regularly rehanging the exhibitions, placing the works in new constellations and contexts. The collection includes significant works by artists such as Matthew Barney, Paul Chan, Trisha Donnelly, Nicole Eisenman, Ida Ekblad, Félix González-Torres, Rachel Harrison, Damien Hirst, Jeff Koons, Glenn Ligon, Sigmar Polke, Cindy Sherman, Børre Sæthre, and Wolfgang Tillmans.

Acknowledgments

Astrup Fearnley Museet would like to warmly thank Frida Orupabo, the museum's staff, Museum Board, and everyone involved in this exhibition and catalog as well as our sponsors, The Thief, Stadsporten AS, Sparebankstiftelsen DNB, and main sponsor, EGD Holding AS, for their ongoing support. Astrup Fearnley Museet is generously supported by Foundation Thomas Fearnley, Heddy and Nils Astrup, and Foundation Hans Rasmus Astrup. We are very appreciative of the assistance of Ben Loveless at Galerie Nordenhake and Lerato Bereng at Stevenson.

Astrup Fearnley Museet Staff

Executive Director and Chief Curator: **Solveig Øvstebø**
Education Coordinator: **Marthe A. Andersen**
Operation Manager: **Jens-Morten Dahl**
Head of Education: **Inger Fure Grøtting**
Facilities Coordinator: **John Hansen**
Digital Content Producer: **Helle Holm**
Archivist: **Hege Kjeldsen**
Museum Host Manager and Administration Coordinator: **Umut Kücükerman**
Curator: **Owen Martin**
Registrar and Collection Manager: **Hanne Hagen Eriksen**
Education Coordinator: **Marianne Reve**
Head of Finance and Administration: **Liv Borgny Rømo**
Designer: **Sandra Stokka**
Commercial Manager: **Véronique Svarstad**
Text and Web Editor: **Renate Thorbjørnsen**
Exhibition Producer: **Einride Torvik**
Shop and Art Club Assistant: **Liv Astrid Thue**
Assistant to Director: **Ine Elisabeth Lindholt Vestengen-Cox**
Head of Communication: **Stein-Inge Århus**

Educators: **Mikael Munz Bakketun, Stine Marie Korsfur, Marte Mestad, Karen Nikgol, Evelin Sofia Sillé, Anne Weyer-Larsen**

Hosts: **Rebecca Askedølen, Pailin Berg, Erik Bromö, Sofie Brønner, Linn Bye, Anna Bove Eiler, Tiril Erdal, Ole-André Greger Eriksen, Maria Bårdsdatter Foslie, Carina Marwell Hansen, Una Hanssen, Linn Hovde Hestnes, Hanne Røstad Karlsen, Julie Margrethe Klevmark, Stine Marie Korsfur, Kaja Kulbraaten, Camilla Laudal, Kjersti Maaø Landsjøåsen, Embla Alvrun U.V. Moe, Karen Nikgol, Jonatan Nilsson, Fanny Emilie Nordheim, Frida Nyhus, Viktor Pedersen, Elise Petersen, Hilde Katerina Pytkowski, Aurora Romano, Sheila Mai Salas, Annine Slettebø, Kristiina Veinberg**

Front of House: **Maya Craig, Marcus Johan Karstensen, Marte Mestad, Hanna Meyer Thuestad, Torkil Ranvik, Victoria Skansen, Tuva Svendsen, Synne Teige, Kristin Tilrem, Elisa Turcato Bakken, Madelon Verbeek**

Technicians (regularly worked with): **Luis Alves, Per Christian Brath, Sofie Brønner, Vidar Ericsson, Anne Fløttum, Anders Grønlien, Mattias Hellberg, Kjartan Helleve, Roger Høyer, Kai Kobi, Clemens Koch, Pablo Lecroisey Lara, Young Lunde, Hanna Sjöstrand, Gunnhild Torgersen, Kristiina Veinberg, Ole Øverdahl**

Museum Board: **Anna Catharina Astrup (Chair), Cecilie Astrup, Knut Brundtland, Jens-Morten Dahl, Erling Kagge, Rolf Johan Ringdal**

Note: correct at the time of publishing

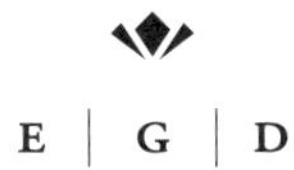

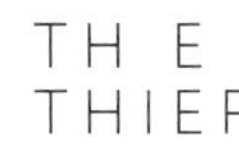

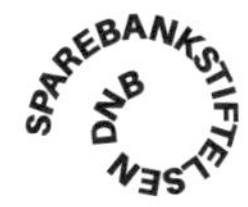

STADSPORTEN®

Published on the occasion of the exhibition *Frida Orupabo: On Lies, Secrets and Silence* at Bonniers Konsthall 28.08.2024—10.11.2024 and Astrup Fearnley Museet 7.2.2025—27.4.2025.

The publication is co-financed by Stiftung Niedersachsen. A special bilingual edition containing translations of the texts into German is available in connection with the awarding of the Spectrum—International Prize for Photography of the Stiftung Niedersachsen to Frida Orupabo on 4 April 2025 at the Sprengel Museum Hannover.

Jointly published by:

Bonniers Konsthall
Torsgatan 19
SE-113 90 Stockholm
www.bonnierskonsthall.se

Astrup Fearnley Museet
Strandpromenaden 2
0252 Oslo
www.afmuseet.no

SKIRA
Skira editore
Via Agnello 18
20121 Milan
skira-arte.com

ISBN 978-88-572-5310-7

Curators and editors:
Yuvinka Medina, Owen Martin

Book design:
Gabrielle Guy

Project manager and proofreader:
Bettina Schultz

Printed and bound in Italy
First edition

Distributed in the USA, Canada, Central & South America by:
ARTBOOK | D.A.P.
75 Broad Street, Suite 630
New York
NY 10004, USA

Distributed elsewhere in the world by:
Thames and Hudson Ltd.
181A High Holborn
London WC1V 7QX
United Kingdom

Photo credits:

Jean-Baptiste Béranger: pp. 47–48, 51–53, 89–92, 110–113 ,124–125. Courtesy of the artist and Bonniers Konsthall, Stockholm
Gerhard Kassner: pp. 26 (left), 33, 35–36, 39–40, 55–56, 58–64, 67, 70–73, 79, 87, 95–99, 102–103, 114–117, 119. Courtesy of the artist and Galerie Nordenhake Berlin, Stockholm, Mexico City
Nina Lieska: p. 22 (left). Courtesy of the artist and Stevenson, Johannesburg, Cape Town, Amsterdam
Carl Henrik Tillberg: p. 29. Courtesy of the artist and Galerie Nordenhake Berlin, Stockholm, Mexico City
Mario Todeschini: pp. 21, 22 (right), 23. Courtesy of the artist and Stevenson, Johannesburg, Cape Town, Amsterdam

pp. 20, 26 (right), 27. Courtesy of the artist and Galerie Nordenhake Berlin, Stockholm, Mexico City

Images on pp. 3–6, 129–140:
Details from *Cloud of Confusion* (2024)

Images on pp. 157–160:
Details from *Trauma Catches Up* (2024)

Front and back cover:
Details from *Trauma Catches Up* (2024)

Inside front cover:
Details from *Trauma Catches Up* (2024) and an outtake from *Cloud of Confusion* (2024)

Inside back cover:
Details from *Trauma Catches Up* (2024) and *Cloud of Confusion* (2024)

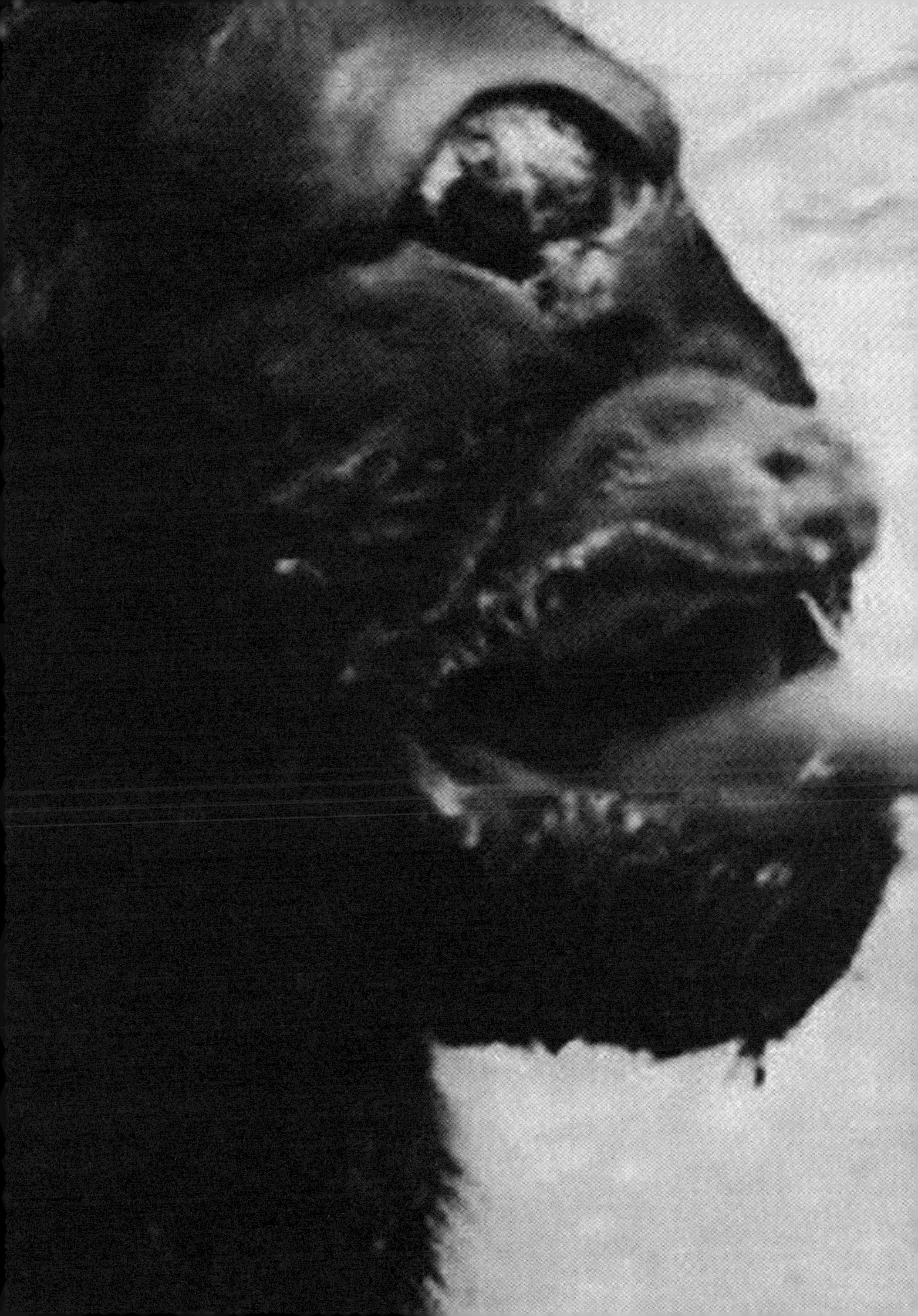

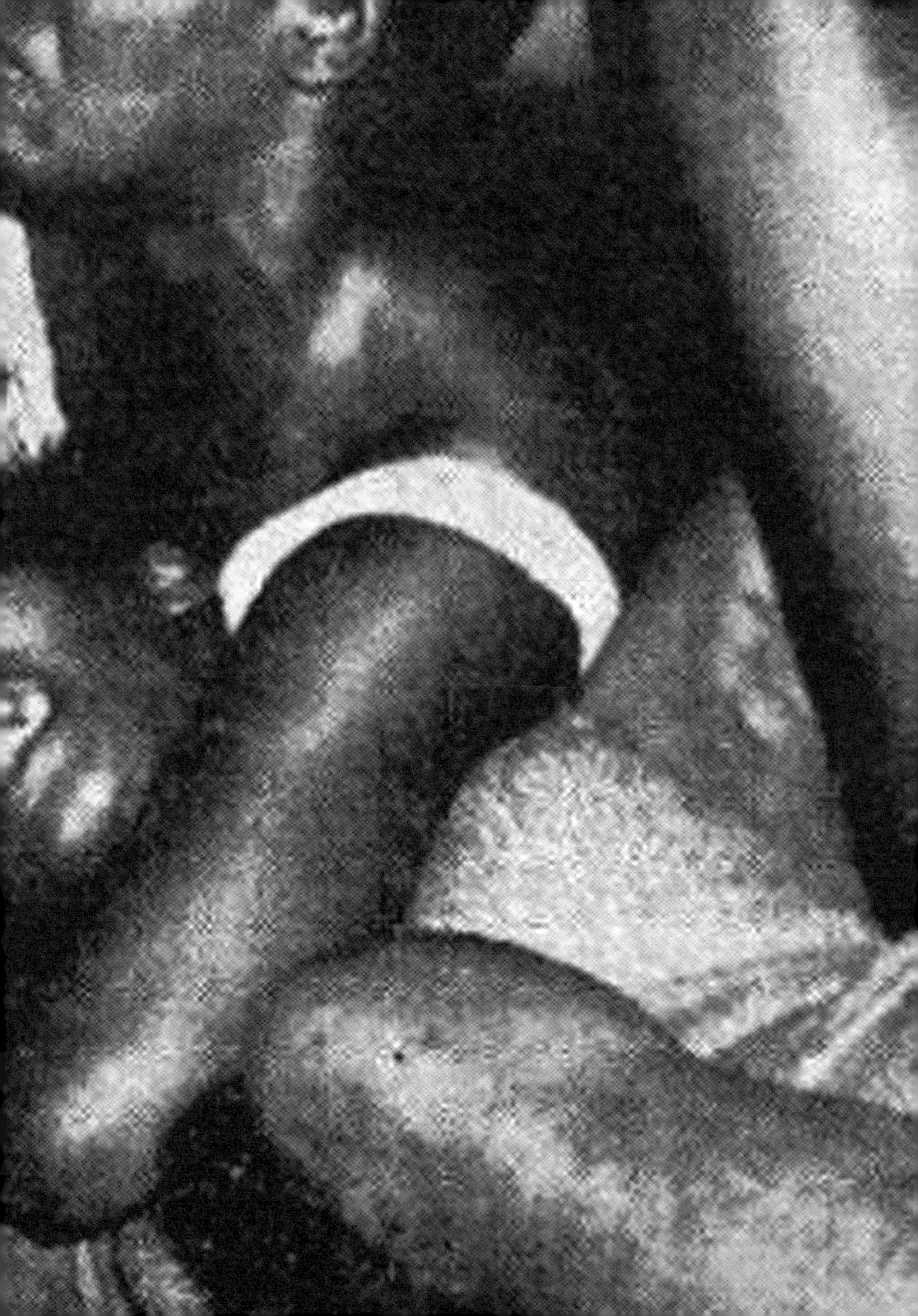

worry

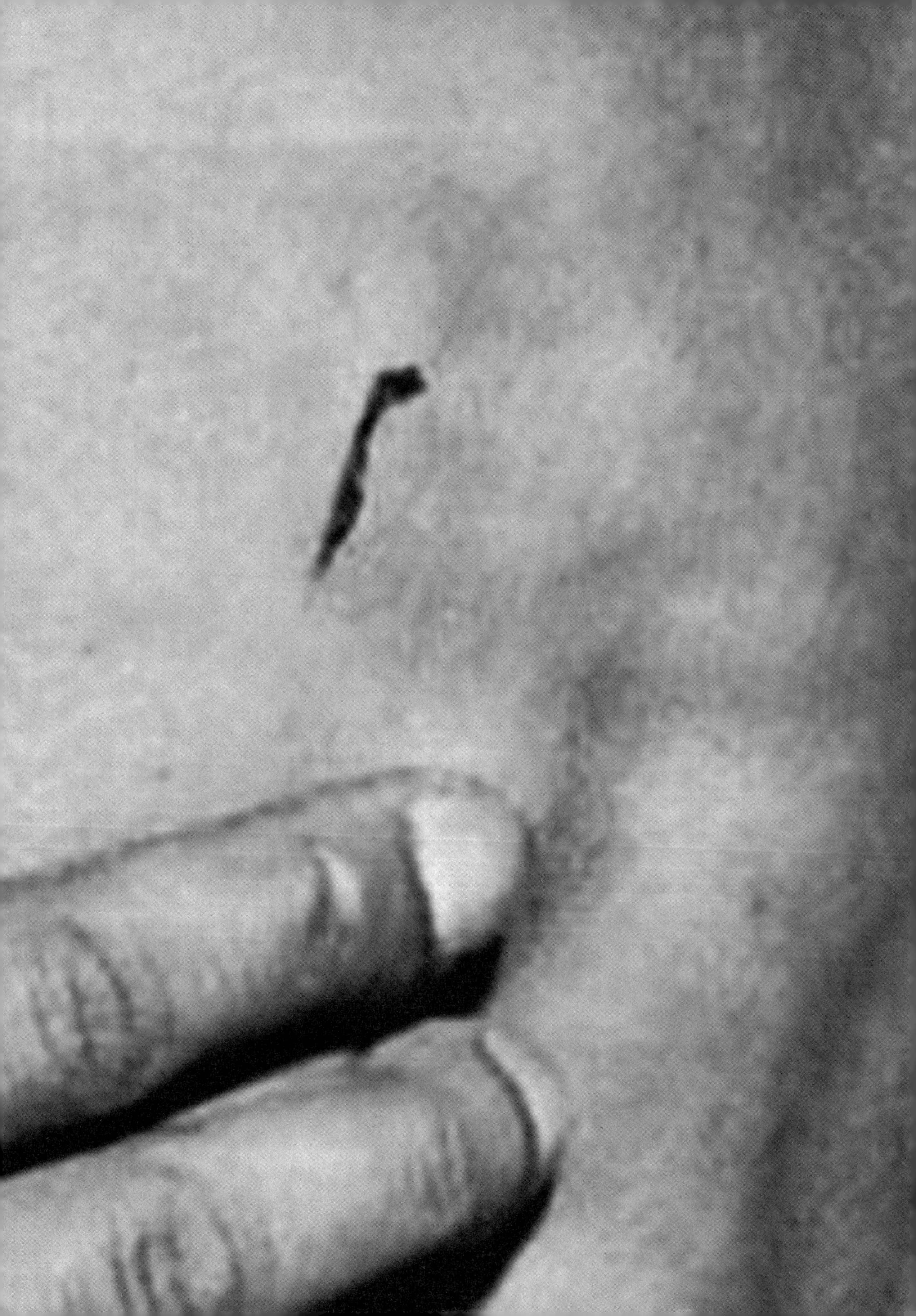